NORTHERN IRELAND, SCOTLAND AND WALES

THE BRITANNICA GUIDE TO COUNTRIES OF THE EUROPEAN UNION

THE UNITED KINGDOM: NORTHEN IRELAND, SCOTLAND, AND WALES

Edited by Jeff Wallenfeldt, Manager, Geography

Britannica
Educational Publishing

IN ASSOCIATION WITH

ROSEN
EDUCATIONAL SERVICES

Published in 2014 by Britannica Educational Publishing
(a trademark of Encyclopædia Britannica, Inc.)
in association with Rosen Educational Services, LLC
29 East 21st Street, New York, NY 10010.

Copyright © 2014 Encyclopædia Britannica, Inc. Britannica, Encyclopædia Britannica, and the Thistle logo are registered trademarks of Encyclopædia Britannica, Inc. All rights reserved.

Rosen Educational Services materials copyright © 2014 Rosen Educational Services, LLC. All rights reserved.

Distributed exclusively by Rosen Educational Services.
For a listing of additional Britannica Educational Publishing titles, call toll free (800) 237-9932.

First Edition

Britannica Educational Publishing
J.E. Luebering: Director, Core Reference Group
Marilyn L. Barton: Senior Coordinator, Production Control
Adam Augustyn: Assistant Manager, Core Reference Group
Steven Bosco: Director, Editorial Technologies
Lisa S. Braucher: Senior Producer and Data Editor
Yvette Charboneau: Senior Copy Editor
Kathy Nakamura: Manager, Media Acquisition
Jeff Wallenfeldt: Manager, Geography

Rosen Educational Services
Nocholas Croce: Senior Editor
Nelson Sá: Art Director
Cindy Reiman: Photo Manger
Brian Garvey: Designer, Cover Design
Introduction by Richard Barrington

Library of Congress Cataloging-in-Publication Data

The United Kingdom : Northern Ireland, Scotland, and Wales/edited by Jeff Wallenfeldt. — First edition.
     pages cm. — (The Britannica guide to countries of the European Union)
"In association with Britannica Educational Publishing, Rosen Educational Services."
Includes bibliographical references and index.
ISBN 978-1-62275-055-9 (library binding)
1. Northern Ireland—Juvenile literature. 2. Scotland—Juvenile literature. 3. Wales—Juvenile literature. 4. Great Britain—Juvenile literature. I. Wallenfeldt, Jeffrey H.
DA27.5.U455 2013
941—dc23

2013002961

Manufactured in the United States of America

On the cover: A composite image of the Wales Millennium Centre *(left)* and a nearby fountain *(right)* in Cardiff Bay, Wales, United Kingdom. © *iStockphoto.com/Darryl Sleath,* © *iStockphoto.com/Ian Jeffery*

Cover, p. iii (map contour and stars), back cover, multiple interior pages (stars) ©iStockphoto.com/pop_jop; cover, multiple interior pages (background graphic) Mina De La O/ Digital Vision/Getty Image

CONTENTS

| Introduction | xii |

Chapter 1: Northern Ireland: The Land and Its People — 1
Relief	3
Drumlin	5
Drainage	6
Soils	6
Climate	6
Plant and Animal Life	7
Ethnic Groups and Language	7
Religion	8
Settlement Patterns	9
Carrickfergus	10
Demographic Trends	11

Chapter 2: The Northern Irish Economy — 12
Agriculture, Forestry, and Fishing	12
Resources and Power	14
Manufacturing	14
John DeLorean	15
Finance	16
Trade	16
Services	16
Labour	17
Transportation	17

Chapter 3: Northern Irish Government and Society — 18
Good Friday Agreement	20
Local Government	21
Justice	21
Political Process	22
Unionist Parties	22
Nationalist Parties	23
The Alliance Party of Northern Ireland	23
Security	24
Royal Ulster Constabulary	24

Health and Welfare	25
Housing	26
Education	26

Chapter 4: Northern Irish Cultural life — 27
Daily Life and Social Customs	28
The Arts	28
Van Morrison	30
Cultural Institutions	31
Sports and Recreation	31
George Best	32
Media and Publishing	32

Chapter 5: Early and Early Modern Ulster — 33
Mythic History	33
Gaelic Irish and Anglo-Normans (c. 600–c. 1300)	34
English and Scottish Plantations	35
Hugh O'Neill, 2nd Earl of Tyrone	36
Religion and Social Structure	36

Chapter 6: The 18th Century and Beyond — 38
Ulster in the 18th Century	38
Orange Society	40
Home Rule	40
Precarious Coexistence	42
Disintegration of Stability	43
Bloody Sunday	44
Power-Sharing Agreements and the Establishment of a Fragile Peace	45

Chapter 7: Scotland: The land and Its People — 48
Relief	52
Loch Ness	53
Drainage	54
Soils	54
Climate	55

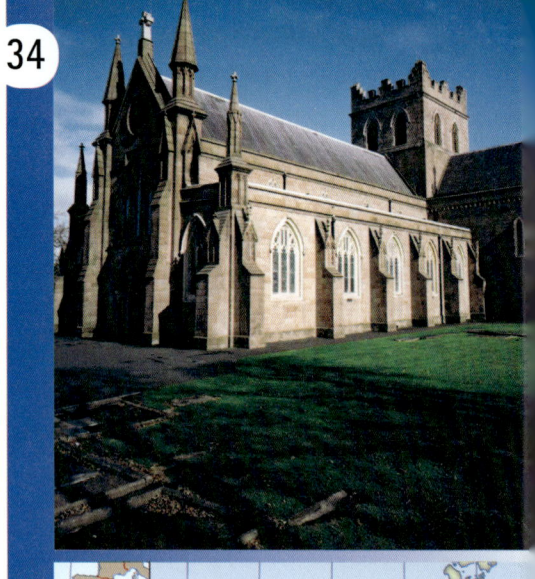

Plant and Animal Life	55
Ethnic Groups	56
Languages	56
Religion	57
Church of Scotland	57
Settlement Patterns	58
Demographic Trends	59

Chapter 8: The Scottish Economy — 60

Agriculture, Forestry, and Fishing	60
Mad Cow Disease	62
Resources and Power	63
Manufacturing	65
Tweed	66
Finance	66
Services	67
Transportation	67

Chapter 9: Scottish Government and Society — 69

Local Government	71
Justice	72
Political Process	72
J. Keir Hardie	73
Security	74
Health and Welfare	75
Housing	75
Education	75
University of Edinburgh	76

Chapter 10: Scottish Cultural Life — 78

Daily Life and Social Customs	78
Kilt	79
Haggis	80
The Arts	80
Robert Burns	81
Cultural Institutions	82
Sports and Recreation	83
Royal and Ancient Golf Club of St. Andrews	83
Media and Publishing	83

Chapter 11: Early Scotland — 85
- Ancient Times — 86
  - Roman Penetration — 86
  - Christianity — 88
  - The Norse Influence — 88
- The Unification of the Kingdom — 89
  - *Macbeth* — 90
  - The Development of the Monarchy — 91
  - David I (1124–53) — 91
  - Medieval Economy and Society — 93
  - David I's Successors — 94
- The Wars of Independence — 95
  - Competition for the Throne — 95
  - *Sir William Wallace* — 96
  - Robert I (1306–29) — 97
  - David II (1329–71) — 98

Chapter 12: From the 15th Century to the Age of Revolution — 100
- The Early Stewart Kings — 100
- 15th-Century Society — 102
  - *The Book of Deer* — 103
- James IV (1488–1513) and James V (1513–42) — 104
- Mary (1542–67) and the Scottish Reformation — 105
- James VI (1567–1625) — 107
- Charles I (1625–49) — 109
- Cromwell — 111
- The Restoration Monarchy — 111

Chapter 13: Scotland Since the 18th Century — 113
- The Act of Union and Its Results — 113
- Jacobitism in the Highlands — 114
- The Scottish Enlightenment — 115
  - *David Hume* — 116
- 19th-Century Scotland — 117
- The Industrial Revolution — 118
- Politics and Religion — 118
- The Highlands — 119
- World War I and After — 120

World War II and After	121
Stone of Scone	122
North Sea Oil and the Rise of Scottish Nationalism	123
The Establishment of a Scottish Parliament	124

Chapter 14: Wales: The Land and Its People — 126

Relief	128
Snowdonia National Park	129
Drainage	130
Soils	130
Climate	131
Plant and Animal Life	131
Ethnic Groups and Languages	131
Religion	132
Settlement Patterns	132
Caernarfon	133
Demographic Trends	135

Chapter 15: The Welsh Economy — 136

Agriculture, Forestry, and Fishing	136
Milford Haven	137
Resources and Power	137
Manufacturing	137
Services	138
Transportation	138

Chapter 16: Welsh Government and Society — 139

Local Government	140
Justice and Security	140
Political Process	140
Neil Kinnock	141
Health and Welfare	141
Housing	142
Education	142

Chapter 17: Welsh Cultural Life — 144

Daily Life and Social Customs	145

Music, Literature, and Film	145
Dylan Thomas	146
Richard Burton	147
Visual Arts	148
Cultural Institutions	149
Sports and Recreation	150
Media and Publishing	150

Chapter 18: Wales Before the Norman Conquest — 151
Roman Wales (1st–4th Centuries)	151
The Founding of the Kingdoms	152
Early Christianity	152
Political Development	153
Hywel Dda	154
Early Welsh Society	155

Chapter 19: Wales in the Middle Ages — 157
Norman Infiltration	157
Gwynedd, Powys, and Deheubarth	158
Llywelyn ap Iorwerth	160
The Edwardian Settlement	161
Rebellion and Annexation	162
Owen Glendower	162

Chapter 20: Wales from the 16th to the 21st Century — 164
Union with England	164
The Reformation	165
Social Change	166
Politics and Religion, 1640–1800	166
The Growth of Industrial Society	168
Rebecca Riots	169
Political Radicalism	170
The 20th Century and Beyond	171

Conclusion	174
Glossary	175
Bibliography	177
Index	180

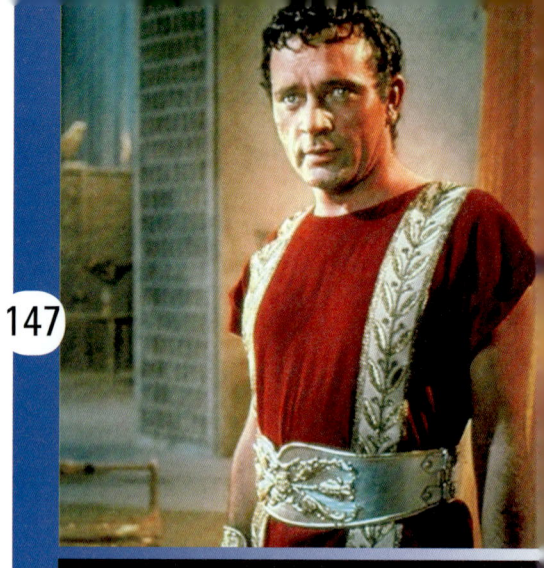

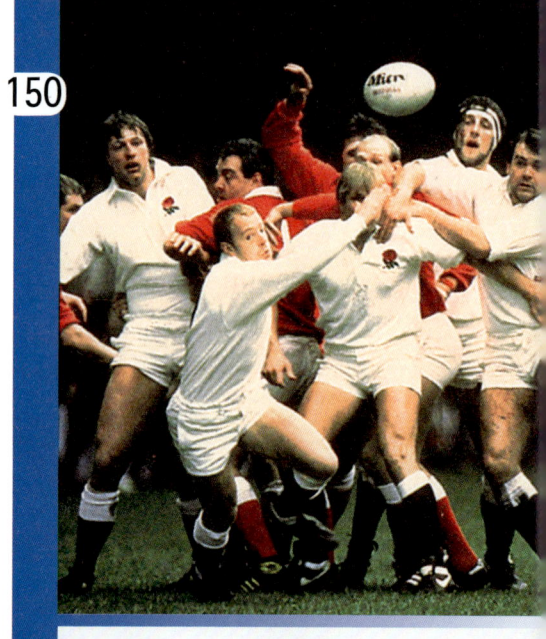

INTRODUCTION

UNITED KINGDOM

- Shetland Islands
- Orkney Islands
- Hebrides
- Scotland
  - Glasgow
  - Edinburgh
- North Atlantic Ocean
- North Sea
- Northern Ireland
  - Belfast
- Ireland
- Irish Sea
- St. George's Channel
- Liverpool
- Wales
  - Cardiff
- England
  - Oxford
  - London
  - Brighton
- Straight of Dover
- English Channel
- France

Creative Jen Designs/Shutterstock.com

While Northern Ireland, Scotland, and Wales have long been joined with England in forming the United Kingdom, it would be a mistake to think of these places as one homogeneous country. Northern Ireland, Scotland, and Wales all have their own identity and cultural personality, making them not only distinct from England but also distinct from each other. Indeed, one thing they do share is a fierce determination to maintain a separate and unique national character, and this strong pride has periodically stirred longings for independence that have led to political action that has challenged the makeup of the United Kingdom.

How Northern Ireland, Scotland, and Wales evolved such strong identities and how they have overcome frequent tensions to participate productively in the United Kingdom are two of the most fascinating aspects of this book. The story is all the more compelling because each of the three has made its mark indelibly on the world's history and culture.

Northern Ireland is a particularly interesting case because being part of the United Kingdom has separated it politically from the rest of the island of Ireland, of which it comprises about one-sixth. Northern Ireland and its larger neighbour, the republic of Ireland, have been separate political entities since the 1920s. Though the separation is political, religion has played no small role. The majority of Northern Ireland's citizens are Protestant, which distinguishes it from the republic of Ireland, which is predominantly Roman Catholic. In Northern Ireland, the coexistence between the Protestant majority and a growing Catholic minority has long been uneasy.

Political and religious tensions have frequently bubbled over into violence, which has hampered the development of Northern Ireland's economy. The economy also suffered from the fact that many of the traditional heavy industries that developed in Northern Ireland in the 19th century—textile manufacture and shipbuilding in particular—went into decline in the later 20th century. As a result of these ongoing economic woes, Northern Ireland has been heavily subsidized by the British government and receives additional assistance from the European Union.

For much of its history, Northern Ireland has been largely governed from London by the British government and Parliament, to which Northern Ireland—like Scotland and Wales—elects representatives. However, in recent years self-government has increased dramatically in Northern Ireland, a trend that has depended on the ability of its often bitterly divided political factions to work together.

As often has been the case elsewhere in the world, the climate of tension in Northern Ireland has contributed to a vibrant cultural scene, which encompasses the contributions of novelist C.S. Lewis, poet Seamus Heaney, playwright Brian Friel, and singer-songwriter Van Morrison. Indeed, religious and political tension tend to be recurring themes in Northern Ireland's art.

Although Northern Ireland has existed as a political entity only since the 1920s, the history of the region reaches back many centuries. What is now Northern Ireland evolved out of the ancient Irish province of Ulster, the northernmost of Ireland's four traditional provinces (the others being Leinster, Munster, and Connaught).

Ancient Ulster extended from the northern and northeastern coasts of Ireland south to what is now County Louth and west to what is now County Donegal. About the beginning of the Common Era, when the ancient provinces of Ireland were first taking permanent shape, Ulster had its capital at Emain Macha, near Armagh. Christianity began to take hold in the region in the 5th century. Though Ulster was dominated for centuries by the O'Neill dynasty, by the 11th century the O'Neills' rule was challenged, first by other Irish nobles, and later by Normans from England and Wales. At first the English grip on Ulster was fairly loose, but it tightened significantly in the 16th and 17th centuries with the plantation (forced settlement) of Scottish and English immigrants and the extension of English law.

The English also introduced what was to have an enduring impact on Ulster's history—the Protestant religion. Protestantism took root in Ulster, but Catholicism remained dominant in the rest of Ireland.

As time went on, a movement for self-government in Ireland gained strength and became a prominent and divisive topic of both Irish and British politics in the late 19th and early 20th centuries. The predominantly Protestant counties of Ulster, however, feared domination by the Catholic south, and many Ulstermen became "unionists" determined not to sever their links with the United Kingdom. When the rest of the island began its journey towards independence as the republic of Ireland, six of Ulster's nine counties remained in the United Kingdom. This left Northern Ireland Irish, yet not part of Ireland, and within the United Kingdom. Yet geographically (and in many ways culturally) it remained separate from the United Kingdom. Decades of struggle within Northern Ireland would culminate in violence, the so-called "Troubles" of the 1970s, from which Northern Ireland would emerge with relative peace and power-sharing rule.

Unlike Northern Ireland, Scotland, which occupies the northern-most third of the island of Great Britain, is connected geographically with England, yet its national character and history are colourfully distinct from those of its southern neighbours. Its northerly location gives Scotland a harsh climate, which has been a challenge to its people and economy through the centuries. This climate, however, is far from the only difficulty Scotland has faced. For much of its history, Scotland was torn by conflict between the Celtic Scots of the Highlands and the Anglo-Saxons of the Lowlands. Indeed it was not until the 20th century that those groups finally seemed to see the value of their common culture and sense of tradition.

Modern Scotland has successfully made the transition from an economy dependent on declining heavy industries to one based on thriving sectors such as energy and technology. Scotland's economic self-sufficiency has increasingly gone hand in hand with a growing spirit of independence. This independence led to the 1997 referendum that resulted in the creation of a separate Scottish Parliament in Edinburgh that shares authority with the British Parliament. Internal matters such as housing and education are governed by the Scots body, while broader responsibilities such as defense and trade are handled in London. The degree of Scottish autonomy and whether Scotland should be fully independent remain topics of lively debate.

Scotland has always maintained a unique cultural identity. Whether it is tartans and kilts, whisky and bagpipes, or the instantly recognizable burr of Scottish pronunciation, there are a number of highly distinct cultural signatures that are instantly associated with Scotland. This volume considers that rich cultural legacy as well as a history filled with larger-than-life heroes and high drama.

A very tangible symbol of Scottish independence can be found in Hadrian's Wall, which dates from the second century CE and remains partially intact today. This is where the invading Romans drew the line marking the northern reach of their conquest of Britain; having found Scotland too wild to successfully occupy, the Romans chose instead to wall it off from their settlements to the south.

To the north of Hadrian's Wall, four distinct peoples—the Picts, Scots, Angles, and Britons—gradually merged into one Scottish kingdom. Yet another influence came from the Vikings, whose initial raids into Scotland began late in the 8th century and whose occupation of what are today some of the Scottish isles continued well into the 15th century.

Out of these different influences, a unified Scottish monarchy developed. Meanwhile, a theme was emerging that would recur throughout Scottish history: Scotland and its leaders would both develop close ties with English rulers and frequently battle them for independence. These battles yielded figures who remain heroes today, such as William Wallace and Robert the Bruce, but the story is more complicated than simply Scots against English. Disputes over succession between rivals to the Scottish throne sometimes created an opening for English rulers to attempt to assert authority over Scotland. Yet another complicating influence was brought to bear when Scotland enlisted France as an ally against the English.

Ironically, unification of the English and Scottish thrones came not by English conquest of Scotland but when Elizabeth I of England named James VI of Scotland to succeed her as James I of England in 1603. Even this unification of the crown did not represent full political union between the two nations, which was not completed until the Act of Union in 1707.

Despite periodic resistance, the link between England and Scotland has endured, and in the 18th century political intrigue gave way to the Scottish Enlightenment, a period of extraordinary intellectual achievement that produced figures who are still seen as giants in their fields, including philosopher David Hume, economist Adam Smith, and poet Robert Burns. In the centuries that followed, Scotland would continue to produce leading figures in philosophy, literature, and science. In short, even while Scotland was no longer independent from England, it increasingly put a uniquely Scottish imprint on the world.

Compared with its Northern Irish and Scottish companions in the United Kingdom, Wales has a somewhat quieter and less bloody history. Nonetheless, this nation also retains a distinct cultural heritage.

Wales bulges out from the west side of the island of Great Britain, and through the centuries its rugged mountains and deep valleys helped it maintain a physical isolation from neighbouring England, though politically the two have been joined for centuries. The geographic isolation of many parts of Wales nurtured a distinct culture. Originally, its people were Celts, though Saxons and Normans from England began entering Wales early in its history. Although the Celtic-derived Welsh language would eventually give way to English as Wales's dominant tongue (especially during the 20th century), Welsh is still spoke by about one-fifth of the population. Moreover there are active efforts to preserve its use, including the Welsh Language Act (1993), which established in principle the equality of Welsh and English in Wales.

In the industrial age, the Welsh economy became largely based on coal mining, but as heavy industry declined, Wales diversified its economy. Today tourism is especially important as both the striking Welsh countryside and the unique local culture remain attractions for visitors from the rest of the United Kingdom and throughout Europe.

Historically, the experience of the Celtic Welsh tribes was similar to that of many local peoples throughout Europe, with among the first influences from the outside world coming from Roman occupation and later from the introduction of Christianity. Despite these shared influences, however, for the first millennium of the Common Era the people of Wales were anything but unified. Instead, the land that is now Wales was dotted with independent and often competing kingdoms, whose divisions were further complicated by disputes over ruling succession. Generally, the only thing that united these different factions was resistance to domination by England, which came nonetheless in the late 13th century with occupation under Edward I.

Union with England was formally completed in the 16th century during the reign of Henry VIII, who incorporated the government of Wales into that of England, while granting Welshmen the same legal status as English citizens. Wales and England remain closely linked today, though through the centuries there has been a persistent movement to maintain a separate Welsh identity, often centred on efforts to preserve the Welsh language.

Recent years have seen a tangible step towards greater autonomy through the creation of a Welsh assembly. This assembly does not have the same scope of authority as the Scottish Parliament, so thus far the movement towards potential autonomy is not as far along in Wales as it is in Scotland.

Ironically, though Northern Ireland, Scotland, and Wales have all chafed to some degree at being part of the United Kingdom, the late 20th century saw them become part of an even broader cooperative organization in the European Union. This organization earned a Nobel Peace Prize in 2012 for its work in fostering cooperation among nations, providing an example of what individual countries have to gain when they choose to work together.

Whether Northern Ireland, Scotland, and Wales remain joined with England in the United Kingdom, or whether their respective independence movements advance still further remains to be seen. This book describes the histories and unique cultural identities that make the pull of independence so strong in these countries, and thus provides a background for a better understanding of how events play out in the years ahead.

CHAPTER 1

NORTHERN IRELAND: THE LAND AND ITS PEOPLE

Lying in the northeastern quadrant of the island of Ireland, on the western continental periphery often characterized as Atlantic Europe, Northern Ireland is sometimes referred to as Ulster, although it includes only six of the nine counties that made up that historic Irish province. Northern Ireland has long witnessed generations of newcomers and emigrants, including Celts from continental Europe and Vikings, Normans, and Anglo-Saxons. In the 17th century, the period of the so-called Ulster plantation, thousands of Scottish Presbyterians were forcibly resettled and English military garrisons built, arrivals that would institutionalize the ethnic, religious, and political differences that eventually resulted in violent conflict.

Beginning in the 1920s, when it was officially separated from Ireland, Northern Ireland has long been tormented by sectarian violence. Notwithstanding the success of peacemaking efforts that began in earnest in the mid-1990s, Northern Ireland is still often best navigated by those who are skilled in the shibboleths and cultural codes that demarcate its peoples, governing which football (soccer) team to cheer

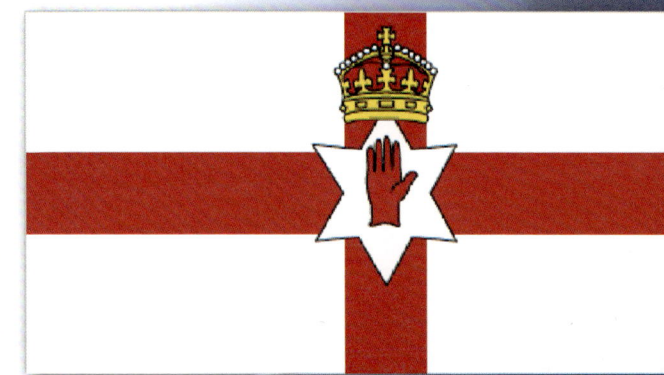

The North Channel coast south of Torr Head, Northern Ireland. © Michael Jennet/Robert Harding Picture Library

Northern Ireland

for, which whisky to drink, and which song to sing. The complexity of these political markers is captured in the graffito once scrawled on Belfast walls that read "If you are not confused you don't understand the situation." But, more recently, Northern Ireland's political fortunes have changed for the better, and with that change has come a flourishing of the arts, so that increasingly outsiders associate the country not with violent politics but with the poems of Seamus Heaney, the music of Van Morrison, and other contributions to world culture.

The capital is Belfast, a modern city whose historic centre was badly damaged by aerial bombardment during World War II. Once renowned for its shipyard—the *Titanic* was built there—Belfast has lost much of its industrial base. The city—as with Northern Ireland's other chief cities Londonderry (known locally and historically as Derry) and Armagh—is graced with parks and tidy residential neighbourhoods. More handsome still is the Northern Irish countryside—green, fertile, and laced with rivers and lakes, all of which have found lyrical expression in the nation's folk and artistic traditions.

Northern Ireland occupies about one-sixth of the island of Ireland and is separated on the east from Scotland, another part of the United Kingdom, by the narrow North Channel, which is at one point only 13 miles (21 km) wide. The Irish Sea separates Northern Ireland from England and Wales on the east and southeast, respectively, and the Atlantic Ocean lies to the north. The southern and western borders are with the republic of Ireland.

RELIEF

Northern Ireland can be thought of topographically as a saucer centred on Lough (lake) Neagh, the upturned rim of which forms the highlands. Five of the six historic counties—Antrim, Down, Armagh, Tyrone, and Londonderry—meet at the lake, and each has a highland region on the saucer's rim. To the north and east the mountains of Antrim (physiographically a plateau) tilt upward toward the coast. They reach an elevation of 1,817 feet (554 metres) at Trostan, with the plateau terminating in an impressive cliff coastline

Part of the Mourne Mountains astride Down district and Newry and Mourne district, Northern Ireland. G.F. Allen—Bruce Coleman

The United Kingdom: Northern Ireland, Scotland, and Wales

of basalts and chalk that is broken by a series of the glaciated valleys known as glens, which face Scotland and are rather isolated from the rest of Northern Ireland. The rounded landscape of drumlins—smooth, elongated mounds left by the melting ice of the final Pleistocene glaciation—in the southeast is punctuated by Slieve Croob, which rises to 1,745 feet (532 metres), and culminates in the Mourne Mountains, which reach an elevation of 2,789 feet (850 metres) at Slieve Donard (Northern Ireland's highest point) within 2 miles (3 km) of the sea. This impressive landscape of granite peaks is bounded by Carlingford Lough to the south.

The scenery to the south of Lough Neagh is gentler, but the land rises to 1,886 feet (575 metres) in Slieve Gullion near the border with Ireland. West of Lough Neagh the land rises gently to the more rounded Sperrin Mountains; Sawel, at 2,224 feet (678 metres), is the highest of several hills over 2,000 feet (610 metres).

DRUMLIN

Drumlins are oval or elongated hills believed to have been formed by the streamlined movement of glacial ice sheets across rock debris, or till. They take their name from the Gaelic word *druim* ("rounded hill," or "mound"). Drumlins are generally found in broad lowland regions, with their long axes roughly parallel to the path of glacial flow. Although they come in a variety of shapes, the glacier side is always high and steep, while the lee side is smooth and tapers gently in the direction of ice movement. Drumlins can vary widely in size, with lengths from 1 to 2 km (0.6 to 1.2 miles), heights from 15 to 30 metres (50 to 100 feet), and widths from 400 to 600 metres.

Drumlin near a beach in Clew Bay, County Mayo, Ireland. Brendanconway

> Most drumlins are composed of till, but they may vary greatly in their composition. Some contain significant amounts of gravels, whereas others are made up of rock underlying the surface till (rock drumlins). Drumlins are often associated with smaller, glacially streamlined bedrock forms known as roches moutonnées.
>
> Drumlins are commonly found in clusters numbering in the thousands. Often arranged in belts, they disrupt drainage so that small lakes and swamps may form between them. In addition to being found in Northern Ireland and the Irish republic, large drumlin fields are also located in central Wisconsin, central New York, northwestern Canada, and southwestern Nova Scotia.

The far southwest, the historic County Fermanagh, is focused geographically on the basin of Lough Erne, in a drumlin-strewn area ringed by hills more than 1,000 feet (300 metres) high.

DRAINAGE

Much of the landscape of Northern Ireland is gentle, and in most low-lying areas it is covered with swarms of drumlins that have played havoc with the local drainage and are interspersed with marshy hollows. Glaciation also gave the land its main valleys: those of the River Bann (which drains Lough Neagh to the Atlantic Ocean) in the north, the River Blackwater in the southwest, and the River Lagan in the east. All these valleys have been important routeways, but none have been more important than the Lagan, penetrating from Belfast Lough to the very heart of Ulster.

SOILS

Soils are varied. Although much glacially transported material covers the areas below 700 feet (215 metres) in elevation, the nature of the soil is predominantly influenced by the underlying parent rock. Brown earth soils, forming arable loams, are extensive and are derived from the ancient Silurian rocks of the southeast—some 420 million years old—and from the more recent basalts of the northeast. There are peaty gleys and podzols in the Sperrins, and the impeded drainage of much of the southwest gives rise to acidic brown soil. Peat soils are common, particularly in the hollows lying between the drumlins, and hill peat is widespread throughout Northern Ireland. Although it is of no great commercial value, peat traditionally has been a source of fuel for the peasant farmer and is still cut extensively.

CLIMATE

Northern Ireland's climate is temperate and maritime; most of its weather comes from the southwest in a series of low-pressure systems bringing the rain and clouds that often lend character to the landscape.

Because Northern Ireland is near the central track of such lows, it often experiences high winds. In the north and on the east coast, particularly, severe westerly gales are common. Above the 800-foot (245-metre) level, distorted trees and windbreaks testify to the severity of the weather. Annual rainfall decreases from west to east, although the hills accentuate the amount to some 80 inches (2,000 mm) in parts of the west, and there is as little as 32.5 inches (825 mm) at Lough Neagh and the extreme southeast. A relatively dry spring gives way to a wet summer and a wetter winter. Daily conditions generally are highly changeable, but there are no extremes of heat and cold. The region is exposed to the ameliorating effects of the North Atlantic Current, a northeastward extension of the Gulf Stream. Average January temperatures vary from 38°F (3.3°C) on the north coast to 35°F (1.7°C) in the east; in July temperatures of 65°F (18.3°C) are common. In late spring and early summer the east has slightly lower temperatures accompanied by coastal fog. These mild and humid climatic conditions have, in sum, made Northern Ireland a green country in all seasons.

PLANT AND ANIMAL LIFE

The general features of the vegetation of Northern Ireland are similar to those in the northwest of Britain. The human imprint is heavy on the landscape and is particularly evident in the absence of trees. Most of the land has been plowed, drained, and cultivated for centuries. Above the limit of cultivation, rough pastures are grazed extensively, and beyond them lies a zone of mountain vegetation. Only about 5 percent of the land is now under forest, and most of this has been planted by the state. Young trees in these plantations are economically unimportant, but locally they help to diversify the landscape.

The fauna of Northern Ireland is not very different from that of Great Britain. There are, however, fewer species of mammals and birds. Only two mammals—the Irish stoat and the Irish hare—and three species of birds are exclusively Irish. The region is rich in fish, particularly pike, perch, trout, and salmon; the first is the only fish introduced in historic times.

As the result of ongoing concern with conservation, there are some 40 nature reserves and several bird sanctuaries controlled by the Ulster Wildlife Trust and by the Department of the Environment.

ETHNIC GROUPS AND LANGUAGES

The cultural differences that underlie many of Northern Ireland's contemporary social problems have a long and troubled history. The region has had lasting links with parts of western Scotland, strengthened by constant population movements. After the Tudor invasions and particularly after the forced settlements, or plantations, of the early 17th century, English and Scottish elements were further differentiated from the native Irish by their Protestant faith. Two distinct and often antagonistic groupings—the indigenous Roman Catholic Irish and the immigrant Protestant English and Scots—date from that period, and they have played a significant role in molding Northern Ireland's development. The settlers dominated County Antrim and northern Down, controlled the Lagan corridor toward Armagh, and also formed powerful minorities elsewhere.

This situation contributed to the decline of spoken Irish (Gaelic), and it is reflected in the contemporary distribution of religions. The accents with which Northern Irish people speak English are regionally distinctive. The northeastern dialect, dominating the historic counties of Antrim and Londonderry and parts of Down, is an offshoot of central Scottish dialect. The remainder of the area, including the Lagan valley, has accents derived from England, more particularly from Cheshire, Merseyside, Greater Manchester, and southern Lancashire, as well as the West Country counties of Gloucestershire, Avon, Somerset, and Devon. The towns show more of a mixture and an overlay of standard English.

Northern Ireland's political divisions are partly reflected through language. Although English is near-universally spoken by everyone in the six counties, Irish also is spoken by a small but significant and growing proportion of the population and is an important element of the cultural identity for many northern nationalists (Roman Catholics who support unification with Ireland)—even those with limited knowledge of the language. Unionists (Protestants who support Northern Ireland's status as a constituent element of the United Kingdom), on the other hand, tend to distrust and dismiss Irish as a cultural expression of political divisiveness.

RELIGION

The demographic balance between Protestants and Roman Catholics in Northern Ireland is becoming increasingly delicate. Catholics now make up about two-fifths of the population, and their slightly higher birth rate has led to speculation that they eventually will become the larger of the "two communities." Although Protestants continue to be a majority, they are perhaps best thought of as a "majority of minorities," in that the Protestant community comprises a mosaic of distinct denominations that vary enormously in size. The most substantial Protestant denomination in Northern Ireland, the Presbyterians, makes up more than one-fifth of the population. About one in six people belong to the next biggest Protestant denomination, the Anglican Church of Ireland. The remainder of the Protestant population is fragmented among dozens of smaller religious groupings.

Protestant and Catholic communities are not distributed evenly. During the political violence of the last third of the 20th century, many Protestants moved away from western and border areas of Northern Ireland. As a result, the historic counties of Londonderry, Fermanagh, and Tyrone now have marked Catholic majorities, while the traditional concentration of Protestants in the eastern reaches has increased. One important exception to this rule is Belfast on the eastern seaboard, where Catholics have become the majority. During the "Troubles"—the term used euphemistically to describe the violence between Catholics and Protestants in Northern Ireland—many wealthy Protestants from Belfast relocated to the pastoral environs of northern Down while their less privileged counterparts moved to the bleak estates that sprung up in the satellite towns that ring the city.

Northern Ireland is also marked by stark patterns of residential segregation. Even when Catholics and Protestants reside in the same part of the region, they tend to live separately from one another. Indeed, about half the Northern Irish live in districts in which nine-tenths or more of residents are drawn from one of the two communities. This segregation, especially evident in Belfast, is even more pronounced in poorer neighbourhoods. The hostilities between adjacent working-class districts composed of different ethnoreligious communities have led to the creation of "peace lines," essentially permanent structures aimed at keeping the warring factions apart. The complex sectarian geography of Northern Ireland places often severe constraints upon the physical mobility of working-class residents in particular and has an important impact upon the manner in which everyday life is organized and experienced. In the interest of self-preservation, young people learn early to recognize the various cues that indicate ethnoreligious identity.

SETTLEMENT PATTERNS

The traditional regions of Northern Ireland correspond closely to the main topographic elements, although they are also the outcome of the cultural evolution of the area. In the north and east the influence of the Scots and English has been paramount. West of Lough Neagh and in the fastness of the Mourne Mountains and of Slieve Gullion, as well as in the more distant Lough Erne region, indigenous elements have maintained a distinctiveness. Such relatively isolated pockets as the glens of the northeast coast and Kilkeel on the southeast coast retain a local consciousness that gives colour and interest to the human geography of Northern Ireland.

The predominant impression of Northern Ireland's landscape is of scattered and isolated farms. Occasional relics of tiny hamlets, or clachans, show that peasant crofts once were huddled together and worked by kinship groups in an open-field system. Between the end of the 18th and the middle of the 19th century, most of the land was enclosed and the scattered strips consolidated, partly as a policy of the landlords but finally because of the decline in rural population after the Potato Famine of the 1840s. The end result was the orderly, small square fields that dominate the contemporary landscape. Some landlords rearranged their tenants' land in narrow ribbons, from valley bottom to mountain pasture, giving a characteristic ladder of fields with the farms strung along the road on the valley side. Drumlins also have had an effect on siting; houses are found away from the peaty bottomlands but below the windswept skyline. Most farmhouses are small, and a few are still thatched. The occasional larger farm often has a Georgian house—simple and dignified, a reflection of the age of consolidation.

Small market towns rather than villages are common. Built by the English and Scottish planters or by the landlords of the 18th century, they have a foreign touch of orderliness and urbanity. Many are grouped around a "diamond" (meeting place), which is used as a marketplace. Some of these towns acquired a mill in the 19th century, but in few cases has this changed the essentially rural context.

Few of the market centres have grown into substantial towns. In the western half of Northern Ireland, regional services and administration have enlarged Omagh and Enniskillen. Some towns have grown with the introduction of industry, particularly Dungannon, which specializes in fabrics, and Carrickfergus, now noted for aluminum castings and telecommunications cables.

CARRICKFERGUS

The town of Carrickfergus (Irish: Carraig Fhearghais) sits on the northern shore of Belfast Lough. Its name, meaning "rock of Fergus," commemorates King Fergus, who was shipwrecked off the coast about 320 CE. Because of its strategic position on a rocky spur above the harbour, Carrickfergus Castle, a perfectly preserved relic of the Norman period, has played a large part in Irish history. It was besieged and taken by the Scot Edward Bruce, brother of King Robert I the Bruce, in 1316, but reverted to English rule in 1318 and remained an isolated stronghold of the English crown. In the English Civil Wars (1642–51) the castle was one of the chief places of refuge for the Protestants of Antrim; in 1642 the first presbytery held in Ireland met there. It was later held by partisans of the English king James II but was surrendered in 1689 to the duke of Schomberg, and in 1690 William III landed there on his expedition to Ireland.

Although chartered since the reign of Elizabeth I, the corporation of Carrickfergus town was superseded in 1840 by a board of municipal commissioners. Carrickfergus was the county town (seat) of Antrim until 1850. The parish Church of St. Nicholas, begun by John de Courci at the end of the 12th century, is renowned for its monument (1625) to Lord Chichester, lord deputy of Ireland (1604–14). Carrickfergus district is bordered by Newtownabbey district to the west and Larne district to the north. Its northwestern section is hilly terrain, sloping southward to the flat shores of Belfast Lough.

Armagh is an ecclesiastical centre with two cathedrals, while Lisburn, Lurgan, and Portadown, all in the Lagan valley, form an extension of the Belfast industrial complex, their size a product of the textile industry. Bangor is a resort and a residential outlier of Belfast. Londonderry, a centre for shirtmaking, was the heart of the Lough Foyle lowlands until the hinterland that it served was split by the partition of Ireland, but it remains the main focus of the west. The size of Belfast, at the head of Belfast Lough on the northeast coast, underlines its dominance of the region, as well as its significance as an industrial centre and major port. Shipbuilding, linen manufacturing, and engineering have declined in Belfast, but shipping remains a major employer, and the aircraft industry has gained in importance. The city is also the centre of government, finance, education, and culture. Reflecting Belfast's 19th-century origin, most of the streets are inextricably and bleakly mixed with mills and factories, while the reclaimed land at the head of Belfast Lough is given over entirely to industry.

DEMOGRAPHIC TRENDS

In terms of population, Northern Ireland is the smallest part of the United Kingdom, and its demographic profile differs from that of Great Britain in a number of ways. Although the Northern Irish birth rate declined over the last two decades of the 20th century, it remains relatively high by British standards. Since partition, emigration from Northern Ireland has tended to outpace immigration; however, the net outflow of people from the region has been relatively small, especially when compared with the mass emigration that has typified Ireland in various periods. The combination of a relatively high birth rate and negligible out-migration has contributed to a gradual rise in the population of Northern Ireland. The population of Northern Ireland is comparatively young in relation to that of the rest of the United Kingdom.

CHAPTER 2

THE NORTHERN IRISH ECONOMY

Northern Ireland's economy is closely bound to that of the rest of the United Kingdom. Although historically the economic links between Northern Ireland and its closest neighbour, the republic of Ireland, were remarkably underdeveloped, trade between the two has grown substantially. Compared with the rest of the United Kingdom, the economy of Northern Ireland has long suffered, largely a result of political and social turmoil. To spur economic development, in the 1980s the British and Irish governments created the International Fund for Ireland, which disburses economic assistance to the entire island, with significant resources going to Northern Ireland. Northern Ireland also receives economic assistance from the European Union.

AGRICULTURE, FORESTRY, AND FISHING

While agriculture historically played an important part in the economy of Northern Ireland, its significance has declined greatly over recent decades. As in other developed societies, the introduction of new technologies has accelerated a process of consolidation, and there are now fewer but substantially larger and more productive farms. In the process, agriculture has become a relatively insignificant source of employment. At the beginning of the 21st century, less than 5 percent of people in Northern Ireland earned a living from the land, though about three-fourths of the total land area was used for agriculture, forestry, and livestock.

Sheep grazing on the Antrim coast. Milt and Joan Mann/Cameramann International

Northern Ireland's frequent rainfall, humidity, and prospect of wet harvests discourage arable farming, but local conditions produce good grass and rich pasture. Nearly all grassland is plowed, and there is little "rough grazing." Mixed farming was traditionally universal, but there has been a considerable movement toward specialization. Nearly half the farms concentrate on sheep and beef, and about one-fifth specialize in dairying. Principal crops include potatoes, barley, wheat, and oats; turnips are grown to feed livestock. The production of grass seed and seed potatoes for export is also important. To the south of Lough Neagh lies a rich orchard country, and apple growing and market gardening are constant features of the landscape. Most of the agricultural land is held by the occupiers in fee simple, but there persists the peculiar feature of conacre, a system of short (11-month) lets, on a portion of the agricultural land. About two-thirds of the farmers are "working owners."

Forestry is not an important industry in Northern Ireland, as much of the native forests were cleared by the end of the 19th century. At the beginning of the 20th century, with about 1 percent of the land forested, the government encouraged reforestation. In 1919 the Forestry

Commission was established to develop policy, and afforestation efforts occurred throughout much of the 20th century. By the end of the century, about 200,000 acres (81,000 hectares) were forested, with about three-fourths of the woodland administered by the Forestry Service. Most of the limited timber production, which accounts for a tiny fraction of employment and gross domestic product (GDP), occurs on state-owned lands.

Ocean fishing is more or less confined to the northern Irish Sea and is limited to trawlers that operate primarily from the ports of Kilkeel, Ardglass, and Portavogie. Prawns, cod, whiting, and herring are among the main catches. There has been increasing development of marine farming, particularly for oysters. Inland, salmon and eel fishing is traditional, the latter concentrated where the River Bann leaves Lough Neagh.

RESOURCES AND POWER

Northern Ireland is not rich in minerals, and mining contributes little to the economy. Less than 1 percent of workers are employed in mining. Among the minerals found are basalt, limestone, chalk, clay, salt, and shale, and there is some iron ore, bauxite, and coal. Hydroelectric resources are not significant, and peat is used as a domestic source of fuel. There are also limited petroleum and natural gas reserves. In the early 21st century an electrical interconnector with Scotland was built to connect Northern Ireland to the European grid, and the interconnector with the grid in the Irish republic was restored. Indeed, in 2007 the Single Electricity Market (SEM) began operation, providing a single wholesale market for electricity for the whole island of Ireland. The Scotland to Northern Ireland natural gas transmission pipeline (SNIP) provides an important industrial and domestic energy source. A gas pipeline completed in 2006 runs from Dublin to Antrim, and another (completed in 2004) connects Derry with a point near Carrickfergus.

MANUFACTURING

During the 19th century the counties that would eventually form Northern Ireland underwent a rapid process of industrialization. In the decades before World War I, the Lagan valley formed with Merseyside and Clydeside a network that was the heart of the British imperial economy. Belfast became the site of many linen mills, rope factories, and heavy engineering concerns. For a time the city produced a greater tonnage of shipping than any other port in the world.

The 20th century, in contrast, was marked by a slow though inexorable industrial decline. Although this trend was reversed somewhat by the outbreak of World War II, the structural weakness of Northern Irish manufacturing became increasingly apparent in the decades that followed. In the mid 1960s the government offered inducements to multinational corporations to invest in Northern Ireland, but, while many foreign companies agreed to establish factories there, the new approach failed to stem the collapse of the manufacturing sector in the last decades of the century.

Two principal factors are responsible for the deindustrialization of Northern Ireland. First, the sustained political violence that overtook the region in the late 1960s has undermined local manufacturing. Ultimately, the executives of multinational corporations have proved reluctant to establish branch plants in a part of the developed world that has become synonymous with political upheaval. Second, the industrial collapse of Northern Ireland must be seen in the wider context of the reconstruction of the global economy. Since the oil price rises of the early 1970s, Western corporations have systematically closed factories in developed societies and transferred production to low-wage economies in the less-developed world.

Like the economic life of many other developed countries, that of Northern Ireland has essentially become postindustrial. Indeed, many of the factories that drove Northern Ireland's industrial economy at its height now stand idle or await conversion to luxury apartments. The shipyards in Belfast stumble from one threatened closure to the next. At the end of the 20th century the manufacturing sector that once employed more than half the Northern Irish workforce provided work for less than one in five.

JOHN DELOREAN

The American automobile manufacturer and entrepreneur John DeLorean (born January 6, 1925, Detroit, Michigan, U.S.—died March 19, 2005, Summit, New Jersey) established the DeLorean Motor Co. near Belfast in the late 1970s. In 1981 it produced the stainless-steel gull-winged DeLorean DMC-12 sports coupe, which sparked the imagination of millions of filmgoers after being featured as a time machine in the blockbuster movie *Back to the Future* (1985). Nevertheless, DeLorean's tenure as an independent carmaker was brief, and the plant closed in 1982, having produced fewer than 10,000 vehicles.

That year DeLorean was charged with conspiring to distribute $24 million in cocaine in an attempt to salvage his flailing company, but he was later acquitted of criminal charges. He was also accused of embezzlement, defaulting on loans, tax evasion, and defrauding investors in his company (including comedian Johnny Carson) out of millions of dollars. Although DeLorean was cleared of the fraud charges, he declared bankruptcy in 1999.

A rising star in the automotive industry, DeLorean had helped to revitalize Packard before leaving in 1956 to join General Motors. While at GM, DeLorean launched (1964) the highly successful Pontiac GTO and advanced to become at age 40 the youngest general manager in GM's history. The innovative DeLorean claimed more than 200 automotive patents.

FINANCE

Unified fiscally with the United Kingdom, Northern Ireland's official currency is the British pound sterling. The three primary revenue sources include a share of the United Kingdom's revenue from customs and excise, income, value-added, and capital gains taxes, as well as the national insurance surcharge; nontax revenue collected locally, such as rates (contributions toward the cost of government services) and property taxes; and specific and nonspecific payments from the United Kingdom, which have become increasingly important since the onset of political unrest in the late 1960s. At the beginning of the 21st century, subsidies from the British Treasury accounted for nearly one-third of Northern Ireland's GDP.

TRADE

Most of Northern Ireland's imports come from, and exports go to, other parts of the United Kingdom. The republic of Ireland is Northern Ireland's primary external trading partner and its leading export market. However, Northern Ireland has consistently run a trade deficit with its southern neighbour. Other major trading partners include Germany, France, the Netherlands, and the United States. In the first decade of the 21st century, exports generally decreased to the European Union but increased to the rest of Britain, the republic of Ireland, and the rest of the world. Among the country's principal exports are food and beverages, transport equipment, computer, electrical, and optical equipment, and chemicals and chemical products.

SERVICES

As manufacturing dwindled in significance, the service sector emerged as the linchpin of the Northern Irish economy and now provides about three-fourths of jobs. Retailing, financial services, and real estate are particularly important sources of local private employment; however, the growth of the tertiary sector is also largely due to the expansion of public services that began in the early 1970s. Indeed, it has been suggested that as many as two out of three in the Northern Irish workforce are employed directly or indirectly by the state, especially in the fields of health, education, administration, and security. Because of the political violence that plagued Northern Ireland, for much of the late 20th century the tourist industry was virtually nonexistent. With the signing of the peace agreement between nationalists and unionists in the late 1990s, however, the tourist industry became an important job creator and revenue generator. By the first decade of the 21st century, tourism accounted indirectly for nearly 5 percent of GDP and employment. The vast majority of tourists come from other areas of the United Kingdom and Ireland, and a significant number also visit from the United States, Canada, and Australia.

LABOUR

Local trade unions are affiliated with the Irish Congress of Trade Unions through its Northern Ireland Committee. Most union members belong both to unions associated with this organization and to British-based unions affiliated with the Trades Union Congress.

TRANSPORTATION

One of the more noteworthy features of the countryside of Northern Ireland is a close network of well-maintained roads that connects all parts of the region. Public road transport outside the Belfast municipal service has been nationalized since 1935, and since 1968 the Northern Ireland Transport Holding Company (formerly the Ulster Transport Authority) has also controlled the railways, bus companies, and Belfast airport. The railways diminished rapidly—from 824 miles (1,326 km) to about one-fourth that figure—in the economic reorganization following nationalization. Inland waterways have almost disappeared, although a little commercial traffic still uses the Lower Bann Navigation to Coleraine, and there is some recreational sailing.

Northern Ireland is well connected to the other regions of the United Kingdom by both sea and air. Belfast is one of the major ports in Britain and Ireland and has several miles of quays with modern container-handling facilities. Larne and Derry are the other ports of significance. Coleraine and Warrenpoint handle some freight, and Larne and Belfast handle passenger transport. The Belfast International Airport, near Aldergrove, has regular air service to major cities in Britain, Europe, and North America. The smaller George Best Belfast City Airport has become increasingly popular with commuters traveling to Great Britain and elsewhere.

CHAPTER 3

NORTHERN IRISH GOVERNMENT AND SOCIETY

Because Northern Ireland is a constituent element of the United Kingdom, its head of government is the British prime minister, and its head of state is the reigning monarch. Although the 1920 Government of Ireland Act envisaged separate parliaments exercising jurisdiction over southern and northern Ireland, the architects of the partition anticipated that the new constitutional entity to be known as Northern Ireland would prove too small to be viable and would be rapidly absorbed into a united Ireland. However, because the northern Protestants staunchly opposed the idea of being governed from Dublin, the Irish border has persisted into the 21st century.

The political powers devolved to the new legislature in Belfast by the act of 1920 were considerable (including control of housing, education, and policing), but the new government had little fiscal autonomy and became increasingly reliant upon subsidies from the British government. The form and practice of the new parliament in Belfast mirrored that of Westminster in many respects; for example, the legislature consisted of a Senate and a House of Commons. Under the terms of the partition settlement, London retained control in matters relating to the crown, war and peace, the armed forces, and foreign powers, as well as trade, navigation, and coinage.

When the Irish Free State formally seceded from the British Empire and constituted itself as an independent state in 1949, the British government sought to allay the fears of Protestants in the north by passing legislation stating that

Northern Ireland was and would remain an integral part of the United Kingdom. The Act of Union, which entered into force in 1801, abolished the Irish Parliament and provided for Irish representation in the British Parliament. After the partition of Ireland in 1922, Northern Ireland continued to send representatives to Westminster. Over the years the number of members of Parliament (MPs) elected in Northern Ireland has grown to 18. Northern Ireland also elects delegates to the European Parliament (the legislative branch of the European Union).

In response to a deteriorating political climate in Northern Ireland and to years of horrific levels of communal violence, in March 1972 the British government of Edward Heath suspended the Belfast parliament and Home Rule and began governing the region directly through the secretary of state for Northern Ireland. From the outset the British government sought political settlements that would foster stability and enable the restoration of a revised version of devolved power in the region. However, for more than 25 years a series of attempts to introduce either a power-sharing executive or a new assembly proved unsuccessful.

Nevertheless, political settlements continue to be proffered. On April 10, 1998, the Good Friday Agreement (Belfast Agreement) was signed by representatives of various political factions in Northern Ireland, paving the way, many thought, for the end to the theretofore intractable Troubles. Moreover, referenda based on the agreement were

Parliament Buildings at Stormont, east of Belfast. G.F. Allen/Bruce Coleman, Inc.

passed overwhelmingly on both sides of the Irish border, with about 95 percent of Irish voters and 70 percent of Northern Irish voters endorsing the agreement. While the Good Friday Agreement envisaged changes on many fronts, its central concern was political accommodation between Protestants and Catholics in Northern Ireland.

Under the terms of the initiative, the 108-member assembly established in Belfast is obliged to operate along consociational lines, and the executive includes both unionists (Protestants who support continued British rule of Northern Ireland) and nationalists (Catholics who support a united Ireland). There are six representatives from each of the 18 constituencies in Northern Ireland. The assembly sits at Parliament Buildings, Stormont Estate, in Belfast. The legislature selects a first minister and a deputy

GOOD FRIDAY AGREEMENT

By the mid-1960s the demographic majority that Protestants enjoyed in Northern Ireland ensured that they were able to control the state institutions, and these powers were at times used in ways that disadvantaged the region's Roman Catholic minority (though the extent and even the existence of discrimination in Northern Ireland remain a matter of intense debate). An active civil rights movement emerged in the late 1960s, and incidents of communal violence ensued, which led the British government to send troops to assist in quelling the urban violence. Bombings, assassinations, and rioting between Catholics, Protestants, and British police and troops continued into the early 1990s. A tentative cease-fire was called in 1994, but sporadic violence continued.

Multiparty talks—involving representatives of Ireland, various political parties of Northern Ireland, and the British government—resumed in June 1996 and eventually culminated in the signing in Belfast on April 10, 1998 (that year's Good Friday), of an agreement that called for the establishment of three "strands" of administrative relationships. The first strand provided for the creation of the Northern Ireland Assembly, which would be an elected assembly responsible for most local matters. The second was an institutional arrangement for cross-border cooperation on a range of issues between the governments of Ireland and Northern Ireland. The third called for continued consultation between the British and Irish governments. In a jointly held referendum in Ireland and Northern Ireland on May 22, 1998—the first all-Ireland vote since 1918—the agreement was approved by 94 percent of voters in Ireland and 71 percent in Northern Ireland. However, the wide disparity between Catholic and Protestant support in Northern Ireland (96 percent of Catholics voted in favour of the agreement, but only 52 percent of Protestants did) indicated that efforts to resolve the sectarian conflict would be difficult.

The most severe evidence of division came just four months after the agreement was signed, in August 1998, when a splinter group of the Irish Republican Army (IRA), the Real IRA, killed 29 people in a bombing in the town of Omagh. Moreover, the IRA's failure to decommission its weapons delayed the formation of the Northern Ireland Executive (a branch of the Northern Ireland Assembly), in which Sinn Féin, the political wing of the IRA, was to have two ministers.

On December 2, 1999, the Republic of Ireland modified its constitution, removing its territorial claims to the whole of the island of Ireland, the United Kingdom yielded direct rule of Northern Ireland, new agreements between Ireland and the United Kingdom and between Ireland and Northern Ireland entered into force, and, symbolically, Irish Pres. Mary McAleese had lunch with Queen Elizabeth II.

first minister, both of whom need the support of a majority of unionist and nationalist legislators. Moreover, legislation can be passed in the assembly only if it has the support of a minimum proportion of both unionist and nationalist members.

Initially at least, the powers exercised

by the new assembly were slated to be relatively minor. Control over key issues such as taxation, policing, and criminal justice were retained by Westminster. Further devolution of authority was dependent on the success of the initiative. While opposition to the agreement existed on both sides, it was especially strong among unionists. The future success of the peace process seemed to hinge on whether the issue of "decommissioning" of paramilitary weapons, particularly by the Irish Republican Army, could be resolved. Although considerable progress was made toward decommissioning, there continued to be significant opposition to the peace process by some segments of the unionist community. In 2002 devolved power was suspended, and Northern Ireland was ruled from London. In subsequent years the more moderate parties that negotiated the Good Friday Agreement were supplanted as Northern Ireland's leading parties, making it more difficult to achieve compromise and the return of power to Northern Ireland. In 2007, however, the more hard-line Roman Catholic Sinn Féin and Protestant Democratic Unionist Party (DUP)—the latter having previously refused even to meet with representatives of Sinn Féin—reached a historic settlement to form a power-sharing government, thereby allowing the return of devolved power to Northern Ireland.

LOCAL GOVERNMENT

The former two-tier system of local government—6 counties and a county borough, 24 urban and 26 rural districts—was replaced in 1973 by a single-tier system, paralleling similar changes in the remainder of the United Kingdom; this structure remained unaffected by the local government reorganization in the rest of the United Kingdom in 1996–98. There are now a total of 26 districts, each with an elected council. The status of Belfast and Derry was maintained in their designation as city councils, and 13 other councils—Antrim, Ards, Ballymena, Ballymoney, Carrickfergus, Castlereagh, Coleraine, Craigavon, Larne, Limavady, Lisburn, Newtownabbey, and North Down—have borough status. The councils are responsible for licensing, parks and recreation, environmental health, waste collection, arts and cultural events, local tourism, and economic development. They have an advisory role on regional services such as planning, education, housing, and health and social welfare.

JUSTICE

In most respects the administration of justice parallels the system in the United Kingdom as a whole and is administered by the Crown Court, the High Court, and the Court of Appeal, with final recourse to the House of Lords. Minor offenses are dealt with by a magistrates' court, and others in county courts supervised by a judge and subject to a jury. The exception is politically motivated crimes ("terrorist offenses"), which are heard by a single Crown Court judge with no jury. In 1995 the independent Criminal Cases Review Commission was created to examine convictions and sentencing as part of the appeal process.

POLITICAL PROCESS

All citizens 18 years of age or older are eligible to vote. For elections to the House of Commons in London, members are elected by plurality vote in single-member geographic constituencies. In contrast, elections to the Northern Ireland Assembly and to the European Parliament are conducted by the single-transferable-vote formula, a form of proportional representation that virtually guarantees representation for the various sectarian parties.

From the outset the political culture of Northern Ireland has been dominated by the "border question," with political aspirations in the region often closely associated with ethnoreligious background. The overwhelming majority of Protestants prefer that the union with Great Britain continue, and they most often vote for those parties dedicated to that end. Political attitudes within the Catholic community tend to be more complex. Opinion polls conducted in Northern Ireland indicate that a substantial minority of Catholics are essentially indifferent to the constitutional future of the region, and it seems likely that those Catholics who have secured significant material gains since the introduction of "direct rule" from Westminster tend to be disinterested in the border question. Most Catholics, however, aspire to a united Ireland and vote accordingly. As a result, the Catholic community as a whole is generally characterized as nationalist. The proportion of representatives from unionist parties in the House of Commons generally has been greater than the overall share of Protestants in Northern Ireland.

UNIONIST PARTIES

The finer details of party political life in Northern Ireland tend to reflect the divisions that exist within the two main communities. For most of the 20th century, unionist politics in Northern Ireland was dominated by the Ulster Unionist Party (UUP), but during the unrest that began in the 1960s the monolith of unionism disintegrated into a bewildering array of parties. Consequently, contemporary Ulster unionism has been defined by its accommodation of a host of competing, often contradictory voices. Indeed, in recent elections unionist voters have been faced with the choice of no fewer than six parties, as well as an endless stream of independents.

Nevertheless, since the 1970s, unionist politics in Northern Ireland has been dominated by two main parties: the UUP, whose support declined in the last decades of the 20th century, and its principal competitor, the DUP, which opposed the Good Friday Agreement and traditionally tends to be less open to political compromise than the UUP, perhaps partly because it is supported by more fundamentalist Protestant denominations; following the 2007 elections, however, the DUP agreed to form a power-sharing government with the nationalist Sinn Féin. Another "loyalist" party, the Progressive Unionist Party (PUP), has ties to the paramilitary Ulster Volunteer Force.

NATIONALIST PARTIES

The political allegiances of nationalists are divided between two rather different parties: the Social Democratic and Labour Party (SDLP), the principal voice of Irish nationalism since the 1970s; and Sinn Féin, often characterized as the political wing of the Irish Republican Army (IRA). Appealing primarily to the Catholic middle class, the SDLP has insisted that a resolution of the conflict in Northern Ireland is dependent on dialogue and compromise. Its strategy—centred on unionists and nationalists sharing power and on closer ties between Belfast and Dublin—has proved persuasive to key players in the peace process outside Northern Ireland. Indeed, many terms of the Good Friday Agreement reflect measures the party has long advocated.

In contrast, Sinn Féin traditionally has argued that the Troubles are merely another example of the problems that British imperialism has visited upon Ireland and that the only solution is departure of the British and unification of the island. The IRA's 1995 cease-fire was a historic move away from its traditional commitment to a military solution to end Britain's sovereignty over Northern Ireland. Subsequently Sinn Féin scored electoral gains, even becoming the largest nationalist party (albeit by a small margin) in national and local elections in 2001.

THE ALLIANCE PARTY OF NORTHERN IRELAND

Of the political parties that have sought to attract voters from both unionist and nationalist communities, only the Alliance Party of Northern Ireland (APNI) has had meaningful impact, though despite its success at the polls it has never become a major player in the political affairs of the region. Although formally supportive of the union, it has drawn backing from roughly equal numbers of unionists and nationalists, largely among middle-class liberals. Ironically, the advancing peace process appears to have eroded support for the APNI, one of the few local parties that has consistently championed negotiation and tolerance. Despite its attempt to remain outside either the nationalist or unionist camps within the Northern Ireland Assembly, in 2001 the APNI registered as a unionist party in order to provide a unionist majority for the first minister, saving Northern Ireland from even greater political turmoil.

SECURITY

Policing is a politically contentious matter. After partition, policing in Northern Ireland was the responsibility of the Royal Ulster Constabulary (RUC), whose officers are overwhelmingly drawn from the unionist community, prompting deep distrust of the force by many nationalists. The Good Friday Agreement called for a reformed and smaller police force able to engage the support of the nationalist community. Published in December 2000, the report of the Patten Commission on policing recommended comprehensive reform of policing practice and structures. Many of its recommendations, including changing the RUC's name to the Police Service of Northern Ireland, have been implemented.

Security forces in Northern Ireland (and the rest of the United Kingdom) have long had extensive powers to combat terrorism. In particular, they have special powers to arrest and interrogate individuals suspected of terrorist offenses. The number of people charged with terrorist or other serious offenses to the public order peaked at more than 1,400 in the early 1970s but had declined by about four-fifths that number by the beginning of the 21st century, as loyalist and IRA prisoners were released under provisions of the Good Friday Agreement.

In August 1969 sustained civil unrest led to the introduction of British troops onto the streets of Londonderry and Belfast, and the British army played a central and controversial role in the political tragedy that unfolded. (Significantly, the army recruited a regiment specifically composed of people from Northern Ireland; initially known as the Ulster Defence Regiment, this force merged with the Royal Irish Rangers in 1992 and was renamed the Royal Irish Regiment.) At the height of the Troubles, heavily armed soldiers and police officers were

ROYAL ULSTER CONSTABULARY

Established in 1922, the Royal Ulster Constabulary (RUC) had a paramilitary character until 1970, when the force was remodeled along the lines of police forces in Great Britain. In 1970 the security of Northern Ireland became the responsibility of the RUC, the British army, and the Ulster Defence Regiment (UDR). The British government has tried to keep the RUC as the chief peacekeeping force in Northern Ireland, while the army and the UDR play as minor roles as possible. Frequent complaints of RUC mistreatment of suspects and prisoners have led to investigations and some changes in procedures, such as closed-circuit monitoring of interview rooms at the Castlereagh interrogation centre at Belfast. As part of the reform implemented following the Belfast (Good Friday) Agreement (1998), the RUC was renamed the Police Service of Northern Ireland in 2001.

a common sight in Northern Ireland, with a peak of about 27,000 British troops garrisoned there. As the possibility of a settlement increased, however, the security forces became a much less visible presence, and in 2007 the army contingent was reduced to 5,000 troops, with the responsibility for security transferred completely to the police.

Throughout the Troubles, the Maze prison, located 10 miles (16 km) west of Belfast at a former Royal Air Force airfield, was a symbolic centre of the struggle between unionists and nationalists. The prison sometimes housed up to 1,700 prisoners, including many of the most notorious paramilitary offenders. The prison population was divided along paramilitary lines, with each prisoner responsible to his "commanding officer." As a result, the prison was the site of many protests and violent activities, including hunger strikes, attempts at mass escape, and murder; it was considered by some to be a "university of terror," where both unionist and nationalist prisoners learned how to commit deadlier terrorist offenses after their release. Under the terms of the Good Friday Agreement, most prisoners—including many who were convicted of murder—were released, and the prison was closed in 2000.

HEALTH AND WELFARE

In Northern Ireland the provision of health care is the responsibility of the Department of Health and Social Services. The Queen's University has a large medical faculty that supports the health service. Northern Ireland is also known for its export of doctors and nurses.

Because it has traditionally been the most underdeveloped region of the United Kingdom, Northern Ireland has had a comparatively high incidence of socioeconomic problems. Although joblessness declined in the 1990s, unemployment has remained high relative to the rest of the United Kingdom, and at the beginning of the 21st century only London, North East England, and Scotland had higher levels of unemployment. Moreover, wages are often lower and working conditions worse in Northern Ireland than in the rest of the United Kingdom. The coincidence of relatively high unemployment and comparatively poor wages has meant that the Northern Irish are more likely than British citizens in general to be dependent upon the state.

As in a number of other Western societies at the end of the 20th century, the gap between the rich and poor in Northern Ireland has widened. In 1979 one-tenth of the population of Northern Ireland resided in households earning less than 50 percent of the national average income; by 1999 this proportion had grown to one in four. As the number of relatively poor people has grown, so, too, has the number of comparatively wealthy, partly because of the rise in the number of management and professional positions in the public sector. Moreover, because housing prices are appreciably lower than the British average, the "new middle classes" in Northern Ireland are able to enjoy lifestyles that would be beyond their means if they lived in most other regions of the United Kingdom.

HOUSING

Substandard housing for the Catholic community was one of the grievances that led to protests by Catholics during the 1960s. At that time, less than two-thirds of Catholic homes—compared with about three-fourths of Protestant homes—had hot water. Moreover, the allocation of public housing units was under the control of Protestant-dominated local councils, which were accused of discriminatory practices. Over the last quarter of the 20th century, significant investments were made in housing, eliminating most inequities. Rates of home ownership increased significantly, especially because of policies implemented by the British government that allowed the sale of public housing units to their tenants. Whereas less than half of all homes were owned by their tenants in the early 1970s, by the end of the century more than 70 percent of homes were owner-occupied.

EDUCATION

While education policy in Northern Ireland has been strongly influenced by trends elsewhere within the United Kingdom, the region's schools remain distinctive. Notably, the model of education practiced in Northern Ireland continues to be selective despite the government's elimination in 2008 of the intelligence ("transfer") tests that were administered to most children at about age 11 to determine the type of post-primary school they could attend—a grammar school (selective) or a secondary school (not selective). These "eleven-plus" examinations had been eliminated earlier in most of the rest of the United Kingdom. Although these standardized tests were eliminated in Northern Ireland, schools were still allowed to use selective exams and procedures for admitting students. Grammar schools in Northern Ireland continue to cater to pupils deemed capable of appreciating an academic education; secondary intermediate schools offer more general and vocational training. Traditionally, Northern Irish schools have also segregated along ethnoreligious lines. Although formally open to all, the state-run schools have tended to attract Protestant children. Pupils from nationalist backgrounds typically have attended schools effectively under the control of the Catholic church. However, there are schools that draw more or less equally from both communities.

Northern Ireland has two universities. The Queen's University of Belfast, established in 1845 as one of three in Ireland, has had a charter since 1908. The University of Ulster was established in 1984 by the merger of the New University of Ulster (at Coleraine) and the Ulster Polytechnic. It has campuses at Coleraine, Jordanstown, Derry, and Belfast.

CHAPTER 4

Northern Irish Cultural Life

Cultural life in Northern Ireland tends to follow the contours of political and sectarian differences and to be marked by any number of shibboleths. For example, Roman Catholics and Protestants may listen to the same song but call it by different names; however, age, gender, and class play at least as large a role as religion in explaining many variations in music, drinking, and social life. Although there is a shared participation in global culture, such as Hollywood movies, football (soccer), and popular music, both the nationalist and unionist communities maintain their own cultural practices. Irish music and dance and the Gaelic games (football and hurling) form a cultural focus in nationalist communities, along with an interest in the Irish language that has led to the establishment of a network of Irish-language schools. In the unionist community, attempts to establish Ulster-Scots as a language have not been successful, and cultural life has been more influenced by trends in the rest of the United Kingdom. Much cultural activity in Protestant working-class communities has centred on the Orange Order and the tradition of marching bands. Both communities have produced internationally known writers, poets, actors, and musicians, many of whom have spoken out forcefully against sectarian violence. Government, through its various agencies, takes a keen interest in promoting cultural practices that transcend sectarian divisions. Cultural life in Northern Ireland tends to be public and oral. Outsiders are struck by the lively social life, the importance of conversation and the witty remark, and the abiding interest in music.

DAILY LIFE AND SOCIAL CUSTOMS

Northern Ireland is in many ways a traditional society. Church attendance is high (but steadily declining), family life is central, and community ties are strong. The daily interactions of most people are confined to members of their own community, whether in urban neighbourhoods or country villages. Dancing, music, and cultural and community festivals proliferate in Catholic communities, particularly in the months following St. Patrick's Day (March 17). Easter and the ancient Celtic Halloween are celebrated by both communities, albeit separately. Poitín (illegal homemade whisky) is sometimes drunk at weddings and funerals.

The centrepiece of Protestant celebrations is the marching season commemorating the Battle of the Boyne, which marks William III's victory in 1690 over the deposed Catholic king James II. A colourful, boisterous tradition, the marches begin about Easter and reach a climax on July 12. They often wind their way into now majority-Catholic communities, and, because of their political overtones, the marches have engendered significant hostility from the Catholic community and regularly embroil the British government in political controversy. Violent clashes between Protestants and Catholics are not uncommon during the marching season.

Everyday life is permeated by political divisions. Complex linguistic codes govern interactions between people, particularly those with strangers in public places. Public space is generally defined as Catholic, Protestant, or mixed—by far the smallest category—and forays across sectarian boundaries are often avoided. Apart from some middle-class and student areas, most neighbourhoods are religiously homogeneous and are often defined by "peace walls," which separate the two communities. These walls are festooned with lively murals and graffiti that represent some of the country's most visible public art. It is in areas where boundaries are fluid and contested and where poverty and deprivation abound, such as North Belfast, that most sectarian conflict occurs. In rural areas there is little direct confrontation, but the bitterness remains; indeed, some of the worst atrocities of the late 20th century took place in the countryside.

As primary and secondary school education remains predominantly parochial, there is little contact between Catholic and Protestant children. The schools have become a focal point for attacks, especially against Catholic children on their way to and from school in North Belfast. These attacks attest to the continued deep sectarian divisions that pervade daily life in Northern Ireland.

THE ARTS

Northern Ireland's Arts Council, a semi-autonomous body, is officially charged with encouraging all aspects of the arts, and the establishment of a government ministry has provided further impetus for artistic development. Local councils also devote a proportion of their budget to the arts. Funds from the National Lottery have been disbursed to build new theatres and arts centres, notably in Londonderry and Armagh. The reopening of the Grand Opera House in 1980 marked an important moment in the revival of the performing arts in Belfast. A new concert venue, the Waterfront Hall, opened in 1998, and a cultural quarter near the city centre has been developed. The city has a number of other theatres and arts centres, and there is also a touring company based at the University of Ulster at Coleraine. Classical music is mainly imported, but Belfast has a symphony orchestra and a youth orchestra and has fostered one of the largest festivals (ranging from classical to pop music) in the United Kingdom.

The sectarian conflict between Catholics and Protestants has left a distinct imprint on the arts; few art forms were untouched by the conflict. The troubled reality of Northern Ireland has been central to drama, poetry, fiction, and the visual arts. The most focused impact of the Troubles was on the visual arts, however. During most of the 20th century, the small and conservative visual art world was dominated by the landscape tradition, and ambitious artists moved to either Dublin or London. From the 1980s, younger artists (along with some of the earlier generation) began to produce a body of art concerned with problems of identity, conflict, and place. During the last two decades of the 20th century, there was a dramatic expansion in the visual arts, as the newer generation explored installation, video, and digital art forms. Lacking a developed art market, however, many artists continued to move to the republic of Ireland, where state support for artists is well established.

A number of poets, playwrights, musicians, and writers have achieved international recognition. Among Northern Ireland's most famous writers is Belfast-born C.S. Lewis, whose *Chronicles of Narnia* series is a classic of modern children's literature, while the Brontë family, which migrated to England from County Down, is remembered there with a cultural centre. The Nobel laureate Seamus Heaney and poets such as Paul Muldoon, Tom Paulin, Medbh McGuckian, Derek Mahon, and Michael Longley have well-established reputations; many of these poets have drawn inspiration from Old Irish work such as the 7th–8th-century epic *Táin bó Cuailnge* ("The Cattle Raid of Cooley"), and Heaney has translated the 12th-century Irish epic poem *Buile Suibhne* ("The Frenzy of Suibhne" or "The Madness of Sweeney"). Playwright Brian Friel and novelists Brian Moore, Bernard MacLaverty, Robert MacLiam Wilson, David Park, and Eoin McNamee have also gained international acclaim.

As with the other arts, Northern Ireland's music tends to be classified

VAN MORRISON

Van Morrison (born George Ivan Morrison, August 31, 1945, Belfast, Northern Ireland) grew up in a working-class Protestant family in Belfast. He took up the saxophone, guitar, and harmonica, and by his mid-teens he was playing in bands. He first gained notoriety as the vocalist and frontman for the group Them. More than a simple entertainer, Morrison helped transform the rock singer into something darker, more profound, and less willingly manipulated by music industry professionals. He sought to model himself on the integrity of the old bluesmen and the willfulness of poets. Leaving Them in 1967, he moved to the United States, and a year later he released the album *Astral Weeks*, an astonishingly original cycle of extended semi-improvised songs with backing from an acoustic group. The record was neither rock nor folk nor jazz, and yet it was something of all three. It came to be recognized as one of the most intense and genuinely poetic works in the history of rock.

Under the continuing influence of the writings of John Donne, William Blake, and William Butler Yeats, Morrison recorded songs such as "Listen to the Lion" (1972) and "Vanlose Stairway" (1982), but his future direction was more clearly indicated by his next album, *Moondance*, which featured a snappy little rhythm-and-blues band and carefully structured songs, including the title song. Subsequent hits included "Wild Night" and "Jackie Wilson Said."

Throughout his career Morrison seemed oblivious to public taste and reaction to him. Instead he explored Celtic roots by collaborating with the Chieftains, developed a lifelong interest in jazz, and wrote songs in a complex, idiosyncratic style suffused with spiritual yearning. Onstage he mixed, matched, and contrasted all these approaches.

as either Roman Catholic or Protestant. Drawing on Scottish, French, English, and Austrian sources, the traditional music that most of the world associates with Ireland is largely the preserve of the nationalists and central to the ceilis, the informal musical gatherings that are so much a part of the Scottish and Irish traditions. While there are pockets of this sort of music in the Protestant community, its musical tradition is centred on marching bands, most of which are more enthusiastic than competent. One distinctive component of the Protestant tradition is the Lambeg drum, made of goatskin stretched over an oak shell. While most well-known Catholic musicians tend to perform in traditional idioms, many Protestants have found success blending local traditions into a more cosmopolitan framework.

The flutist James Galway and pianist Barry Douglas have had tremendous success in classical circles, while the compositions of Elaine Agnew have found a following outside the country. Belfast native Van Morrison is one of rock music's major figures, and the city's Stiff Little Fingers was an influential part of the United Kingdom's punk rock explosion of the late 1970s. Northern Ireland's vibrant musical culture helps to nurture young musicians.

The film industry has had a growing presence in Northern Ireland. Actors Liam Neeson and Stephen Rea are internationally recognizable, and Kenneth Branagh, whose family left Northern Ireland when he was a child, has found success as both an actor and a director. Many films have depicted Northern Irish society and settings, notably Carol Reed's *Odd Man Out* (1947) and *Cal* (1984), directed by Pat O'Connor. Belfast inaugurated an annual film festival in 2000.

CULTURAL INSTITUTIONS

Belfast is the site of the Ulster Museum, the national museum and art gallery. Londonderry and Armagh also have galleries with permanent collections. The Ulster Folk and Transport Museum in Cultra provides a particularly interesting link with the peasant origins of Northern Ireland and includes an open-air folk museum.

Of other cultural institutions, perhaps the most notable is Armagh Observatory. Founded by Archbishop Richard Robinson (Lord Rokeby) in 1790, it has remained an independently governed institution, though it receives considerable state aid. Along with the separate but related Armagh Planetarium, the observatory offers extensive public programs and has one of the few astronomy libraries in Britain and Ireland. A major collection of Irish literature is housed at the Linen Hall Library in Belfast. There also is a major maritime museum, the Harbour Museum, in Londonderry.

SPORTS AND RECREATION

The people of Northern Ireland participate in the same sports that are played throughout the United Kingdom. Most athletes in Northern Ireland compete in the Olympic Games as part of the United Kingdom team (though many Roman Catholics join the national team of the republic of Ireland). Northern Ireland, like the other constituent members of the United Kingdom, fields a separate national team for World Cup football (soccer). Among the most notable footballers from Northern Ireland are Danny Blanchflower, who starred when the Northern Irish reached the World Cup quarterfinals in Sweden in 1958; the flamboyant George Best (called the "fifth Beatle" during his career in England); and the seemingly ageless goalkeeper Pat Jennings, whose career spanned decades from the 1960s to the 1980s. In addition, Rugby Union football is especially popular, and players from the Ulster team join the Irish team for international matches. Moreover, the Gaelic games—including such traditional sports as Gaelic football, hurling, and handball—have gained significant popularity, though confined primarily to the Catholic community. Sport fishing is among the most popular recreations, and the plentiful bream, roach, salmon, and trout attract fishing enthusiasts from

GEORGE BEST

While still a schoolboy, George Best (born May 22, 1946, Belfast, Northern Ireland—died November 25, 2005, London, England) was recommended to Manchester United by a local Belfast football (soccer) scout, who called the youngster a "genius." Best joined the club at age 15, and he made his first-division debut two years later, in 1963. He was an immediate sensation, scoring acrobatic goals and helping United to a league title in his second season. He led the club to another league championship during the 1966–67 season. In 1968 he was named European Footballer of the Year and helped United become the first English club to win the European Cup. Best scored a total of 178 goals in his 466 career games with United.

Called the "Fifth Beatle," the handsome Best had long hair that was an anomaly among footballers but was reminiscent of the "mop tops" of England's preeminent rock and rollers, the Beatles. Like them, Best was a colossal celebrity. His fame transcended the football world—Best was the first of many footballers to become a regular subject of the British tabloids—but it also helped foster a drinking problem that would prove to be his undoing. After a bitter departure from United in 1974, he played for numerous lesser teams in Britain, Spain, Australia, and the United States until 1983. His drinking continued to affect his play, however, and he became as well known for his squandered talent as for his undeniable brilliance. Best underwent a liver transplant in 2002 but ultimately was unable to overcome his alcoholism, and he died from a series of transplant-related infections that his compromised immune system could not combat.

throughout Europe. Northern Ireland's hill-walking courses and excellent beaches might also attract much greater numbers of tourists were it not for the region's political instability.

MEDIA AND PUBLISHING

Northern Ireland is serviced by both state and commercial broadcasting. In addition to relaying its national programming, the British Broadcasting Corporation operates two regional radio services (Radio Foyle and Radio Ulster) and has television studios in Belfast. There are numerous independent radio stations and an independent television service (UTV). Northern Ireland shares the British press, but several daily newspapers (e.g., the *Belfast Telegraph* and the *Irish News*) are published in Belfast.

CHAPTER 5

EARLY AND EARLY MODERN ULSTER

Ireland's northernmost provinces have some geographic distinctness. A diagonal line from the northwestern point of Donegal Bay to the southeastern point of Dundalk Bay marks the narrow waist of the island. A belt of hills, lakes, and forests along this line provides a natural border to the north, discouraging access to or from it. During the early Common Era (in the 5th and 6th centuries), the region had a distinctive culture, known under the Celtic name Ulaid (Latin: Ultonia; English: Ulster). Its political centre was at Emain Macha, or Navan Fort, near the present-day city of Armagh. The most successful Christian missionary in Ireland, the 5th-century Patrick, was predominantly based in the north and associated with its rulers. He established his ecclesiastical centre near Emain Macha, at Armagh, which is still the primatial see of both the Roman Catholic Church in Ireland and the Protestant Church of Ireland.

MYTHIC HISTORY

Ulster is of special importance in the mythic history of Ireland because its rulers and their champions played a prominent role in the rich Irish sagas of the Middle Ages. The Ulster cycle of these tales deals with the exploits of a King Conchobar and the prodigious warriors of the Red Branch, the most celebrated of whom was Cú Chulainn. The best-known tale of this cycle is the *Táin bó Cuailnge* (*The Cattle Raid of Cooley*), which recounts the invasion of Ulster by Queen Medb of Connaught (Connacht, the traditional

St. Patrick's Cathedral (Church of Ireland), Armagh. Tourism Ireland

western province; literally, the "descendants of Conn") in pursuit of a legendary bull. Eventually the men of Connacht are repulsed by the Ulstermen and their spectacular hero, Cú Chulainn.

The oldest manuscript of the *Táin*, known as *The Book of the Dun Cow*, was compiled in the 12th century and contains language dated to the 8th century. However, it is widely assumed that the story existed in oral form for at least several centuries previously and that it includes descriptions of practices current in Celtic society in Ireland or Britain or in continental Europe as long as several centuries before the birth of Christ. If it is mythic with respect to particular persons and events, the *Táin* is nevertheless an invaluable source for the early history of Irish society.

GAELIC IRISH AND ANGLO-NORMANS (C. 600–C. 1300)

The post-mythic history of Ulster dates from the 7th century, when it begins to be available from Latin documents and chronicles created by churchmen. By that time the 100 or more *tuatha* (clans) of the island had loosely grouped themselves into the five provinces of Ulster (Ulaidh), Meath (Midhe, which later dissolved), Leinster (Laighin), Munster (Mumhain), and Connaught (Connacht). By the 8th century, Ulster was dominated by a dynasty called the Uí Néill (O'Neill), which claimed descent from a shadowy figure of the 5th century known as Niall of the Nine Hostages. Divided into a northern and a southern branch, the Uí Néill asserted hegemony as high kings, to whom all other Irish kings owed deference. In the early 11th century the king of Munster, Brian Boru, effectively challenged the high kings of the Uí Néill dynasty and thereby ended Ulster's political dominance in early Irish history.

Munster's dominance was short-lived. In the mid-12th century an incursion of Norman adventurers from England, South Wales, and continental Europe greatly complicated the island's political pattern. The Norman beachhead was in Waterford in the southeast, but from there they struck out both north and west. By 1177 a force of several hundred men under John de Courci, advancing north from Dublin, had established itself in northern County Down and southern County Antrim. They built formidable castles at Downpatrick and Carrickfergus and established the northeast coast as the heart of Norman Ulster. De Courci became so threateningly independent that King John of England created an earldom of Ulster in 1205 and conferred it upon the more submissive Hugh de Lacy, who became known as the earl of Ulster. The title passed to the Norman family of de Burgo, which was joined in the coastal sections of Down and Antrim in the late 13th century by Anglo-Norman families with names such as Mandeville, Savage, Logan, and Bisset. The hinterland of Ulster remained imperviously Gaelic.

ENGLISH AND SCOTTISH PLANTATIONS

During the 16th and 17th centuries, the most isolated and undisturbed part of Ireland was transformed by immigration from Britain. The narrow North Channel separates northeastern Ulster from southwestern Scotland. Whereas in the early Middle Ages there had been a significant eastward migration of people from Ulster to Scotland, a pronounced westward flow of Scots to Ulster began in the 16th century. The crucial preconditions of Ulster's transformation were the expansion of English ambitions in Ireland from the 1530s, the defeat of Hugh O'Neill, 2nd earl of Tyrone, and the lords of the north in the opening years of the 17th century, and the determination of King James I to "plant" six of Ulster's nine counties with immigrant English and Scottish colonists.

A few years after the defeat of the northern earls, an excuse was found to plant the six counties of Ulster, which were judged to have escheated to the crown. Only Monaghan, Down, and

HUGH O'NEILL, 2ND EARL OF TYRONE

Although he was a member of a powerful Ulster family, Hugh O'Neill (born C. 1540—died July 20, 1616, Rome) grew up in London. In 1568 he returned to Ireland and assumed his grandfather's title, becoming the 2nd earl of Tyrone. By cooperating with the government of Queen Elizabeth I, he established his base of power, and in 1593 he replaced Turlough Luineach O'Neill as chieftain of the O'Neills. Skirmishes between Tyrone's forces and the English in 1595 were followed by three years of fruitless negotiations between the two sides.

In 1598 Tyrone reopened hostilities. His victory (August 14) over the English in the Battle of the Yellow Ford on the Blackwater River, Ulster—the most serious defeat sustained by the English in the Irish wars—sparked a general revolt throughout the country. Pope Clement VIII lent moral support to Tyrone's cause, and, in September 1601, 4,000 Spanish troops arrived at Kinsale, Munster, to assist the insurrection. But these reinforcements were quickly surrounded at Kinsale, and Tyrone suffered a staggering defeat (December 1601) while attempting to break the siege. He continued to resist until forced to surrender on March 30, 1603, six days after the death of Queen Elizabeth.

Elizabeth's successor, King James I, allowed Tyrone to keep most of his lands, but the chieftain soon found that he could not bear the loss of his former independence and prestige. In September 1607 Tyrone, with Rory O'Donnell, earl of Tyrconnell, and about 100 northern chieftains, secretly embarked on a ship bound for Spain. The vessel was blown off course and landed in the Netherlands. From there the refugees made their way to Rome, where they were acclaimed by Pope Paul V. This "flight of the earls" signaled the end of Gaelic Ulster; thereafter the province was rapidly Anglicized. Outlawed by the English, Tyrone lived in Rome for the rest of his life.

Antrim were excepted, the first because it had been subjected to a "native" plantation in the 1590s and the latter two because neither was held by the rebel earls and both were already areas of extensive de facto Scottish settlement. Plantation involved confiscated territory being granted to new landowners on the condition that they would establish settlers as their tenants and that they would introduce English law and the Protestant religion. This formalized and encouraged an immigration that had begun before the 17th century and that continued throughout and after it.

RELIGION AND SOCIAL STRUCTURE

Religious differences accentuated the transforming effect of immigration. A halfhearted attempt to propagate Protestantism in Ireland had largely failed by the 1590s among both the Gaelic Irish and the so-called Old English (descendants of the Anglo-Normans). Despite its nominal proscription, the Roman Catholic Church claimed the allegiance of almost the entire population, except the newcomers from Britain. English-born settlers gravitated to the Church of Ireland, a Protestant church modeled on the Church of England. Scottish settlers brought with them the ardent Calvinism that had recently established itself in their homeland. Any affinity that Gaelic Irish and Gaelic Scots might once have shared was offset, in an age of doctrinal extremism and intolerance, by the polarities of their respective religions.

Ulster became a province dominated by Protestant English and Scottish planters. Its landholding aristocracy was largely English, but beneath it lay a yeomanry of substantial tenant farmers drawn from both Scottish and English immigrants. This represented a significant change in the economics of agriculture in Ireland. As a result, the native Irish were disadvantaged and displaced to less-arable and more-marginal landholdings, though many continued as tenants of the new owners. The most violent reaction to this economic and cultural displacement was the rebellion of 1641, which originated in Ulster and took the form of a surprise attack upon English (and later Scottish) settlers. The plantation temporarily collapsed as colonists fled for their lives, but, with the reconquest of Ireland by Oliver Cromwell in the 1650s and the restoration of the Stuart monarchy in 1660, the Ulster plantation was reestablished.

CHAPTER 6

THE 18TH CENTURY AND BEYOND

The plantation of the 17th century made Ulster distinct among the provinces of Ireland because its immigrant British and Protestant population was larger and more concentrated than that of any other region. When in 1689 the Roman Catholic James II, who had been expelled from England by the Glorious Revolution of the previous year, attempted to recover his fortunes in Ireland, he based his forces in Catholic Dublin. His adversary and successor as king of Great Britain, the Protestant William III, made Protestant Belfast his encampment. When James's forces surrounded the new town of Londonderry (Derry), its Protestant inhabitants withstood a long and painful siege rather than capitulate to a Catholic Stuart. At the Battle of the Boyne in 1690, William's forces routed those of James. Although Ulster was the most British and most Protestant part of Ireland, it contained a large population of non-British Catholics and was contiguous with a larger and preponderantly Catholic Ireland.

ULSTER IN THE 18TH CENTURY

In the late 17th and early 18th centuries, Ulster, like many predominantly Protestant regions of Europe, became a refuge for Huguenots, Protestants who fled from France after the revocation of the Edict of Nantes in 1685. Many of these refugees brought commercial and industrial skills that contributed to the development of linen cloth manufacture. Although the linen industry remained traditional and small-scale (and existed in other parts of Ireland as well), it established a foundation for the later industrialization of Belfast and the River Lagan valley in the 19th century.

In 18th-century Ulster there were two elite and two lower classes. One group of elites was predominantly English, contained the most influential landowners, and was Protestant, affiliated with the Church of Ireland; the other was predominantly commercial, contained Scots as well as English, and included Protestants affiliated with various sects, especially Calvinist ones. The two lower classes were divided by religion: one was Catholic, the other Protestant. Among the lower-class Protestants there was substantial emigration to North America in the middle decades of the 18th century. These so-called Scotch-Irish, frustrated by limited economic opportunity in Ulster, became a mainstay of the Middle Atlantic colonies and the Appalachian frontier. The lower-class Protestants who remained in Ulster competed with lower-class Catholics for favourable leases of land and later for favourable jobs. The elites gradually gained the allegiance of the lower-class Protestants by playing upon sectarian fears.

Late 18th-century Ulster exhibited diverse, contrary tendencies. Belfast was the seat of the Society of United Irishmen (founded 1791), whose Enlightenment-inspired members dreamed of an ecumenical nation freed of corrupt Hanoverian monarchy and religious division. However, conditions in County Armagh gave rise to bitter sectarian strife, and a pitched battle between Protestant and Catholic factions at the Diamond (near Loughgall) in September 1795 led to the founding of the Orange Society (later known as the Orange Order), which was devoted to maintaining British rule and Protestant ascendancy. A series of rebellions in the summer of 1798—inspired by the United Irishmen but triggering the sectarian passions of the Catholic peasantry, especially in Leinster—attracted ineffectual French support and brutal British repression. Some 35,000 people died, and confidence in the ability of the relatively independent (since 1782) Irish Parliament to maintain stability was profoundly shaken. The result was the Act of Union of 1800, which ended such autonomy as existed and transferred Irish representation to the British Parliament at Westminster in London.

From at least the end of the 17th century, the population of Ulster had been predominantly Protestant and British, a stark contrast from the rest of Ireland. Economic differences between Ulster and southern Ireland widened in the 19th century as the north underwent a process of industrialization and urbanization centred in Belfast and the Lagan valley. Textile manufacture, both cotton and linen, and a shipbuilding industry that was in many respects an extension of that of Clydeside in southwestern Scotland gave Ulster an economy and culture very different

ORANGE SOCIETY

The Orange Society was formed in 1795 to maintain the Protestant ascendancy in Ireland in the face of rising demands for Catholic Emancipation. It was named for William of Orange, who became King William III of Great Britain. Enmity between Roman Catholics and Protestants had always been endemic in Ireland and was much exacerbated in the 17th century by the introduction into Ulster of Presbyterian settlers, by the rebellion of 1641, and by the war of 1688–91, when the Catholic king James II attempted to maintain in Ireland the power he had lost in England. Intersectarian feeling became especially bad again in the 1790s, especially in County Armagh, where Protestants, known as the "Peep o' Day Boys," attacked their Catholic neighbours. After a major confrontation in 1795, known as the Battle of the Diamond, the Orange Society (later known as the Orange Order and the Loyal Orange Association) was formed as a secret society, with lodges spreading throughout Ireland and ultimately into Great Britain and various British dominions. In 1835, with the Orange Society in mind, the House of Commons petitioned the king to abolish societies that were secret and that excluded persons on the ground of religion. Some official attempts were made to discourage the provocative Orange processions, the most notable of which is held annually on July 12, the anniversary of the Battle of Aughrim, at which William III's generals were finally victorious in Ireland. The Orange Society strengthened resistance in Ulster to the Irish Home Rule Bill of 1912 and has continued as a bastion of Protestant Unionist opinion.

from that of the heavily rural and agricultural south. In the 1880s a Home Rule movement gathered force in Ireland and was embraced by the leader of Britain's Liberal Party, William Ewart Gladstone, portending minority status in a larger self-ruling Ireland to those who were self-consciously Protestant, British, and Ulster and rekindling the anti-Catholic and anti-Irish passions of the Orange Order.

HOME RULE

As prime minister, Gladstone introduced the first Home Rule Bill in Parliament in 1886. Although the measure was defeated in the House of Commons, its mere formulation was sufficient to raise the spectre of the political domination of Irish Protestants, located mainly in the north, by Irish Catholics, spread throughout the island. Orangeism revived explosively and was adroitly exploited by Conservatives, who made "unionism"—preservation of the union of Great Britain and Ireland—its foremost concern.

A second Home Rule Bill, also introduced by Gladstone, was defeated in 1893, during a Liberal interregnum in a period of prolonged Conservative rule. When the Liberals finally returned to power in 1905, their victory foretold another effort to establish a measure of self-government for Ireland.

In 1912 the third, and final, Home Rule Bill twice passed the House of Commons, but both times it was defeated in the House of Lords. Protestant Ulster, under the leadership of a prominent barrister and member of Parliament, Edward Carson, Baron Carson of Duncairn, resisted incorporation into a self-governing Ireland. Oaths were sworn (the Solemn League and Covenant), and paramilitary forces were organized and armed. A civil war in Ireland, between Irish nationalists in the south and unionists in the north, seemed imminent. In 1914 the Home Rule Bill of 1912 passed the Commons for the third time, which, according to the Parliament Act of 1911, made ratification by the House of Lords unnecessary. However, when war broke out in Europe, the British government postponed the operation of the Home Rule Act until after the war, and the Liberal government of H.H. Asquith implied that special provision would be made for Ulster.

Putting aside their political differences, thousands of Irish Catholics and Protestants joined the British fighting forces in World War I. The situation in Ireland was dramatically inflamed, however, by the Easter Rising of 1916 and its immediate and harsh suppression. The south was becoming radicalized, and it began to appear that, however offensive the third Home Rule Bill was for Protestant Ulster, it was too late and too little to satisfy separatist sentiment in Catholic Ireland. In the 1918 election Sinn Féin (the republican party led by Eamon de Valera) ousted the Home Rule Party, refused to take their seats in the Westminster Parliament, and instead established their own alternative parliament, Dáil Éireann, in Dublin, which was supported by the Irish Republican Army (IRA) in the Anglo-Irish War of 1919–21 (Irish War of Independence).

In 1919 the British coalition government of David Lloyd George was obliged to deal with an almost impossible situation in which most of Ireland rejected the union and most of Ulster rejected everything else. The intended remedy was the Government of Ireland Act of 1920, which created two modestly self-governing units: one comprising six of Ulster's nine counties (later to be known as Northern Ireland), the other comprising the three remaining counties of Ulster together with the 23 counties of the rest of Ireland. Although the Protestant majority of the six counties clearly preferred continuation of the union for all of Ireland, it settled for Home Rule for itself, and the Northern Ireland parliament and government began functioning in June 1921. Paradoxically, the Catholic majority of the 26 counties, for whom Home Rule had originally been intended, rejected it as inadequate.

Lloyd George's government then negotiated the Anglo-Irish Treaty of December 6, 1921, with Sinn Féin. The treaty gave the new Irish Free State dominion status within the British Empire, but it also permitted the six counties of Northern Ireland to opt out of the arrangement, which they did.

A boundary commission was established to review the borders between the Irish Free State and Northern Ireland. In 1925 the commission's final report proposed only small territorial adjustments, with parts of Fermanagh, Tyrone, and Armagh being ceded to the Irish Free State and a part of Donegal to Northern Ireland. But these alterations were opposed by both the Northern Irish and Irish Free State governments, and a final report was never issued. Instead, the Boundary Commission agreement of December 3, 1925, confirmed the boundaries of Northern Ireland as those marked by the six counties of Antrim, Armagh, Down, Fermanagh, Londonderry (Derry), and Tyrone.

PRECARIOUS COEXISTENCE

The constitutional revisions of 1920–22 succeeded in creating a parliament in Northern Ireland that was acceptable to the approximately one million Protestant unionists of the six counties. However, they did not provide a remedy for the several hundred thousand Protestant unionists who lived elsewhere in Ireland, many of whom eventually moved to Northern Ireland. More important, they did not satisfy the concerns of the half million Roman Catholic nationalists who resided within the six counties. Under the leadership of James Craig, 1st Viscount Craigavon, who served as prime minister of Northern Ireland from 1921 to 1940, the Northern Ireland parliament was dominated by a Protestant majority, which governed in its own interest and which was dedicated to maintaining the union with Great Britain. Most Roman Catholics were never reconciled to their status within Northern Ireland, though their opposition was politically ineffective, and they suffered discrimination in employment, public housing, education, and social services. In addition, unionists ensured their political hold over Northern Ireland through the manipulation of electoral boundaries, which minimized the representation of Roman Catholics.

Balancing these disadvantages for the Catholic minority was the industrial economy of the north, which had no parallel in the south. By the end of the 19th century, Belfast was Ireland's largest city, with a population of nearly 350,000 and with numerous jobs in the textile industries and in shipbuilding. Although Protestants were overrepresented, often unfairly, in skilled jobs and managerial positions, Belfast's economic magnet drew lower-class Catholics from the impoverished countryside. The city experienced sectarian violence, its housing was highly segregated (with Catholics generally occupying much of the poor housing stock), and religious intolerance was rampant—all of which worsened already difficult living conditions for Catholics—but its economic appeal endured even through the Great Depression of the 1930s and the doldrums of the 1960s and '70s.

Several factors help to explain the relatively minor emigration of Roman Catholics from the north. Not only did they fear that they would be economically worse off in the south, but World War II brought a measure of economic revival, especially in ship and aircraft manufacture. Moreover, the social welfare provisions extended to Northern Ireland after the war by far exceeded the supports and protections available to individuals in the socially conservative south. Northern Catholics did not "vote with their feet," but neither did they accept the stark inequities in Northern Ireland.

DISINTEGRATION OF STABILITY

By the mid-1960s the fragile stability of Northern Ireland had begun to erode. The demographic majority that Protestants enjoyed ensured that they were able to control the state institutions, and these powers were, more often than not, used in ways that disadvantaged the Catholic minority in the region, though the extent and even the existence of discrimination in Northern Ireland remained a matter of heated debate. An active civil rights movement—partly inspired by the achievements of African Americans in the civil rights movement in United States—emerged in the late 1960s, and incidents of communal violence increased. The police occasionally used force to disperse demonstrators from the streets. The coincidence of increasingly strident demands for reform and equally fervent insistence that there should be none produced a deadly dynamic that brought Northern Ireland to the brink of civil war.

The British government sent troops "in aid of the civil power" at Stormont, Northern Ireland's parliament. Rioting and widespread urban violence had exhausted the Royal Ulster Constabulary and undermined its capacity to secure law and order. In 1969 the Provisional movement of the Irish Republican Army (IRA) emerged out of this communal disorder. The IRA acquired arms and explosives and initiated a campaign of bombings and shootings in order to protect Roman Catholics, destabilize Northern Ireland's institutions, weaken British resolve to maintain the union, and achieve Irish unity. In response to the violence, the authorities introduced internment without trial in August 1971 (ended 1975). However, rather than weakening the IRA's campaign, this encouraged its intensification. Protestant unionists responded by forming their own loyalist paramilitary brigades.

In Derry on January 30, 1972, a day that became known as Bloody Sunday, a peaceful but illegal protest by Catholics against the British government's internment policy turned violent, with British troops opening fire and killing 13 Catholic demonstrators (a 14th died several months

BLOODY SUNDAY

On Sunday, January 30, 1972, a demonstration in Londonderry (Derry) by Roman Catholic civil rights supporters turned violent when British paratroopers opened fire, killing 13 and injuring 14 others (one of the injured later died). The incident, which became known as Bloody Sunday, precipitated an upsurge in support for the Irish Republican Army (IRA) and remained a source of controversy for decades, with competing accounts of the events. In June 2010 the Saville Report, the final pronouncement of a government inquiry initiated by British Prime Minister Tony Blair in 1998, concluded that none of the victims had posed any threat to the soldiers and that their shooting was without justification.

Bloody Sunday began as a peaceful—but illegal—demonstration by some 10,000 people organized by the Northern Ireland Civil Rights Association in opposition to the British government's policy of interning suspected members of the IRA without trial. The demonstrators marched toward Guildhall Square in the city centre, but the British army had cordoned off much of the area, prompting most of the marchers to alter their course and head toward Free Derry Corner. However, some of the demonstrators confronted the soldiers, pelting them with stones and other projectiles. British troops responded by firing rubber bullets and a water cannon. Ordered to arrest as many demonstrators as possible, the army proceeded to confront the marchers, and violence erupted.

Who had fired the first shot long remained a point of contention—with the army maintaining that it had fired only after being fired upon and the Roman Catholic community contending that the soldiers had opened fire on unarmed protesters. Never in question was the fact that after less than 30 minutes of shooting, 13 marchers lay dead. Immediately after the incident an inquiry was ordered by British Prime Minister Edward Heath. It was led by Lord Widgery, the lord chief justice of England, who concluded that the demonstrators fired the first shot but that none of those dead appeared to have carried weapons. The Derry coroner, however, was unequivocal, calling the deaths "unadulterated murder," and nationalists campaigned for more than two decades for the government to establish a new inquiry.

The 5,000-page Saville Report found that the first shot in the vicinity of the march had been fired by the British army and that, though there was some firing by republican paramilitaries, it did not provide any justification for the shooting of the civilian casualties. It also found that none of the soldiers had fired in response to attacks by those throwing projectiles and that none of those who were shot had posed any threat to the soldiers. Upon the issuing of the report in 2010, British Prime Minister David Cameron went before Parliament to apologize for the shootings. The following year the British government announced that it would offer financial compensation to relatives of the victims.

later). Bloody Sunday continued to be a matter of considerable controversy—in particular, the army's orders and the role of the IRA in the violence.

The bloodiest year of the "Troubles"—as the sectarian violence was popularly known—was 1972, when 467 people, including 321 civilians, were killed; approximately 275 people were killed each year in the period 1971–76. The violence diminished in the 1980s, when about 50 to 100 political murders and assassinations occurred each year. By the end of the 20th century, more than 3,600 people had been killed and 36,000 injured; of the deaths, more than 2,000 were the responsibility of republicans, 1,000 of loyalists, and more than 350 of security forces. In the last three decades of the 20th century, more than 1,000 members of the security forces also were killed.

In March 1972 Conservative British Prime Minister Edward Heath suspended the constitution and parliament of Northern Ireland, which thereby ended Home Rule (which did not return until 1999) and restored direct rule from London. Among several initiatives to restore Home Rule, the first, known as the Sunningdale Agreement, led to the creation in 1973 of a short-lived assembly in which Catholics were given some political authority. The Sunningdale Agreement also provided for a Council of Ireland linking the two jurisdictions on the island. Nevertheless, violence continued, and the power-sharing executive collapsed after only a few months because of a strike organized by the Ulster Workers' Council, a committee backed by Protestant paramilitaries. The British army remained a major presence, and elements of martial law permeated the operations of the government and the courts.

POWER-SHARING AGREEMENTS AND THE ESTABLISHMENT OF A FRAGILE PEACE

An assembly that was intended to reflect the diversity of political opinion was established in 1982. However, it foundered and dissolved in 1986. Nationalists made clear that they would not accept a settlement solely internal to Northern Ireland, and they pushed for a significant additional all-Ireland arrangement. In response, the British and Irish governments concluded the Anglo-Irish Agreement (1985), which (to the dismay of unionists) marked the first time that the government of Ireland was given an official consultative role in the affairs of Northern Ireland. In the 1990s talks were held between all Northern Ireland's major constitutional parties with the exception of Sinn Féin, the political wing of the Provisional IRA, which was excluded on the grounds that the IRA, like the loyalist paramilitary groups, continued to engage in terrorist activity. Frameworks for all-party peace talks —notably the Downing Street Declaration (1993), issued by the British and Irish prime ministers, John Major and Albert Reynolds, respectively—were put forward. These guaranteed self-determination for the people of Northern Ireland, promised British government recognition of a unified Ireland if a majority of Northern Ireland's people agreed, and committed Ireland to abandoning its constitutional claim to Northern Ireland in the event of a political settlement.

Both the IRA and the loyalist paramilitary groups announced the cessation of military activity in 1994, though sporadic incidents continued. The major stumbling block to all-party talks was the issue of IRA decommissioning (disarmament). Discussions resumed in June 1996 —though Sinn Féin was not immediately a participant because the IRA had ended its cease-fire (reinstated 1997)—and culminated in the Good Friday Agreement (Belfast Agreement), signed in April 1998. Under the terms of this accord, responsibility for most local matters was to be devolved to an elected assembly. There were institutional arrangements for cross-border cooperation on a range of issues between the governments of Ireland and Northern Ireland and for continued consultation between the British and Irish governments. In a jointly held referendum in Ireland and Northern Ireland on May 22, 1998—the first all-Ireland vote since 1918—the agreement was approved by 94 percent of voters in Ireland and 71 percent in Northern Ireland. However, the wide disparity between Catholic and Protestant support for the agreement in Northern Ireland (96 percent of Catholics but only 52 percent of Protestants voted in favour) indicated that efforts to resolve the sectarian conflict would be difficult.

In elections to a new Northern Ireland Assembly held the following month, the Ulster Unionist Party (UUP), the mainstream Protestant party, won 28 seats; the Social Democratic and Labour Party (SDLP), a moderate Catholic party, won 24; Ian Paisley's Democratic Unionist Party (DUP), a hard-line Protestant party that opposed the Good Friday Agreement, won 20; and Sinn Féin won 18. In July UUP leader David Trimble was elected "first minister designate," and the SDLP's Seamus Mallon was elected Trimble's deputy. Less than two months later, a bombing in Omagh by the Real IRA, an IRA splinter group, killed 29—the deadliest such incident since the start of sectarian violence in the 1960s. The IRA's failure to decommission delayed the formation of the Northern Ireland Executive, in which Sinn Féin was to have two ministers. In December 1999 Trimble agreed, on the understanding that the IRA would fulfill its obligations to disarm, that the Northern Ireland Assembly could begin exercising its power. Nonetheless, it was only in 2001, after intense international pressure following the September 11 terrorist attacks in the United States and several suspensions of devolution, that the IRA began the process of decommissioning. However, in October 2002 devolution was once again suspended amid claims that republicans were gathering intelligence information through a spy network that was operating within the government and contrary to the IRA's cease-fire agreement of 1997.

One of the unforeseen consequences of the Good Friday Agreement was a political polarization within both the Protestant and the Roman Catholic communities. For example, Sinn Féin and the hard-line Protestant DUP began to outpoll the more moderate SDLP and UUP. Although Northern Ireland was experiencing its most peaceful era in a generation, sectarian antagonism remained deep and the future of the new institutions uncertain. Still, there was great optimism following the IRA's announcement in July 2005 that it had ended its armed campaign and had disposed of most of its weapons and would pursue only peaceful means to achieve its goals.

Elections to the Northern Ireland Assembly were held in March 2007, and the DUP captured the most votes, winning 36 seats in the 108-member Assembly; Sinn Féin was second with 28 seats. Later that month Gerry Adams and Ian Paisley—the leaders of Sinn Féin and the DUP, respectively—reached a historic agreement to form a power-sharing government. On May 8, 2007, devolution returned to Northern Ireland as Paisley and Sinn Féin's Martin McGuinness were sworn in as first minister and deputy first minister, respectively. Further evidence of the changing reality in Northern Ireland came in August of that year when the British military presence—which for decades had been ubiquitous—was dramatically reduced to 5,000 troops, with all responsibility for security handed over to the police. In June 2008 Paisley retired and was succeeded as leader of the DUP and as first minister by Peter Robinson (who stepped down from the latter position temporarily in 2010 in response to a political scandal). The final plank of the Good Friday Agreement was put in place in March 2010 when the Assembly voted to devolve policing and justice powers to Northern Ireland.

The DUP and Sinn Féin remained in control of the Assembly in the 2011 elections, in which the former increased its representation to 38 seats and the latter added a seat to reach 29. The Alliance also gained a seat, for a new total of eight seats, while the SDLP and UUP lost ground, falling from 16 to 14 seats and from 18 to 16 seats, respectively. Robinson and McGuinness remained at the head of the Executive. The election provided a measure of vindication for Robinson, who had lost his seat in the Westminster Parliament in the 2010 elections. On June 27, 2012, in an encounter widely viewed as having great symbolic importance to the ongoing reconciliation efforts in Northern Ireland, McGuinness, a onetime commander in the IRA, shook hands with Elizabeth II during a visit to Belfast by the British queen.

CHAPTER 7

SCOTLAND: THE LAND AND ITS PEOPLE

The name Scotland derives from the Latin *Scotia*, land of the Scots, a Celtic people from Ireland who settled on the west coast of Great Britain about the 5th century CE. The name Caledonia has often been applied to Scotland, especially in poetry. It is derived from *Caledonii*, the Roman name of a tribe in the northern part of what is now Scotland.

An austere land, subject to extremes of weather, Scotland has proved a difficult home for countless generations of its people, who have nonetheless prized it for its beauty and unique culture. "I am a Scotsman," the poet and novelist Sir Walter Scott wrote in the 19th century; "therefore I had to fight my way into the world." Historically one of Europe's poorest countries, Scotland has contributed much to political and practical theories of progress: forged in the Scottish Enlightenment in the hands of such philosophers as Francis Hutcheson, Adam Smith, and

David Hume, who viewed humankind as a product of history and the "pursuit of happiness" as an inalienable right, this progressive ideal contributed substantially to the development of modern democracy. Scots have also played a vital role in many of the world's most important scientific and technological innovations, with inventors, engineers, and entrepreneurs such as Alexander Graham Bell, James Watt, Andrew Carnegie, and John McAdam extending Scotland's reach far beyond the small country's borders. Few students of English-language literature are unacquainted with historian Thomas Carlyle, poet Robert Burns, and novelist Muriel Spark.

Scotland's relations with England, with which it was merged in 1707 to form the United Kingdom of Great Britain, have long been difficult. Although profoundly influenced by the English, Scotland has long refused to consider itself as anything other than a separate country, and it has bound itself to historical fact and legend alike in an effort to retain

Edinburgh Castle. © Digital Vision/Getty Images

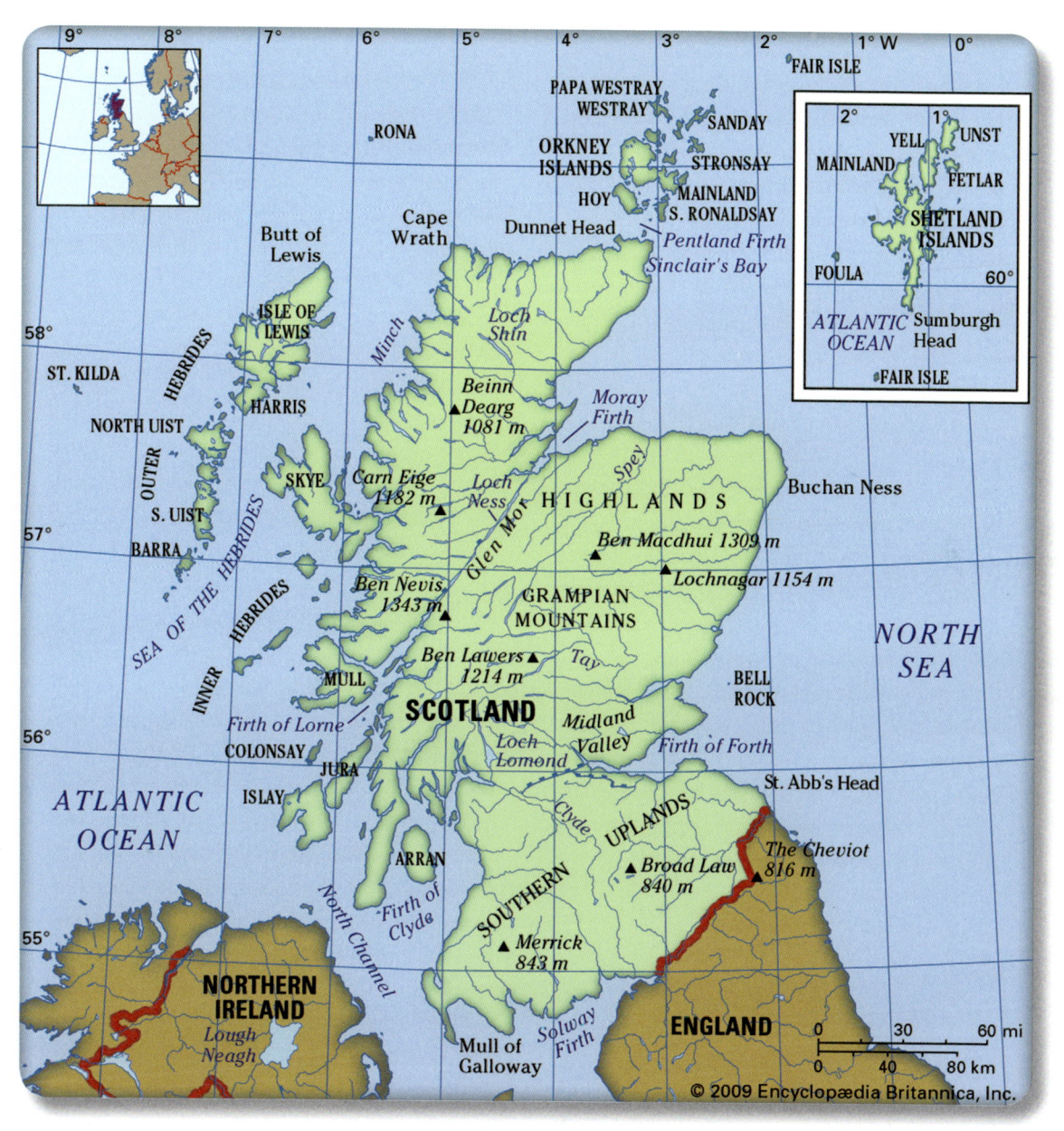

national identity, as well as to the distinct dialect of English called Scots; writing defiantly of his country's status, the nationalist poet Hugh MacDiarmid proclaimed: "For we ha'e faith in Scotland's hidden poo'ers, The present's theirs, but a' the past and future's oors." That independent spirit bore fruit in 1996, when the highly symbolic Stone of Scone was returned to Edinburgh, Scotland's capital, from London, and in 1999 a new Scottish Parliament—the first since 1707—was elected and given significant powers over Scottish affairs.

The most northerly of the four parts of the United Kingdom, occupying about one-third of the island of Great Britain, Scotland is bounded by England to the south, the Atlantic Ocean to the west and north, and the North Sea to the east. The west coast is fringed by deep indentations (sea lochs or fjords) and by numerous islands, varying in size from mere rocks to the large landmasses of Lewis and Harris, Skye, and Mull. The island clusters of Orkney and Shetland lie to the north. At its greatest length, measured from Cape Wrath to the Mull of Galloway, the mainland of Scotland extends 274 miles (441 km), while the maximum breadth—measured from Applecross, in the western Highlands, to Buchan Ness, in the eastern Grampian Mountains—is 154 miles (248 km). But, because of the deep penetration of the sea in the sea lochs and firths (estuaries), most places are within 40 to 50 miles (65 to 80 km) of the sea, and only 30 miles (50 km) of land separate the Firth of Clyde and the Firth of Forth, the two great estuarine inlets on the west and east coasts, respectively.

RELIEF

Scotland is traditionally divided into three topographic areas: the Highlands in the north, the Midland Valley (Central Lowlands), and the Southern Uplands. (The latter two areas are included in the Lowlands cultural region.) Low-lying areas extend through the Midland Valley and along the greater part of the eastern seaboard. The east coast contrasts with the west in its smoother outline and thus creates an east-west distinction in topography as well as a north-south one. The Highlands are bisected by the fault line of Glen Mor (Glen Albyn), which is occupied by a series of lochs (lakes), the largest of which is Loch Ness, famous for its probably mythical monster. North of Glen Mor is an ancient plateau, which, through long erosion, has been cut into a series of peaks of fairly uniform height separated by glens (valleys) carved out by glaciers. The northwestern fringe of the mainland is particularly barren, the rocks of the Lewisian Complex having been worn down by severe glaciation to produce a hummocky landscape, dotted by small lochs and rocks protruding from thin, acidic soil. The landscape is varied by spectacular Torridonian sandstone mountains, weathered into sheer cliffs, rock terraces, and pinnacles.

Southeast of Glen Mor are the Grampian Mountains (also shaped by glaciation), though there are intrusions such as the granitic masses of the Cairngorm Mountains. The Grampians are on the whole less rocky and rugged than the mountains of the northwest, being more rounded and grassy with wider plateau areas. But many have cliffs and pinnacles that provide challenges for mountaineers, and the area contains Britain's highest mountains, reaching a maximum elevation of 4,406 feet (1,343

LOCH NESS

With a depth of 788 feet (240 metres) and a length of about 23 miles (36 km), Loch Ness has the largest volume of fresh water in Great Britain. It lies in the Glen Mor—or Great Glen, which bisects the Highlands—and forms part of the system of waterways across Scotland that civil engineer Thomas Telford linked by means of the Caledonian Canal (opened 1822).

The watershed of Loch Ness covers more than 700 square miles (1,800 square km) and comprises several rivers, including the Oich and the Enrick. Its outlet is the River Ness, which flows into the Moray Firth at Inverness. Seiches (surface oscillations), caused by differential heating, are common on the loch. The sharp rise and fall of the level of the loch is one reason for the scanty flora of the waters; another reason is the great depths of the loch near the shoreline. The abyssal fauna is also sparse.

Like some other very deep lochs in Scotland and Scandinavia, Loch Ness is said to be inhabited by an aquatic monster. Many sightings of the so-called Loch Ness monster have been reported, and the possibility of its existence—perhaps in the form of a solitary survivor of the long-extinct plesiosaurs—continues to intrigue many.

Loch Ness, in the Highlands of Scotland. At the head of the loch is the monastery at Fort Augustus. A.F. Kersting

---

metres) at Ben Nevis. There are some flatter areas—the most striking being Rannoch Moor, a bleak expanse of bogs and granitic rocks—with narrow, deep lochs such as Rannoch and Ericht. The southeastern margin of the Highlands is clearly marked by the Highland Boundary Fault, running northeast to southwest from Stonehaven, just south of Aberdeen, to Helensburgh on the River Clyde and passing through Loch Lomond, Scotland's largest stretch of inland water. The southern boundary of the Midland Valley is not such a continuous escarpment, but the fault beginning in the northeast with the Lammermuir and Moorfoot hills and extending to Glen App, in the southwest, is a distinct dividing line. In some ways the label Lowlands is a misnomer, for, although this part of Scotland is low by

Ben Nevis viewed from Loch Linnhe. Colour Library International

comparison with adjoining areas, it is by no means flat. The landscape includes hills such as the Sidlaws, the Ochils, the Campsies, and the Pentlands, composed of volcanic rocks rising as high as 1,898 feet (579 metres). The Southern Uplands are not as high as the Highlands. Glaciation has produced narrow, flat valleys separating rolling mountains. To the east of Nithsdale the hills are rounded, gently sloping, and grass-covered, providing excellent grazing for sheep, and they open out along the valley of the lower Tweed into the rich farming land of the Merse. To the west of Nithsdale the landscape is rougher, with granitic intrusions around Loch Doon, and the soil is more peaty and wet. The high moorlands and hills, reaching up to 2,766 feet (843 metres) at Merrick, are also suitable for sheep farming. The uplands slope toward the coastal plains along the Solway Firth in the south and to the machair and the Mull of Galloway farther west.

DRAINAGE

Uplift and an eastward tilting of the Highlands some 50 million years ago (during the Eocene Epoch) formed a watershed near the west coast. As a result, most rivers drain eastward, but deeply glaciated rock basins in the northern Highlands form numerous large lochs. There are fewer lochs in the Grampian Mountains, although the area contains the large lochs of Ericht, Rannoch, and Tay. Well-graded rivers such as the Dee, the Don, and the Spey meander eastward and northeastward to the North Sea. The Tay and Forth emerge from the southern Grampians to flow out of the eastern Lowlands in two large estuaries. The Clyde and the Tweed both rise in the Southern Uplands, the one flowing west into the Firth of Clyde and the other east into the North Sea, while the Nith, the Annan, and a few other rivers run south into the Solway Firth. Lochs are numerous in the Highlands, ranging from moraine-dammed lochans (pools) in mountain corries (cirques) to large and deep lochs filling rock basins. In the Lowlands and the Southern Uplands, lochs are shallower and less numerous.

SOILS

With Scotland's diversity in geologic structure, relief, and weather, the character of the soil varies greatly. In the northwest, the Hebrides, the Shetland Islands, and other areas, the soil is poor and rocky, and cultivation is possible only at river mouths, glens, and coastal strips. On the west coast of some Hebridean islands, however, there are stretches of calcareous sand (the machair) suitable for farming. Peat is widespread on moors and hills. Areas with good, arable land have largely been derived from old red sandstone and younger rocks, as in the Orkney Islands, the eastern Highlands, the northeastern coastal plain, and the Lowlands.

CLIMATE

Scotland has a temperate oceanic climate, milder than might be expected from its latitude. Despite its small area, there are considerable variations. Precipitation is greatest in the mountainous areas of the west, as prevailing winds, laden with moisture from the Atlantic, blow from the southwest. East winds are common in winter and spring, when cold, dry continental air masses envelop the east coast. Hence, the west tends to be milder in winter, with less frost and with snow seldom lying long at lower elevations, but it is damper and cloudier than the east in summer. Tiree, in the Inner Hebrides off the west coast, has a mean temperature in winter of 41°F (5°C) in the coldest month (as high as southeastern England), whereas Dundee, on the east coast, has 37°F (3°C). Dundee's mean temperature in the warmest month is 59°F (15°C) and Tiree's 57°F (14°C). There is a smaller range of temperatures over the year in Scotland than in southern England. Precipitation varies remarkably. Some two-thirds of Scotland receives more than 40 inches (1,000 mm) annually, the average for Britain, with the total reaching 142 inches (3,600 mm) in the Ben Nevis area and somewhat more near Loch Quoich farther to the northwest. In the flat Outer Hebrides conditions are less humid, as in the east, where the Moray Firth receives annually less than 25 inches (635 mm) and Dundee less than 32 inches (810 mm). A significant amount of snow falls above 1,500 feet (460 metres) in the Highlands in winter.

PLANT AND ANIMAL LIFE

Lower elevations, up to about 1,500 feet, were once covered with natural forests, which have been cleared over the course of centuries and replaced in some areas by trees, plants, and crops. Survivals of the original forest are found sporadically throughout the Highlands—for example, in the pinewoods of Rothiemurchus in the Spey valley. Grass and heather cover most of the Grampians and the Southern Uplands, where the soil is not so wet and dank as in the northwestern Highlands. Shrubs such as bearberry, crowberry, and blaeberry (bilberry) grow on peaty soil, as does bog cotton. Alpine and Arctic species flourish on the highest slopes and plateaus of the Grampians, including saxifrages, creeping azalea, and dwarf willows. Ben Lawers is noted for its plentiful mountain flora.

Scotland is rich in animal life for its size. Herds of red deer graze in the corries and remote glens; although formerly woodland dwellers, they are now found mainly on higher ground, but roe deer still inhabit the woods, along with sika and fallow deer (both introduced species) in some areas. Foxes and badgers are widespread, but the Scottish wildcat has become critically endangered as a result of disease and interbreeding with domestic cats. Rabbits were once decimated by the disease myxomatosis but have largely recovered to earlier numbers. Pine marten, otters, and mountain and brown hares are among other wild mammals. A few ospreys nest in Scotland, and golden eagles, buzzards, peregrine falcons, and kestrels are the most notable of resident birds of prey. The red grouse, the Scottish subspecies of the willow grouse, has long been hunted for sport. Other species of grouse include the ptarmigan, found only at higher elevations, and the large capercaillie, which has been reintroduced into Scotland's pine woodlands. Large numbers of seabirds, such as gannets, fulmars, guillemots, and gulls breed on cliffs and on the stacks (isolated rocks) around the magnificent coasts. More than one-third of the world's Atlantic, or gray, seals breed in Scottish waters, especially around the Northern and Western Isles, as do numerous common seals; dolphins and porpoises are regularly seen and whales occasionally, especially on the west coast.

ETHNIC GROUPS

For many centuries continual strife characterized relations between the Celtic Scots of the Highlands and the western islands and the Anglo-Saxons of the Lowlands. Only since the 20th century has the mixture been widely seen as a basis for a rich, unified Scottish culture; the people of Shetland and Orkney have tended to remain apart from both of these elements and to look to Scandinavia as the mirror of their Norse heritage. Important immigrant groups have arrived, most notably Irish labourers; there have also been significant groups of Jews, Lithuanians, Italians, and, after World War II, Poles and others, as well as a more recent influx of Asians, especially from Pakistan. The enlargement of the European Union in 2004 led to a dramatic increase in immigration from the countries of Eastern Europe.

LANGUAGES

Scotland's linguistic heritage is complex. The vast majority of the population now speaks English, but both Scottish Gaelic and the Scots language have wide influence. Languages such as Urdu and Punjabi continue to be spoken by immigrant groups, and the Scottish Parliament provides information in different languages to meet these needs.

Gaelic, the Celtic language brought from Ireland by the Scots, is spoken by only a tiny proportion of the Scottish population, mainly concentrated in the Western Isles and the western Highlands, with pockets elsewhere, especially in Glasgow. Interest in Gaelic has increased sharply, especially following the establishment of the new Scottish Parliament in 1999, and its literature has flourished. Scots was originally a form of Old English that diverged from southern forms of the language in the Middle Ages, becoming a separate national tongue by the 15th century. Union with England and other factors caused English gradually to be adopted as the official and standard language; however, Scots survives in the Lowland areas, in a vigorous tradition of poetry and drama, and in aspects of the English spoken by most Scots. Both Gaelic and Scots are recorded and supported by major works of scholarship: the *Linguistic Survey of Scotland* (1975–86), *The Scottish National Dictionary* (1931–75), and *A Dictionary of the Older Scottish Tongue* (1931–2002). The Scottish government has allocated funds to support Gaelic, notably in broadcasting and education, and it also has provided grants to Scots-language organizations. Local education authorities are required to provide for the teaching of Gaelic in Gaelic-speaking areas, and they give guidance on ways to include Scots literature in school curricula.

RELIGION

Scotland is relatively free from ethnic and religious strife. The Church of Scotland, Presbyterian in structure and Evangelical in doctrine, is the established religion and largest communion, though membership has been steadily declining. It is controlled by a hierarchy of church courts, from the kirk session (governing the affairs of a congregation) through the presbytery (covering a group of parishes) to the General Assembly, at which clergy and lay representatives meet annually in Edinburgh to discuss key issues relating to Scottish society.

The Roman Catholic Church is organized into two archdioceses and six dioceses. The Scottish Episcopal Church is also significant, and there are congregations of other denominations, such as

CHURCH OF SCOTLAND

According to tradition, the first Christian church in Scotland was founded about 400 by St. Ninian. In the 6th century, Irish missionaries included St. Columba, who settled at Iona about 563. In 1192 the Scottish church was declared "a special daughter" of the Roman see, subject only to the pope. St. Andrews became an archiepiscopal see in 1472, followed by Glasgow in 1492.

The earliest Scottish Reformers were under Lutheran influence but were subsequently influenced by the Swiss Reformers. The Calvinistic tone of the Scottish Reformation was ascribable to John Knox, who became the leader of the Scottish Reformation. Knox's admiration for John Calvin and for the reformation that Calvin led in Geneva is evident in Knox's Scots Confession, in the *Book of Common Order* (often known as Knox's liturgy), and in the Book of Discipline, the last of which discussed a plan for a godly church and commonwealth. The Scottish Reformers held a parliament in August 1560, which abolished the authority of the pope in Scotland, adopted the Scots Confession, and forbade the celebration of mass.

After the breach with Rome it was uncertain for more than a century whether the church in Scotland would be episcopal or presbyterian in government. Charles I, who ruled Scotland and England, preferred the episcopal form, while the Scottish people insisted on the presbyterian form. The struggle was long and complicated, but, when William and Mary became the English monarchs in 1689, Presbyterianism was permanently established in Scotland by constitutional act.

New problems then developed. In the late 17th century a large group of essentially professional clergymen known as Moderates became influential in the church. They were opposed by the Evangelicals, who held firmly to the traditional Calvinism of the Westminster Confession.

When the British Parliament restored patronage in Scotland in 1712, the people lost the right to elect their pastors to the landowners, which brought the Church of Scotland under the control of the Moderate ministers.

Dissension between the Moderates and the Evangelicals, who had been strengthened by religious revivals and the Sunday school movement, increased from 1833 to 1843. Finally a large group, led by Thomas Chalmers, left the established church and formed, in 1843, a Free Church of Scotland. All but one of the Church of Scotland missionaries and most of its best scholars joined the Free Church.

Gradually, better leadership replaced the Moderate party in the Church of Scotland. Patronage was abolished in 1874, and closer relations with the Free Church developed. In 1921 the state severed its old relation with the Church of Scotland, leaving it the national church but not the established state church. After several years of negotiations, the two churches united in 1929 under the old name of the Church of Scotland.

Subsequently the church continued to be active in missionary work and to take an active part in the Protestant ecumenical movement. Moves to affiliate it with the Church of England were defeated in 1959 and 1971.

the Free Church of Scotland, Baptists, Congregationalists, Methodists, and Unitarians. Faiths other than Christianity are also practiced, especially by ethnic minority groups; for example, Glasgow has several synagogues and mosques and a Buddhist centre.

SETTLEMENT PATTERNS

In earlier times mountains, rivers, and seas divided the Scottish people into self-sufficient communities that developed strong senses of local identity. This sense has been eroded by social mobility, modern transport, broadcasting, and other standardizing influences and by a general shift from rural to urban ways of life. Yet vestiges of regional consciousness linger. The Shetland islanders speak of Scotland with detachment. The Galloway area in the southwest, cut off by hills from the rest of the country, has a vigorous regional patriotism. The Gaelic-speaking people of the Hebrides and the western Highlands find their language a bond of community. The northeast has its own local traditions, embodied especially in a still vigorous Scots dialect, and Borderers celebrate their local festivals with fervour. The most thickly populated rural areas are those with the best farming land, such as in East Lothian and in the northeast.

The Highlands once nourished a large population, but "Highland Clearances" (a series of forcible evictions) and continuous emigration since the 18th century have caused it to dwindle. Now settlements in the Highlands are mostly remnants of crofting townships—that is, irregular groupings of subsistence farms of a few acres each. The old pattern of crofting was one of communities practicing a kind of cooperative farming, with strips of common land allotted annually to individuals. Examples of the old system survive, but now crofters have their own arable land fenced in, while they share the common grazing land. In East Lothian and other areas of high farming, the communal farm has long been replaced by single farms with steadings (farmsteads) and workers' houses. Scotland noticeably lacks those old villages that evolved in England from medieval hamlets of joint tenants. Some planned villages were built by enterprising landowners in the 18th century.

Burghs, often little bigger than villages, were mostly set up as trading centres, ports, or river crossings or to command entrances to mountain passes. Many small towns survive around the east and northeast coast that were once obliged to be self-contained in consumer industries and burghal institutions because they lacked adequate transportation systems. The growth of industry and transport has helped produce urbanization. Edinburgh, Dundee, and Aberdeen are centres of administration, commerce, and industry for their areas, but only central Clydeside, including Glasgow with its satellite towns, is large enough to deserve the official title of conurbation (metropolitan area).

DEMOGRAPHIC TRENDS

While Scotland makes up about one-third of the area of the United Kingdom, it has less than one-tenth of the population, of which the greatest concentration (nearly three-fourths) lives in the central belt. Historically, England has been the main beneficiary of Scottish emigration, especially during economic downturns. Large-scale emigration also placed Scots in such countries as Canada, the United States, and Australia until the late 20th century; despite this phenomenon, however, the size of the Scottish population has remained relatively stable since World War II. The pattern of migration began to reverse when the North Sea petroleum industry brought many people to the northeast and the north, not only from various parts of Scotland and the United Kingdom but also from other countries, notably the United States. Scotland is now increasingly seen as an attractive place to work and live.

CHAPTER 8

THE SCOTTISH ECONOMY

During the 1970s and '80s Scotland's economy shared in acute form the problems besetting many European countries, brought about by rapid changes that included the widespread failure of heavy industries. Unemployment became a serious problem, especially in those areas where major industries had declined. Successive governments made efforts to improve these conditions by a variety of measures. Beginning in the 1980s, Scotland's economy benefited from the exploitation of North Sea petroleum and natural gas and from the development of high-technology and other economic sectors.

Scotland remains a small but open economy and accounts for about five percent of the United Kingdom's export revenue. Its gross domestic product (GDP) per capita is higher than in all other areas of the United Kingdom outside London and England's eastern regions, and its level of unemployment is fairly low. However, wealth in Scotland is not evenly distributed, and the average unemployment rate hides pockets of much higher unemployment in some regions and localities. Although the British government controls Scotland's macroeconomic policy, including central government spending, interest rates, and monetary matters, the Scottish Parliament has power over local economic development, education, and training.

AGRICULTURE, FORESTRY, AND FISHING

Wild animals, birds, and river fishes are of minor importance as an economic resource, but deer and grouse hunting, as well as fishing, provides employment in parts of the Highlands in which other activities are hardly possible. Venison, including meat from deer farms, is exported to the European mainland.

No economic sector made greater progress in the post–World War II period than agriculture in terms of productivity. Mechanization allowed the full-time labour force to fall from about 88,000 in 1951 to roughly one-fourth of that number by the end of the 20th century, but by the early 21st century the number of those employed in agriculture increased to some 65,000 people, and farming was a significant contributor to Scotland's rural economy. Still, though there are thousands of crofts (subsistence farms) in the north, many of them are no longer cultivated. Crofting is a special branch of Scottish agriculture that has to be supplemented by other work, such as forestry, road work, and weaving, as well as in the tourist industry.

Most of Scotland consists of hilly or marginal land, with hill sheep farming predominating, particularly in the Southern Uplands and in the Highlands. In the southwest, dairy farming suits the wetter, milder climate and has a convenient market in the central Clydeside conurbation. The most striking feature of livestock farming has been the rise in the number of cattle and, to a lesser extent, sheep; pig and poultry production has also expanded. However, during the

Highland cattle resting in a field, Scotland. Brand X Pictures/Punchstock

1990s publicity surrounding an outbreak of bovine spongiform encephalopathy (commonly known as mad cow disease) adversely affected cattle farming.

Field crops are mainly found along the eastern seaboard. Barley and wheat are the main cereals; the land devoted to potatoes, though substantial, has declined. Rapeseed production has increased considerably, while oat cultivation has fallen

MAD COW DISEASE

Mad cow disease, formally known as bovine spongiform encephalopathy (BSE), is caused by an infectious agent that has a long incubation period of between two and five years. Signs of the disease include behavioral changes, such as agitation and nervousness, and a progressive loss of muscular coordination and locomotive function. In advanced stages the animal frequently loses weight, shows fine muscular contractions over its neck and body, walks in an abnormal and exaggerated manner, and may isolate itself from the herd. Death usually follows within a year of the onset of symptoms. No treatment or palliative measures are known.

First recognized in cattle in the United Kingdom in 1986, BSE became epidemic there, particularly in southern England. Cases also were reported in other parts of Europe and in Canada. The disease is similar to the neurodegenerative disease of sheep called scrapie. It is thought to have arisen when cattle were fed high-protein supplements made from ruminant carcasses and offal (the trimmings of butchered animals). Although animal remains had been used as a source of dietary supplements for several decades without problems, modifications to the rendering process—specifically, reduction in the temperatures used and discontinuance of certain solvents—in the early 1980s were followed by the outbreak of BSE. The timing of events suggested that the modified process no longer incapacitated the infectious agent. In 1988, on the basis of this inferred connection, the British government banned the use of animal-derived protein supplements. The following year the U.S. Department of Agriculture banned the import of live ruminants from countries known to have BSE, and in 1997 both the United States and Canada implemented bans on the use of animal-derived proteins in ruminant feed. From 1986 to 2008 nearly 185,000 cases of BSE were confirmed in the United Kingdom. In contrast, through February 2008 a total of just 16 cases of BSE were confirmed in North America, with the majority of cases occurring in Canadian-born cattle. Because of heightened awareness of increasing prevalence of BSE in Canadian cattle, Canada enhanced its feed ban in 2007 to prohibit the inclusion of "specified risk materials," as well as animal proteins, from all animal feeds.

BSE, scrapie, and similar diseases in other species, such as Creutzfeldt-Jakob disease and kuru in humans, are categorized as transmissible spongiform encephalopathies. They are so named because the brain tissue of organisms with the disease becomes pitted with holes in a spongelike pattern. The cause of these diseases is attributed to an unusual infectious agent called a prion. The prion is a modified form of a normally harmless protein found in the brain of mammals and birds. In its aberrant form, however, the prion protein builds up in nerve cells as it multiplies. This accumulation somehow damages these cells and leads to the characteristic neurodegeneration. It is suspected that there also exists an atypical strain of BSE, which arises spontaneously (as opposed to orally through the ingestion of contaminated feed) and leads to a distinct prion disease characterized by a lack of pitted holes in the brain.

After the emergence of BSE, concern grew over a possible relationship between the animal disease and the occurrence of Creutzfeldt-Jakob disease in people. Beginning in the mid-1990s a new variant form of Creutzfeldt-Jakob disease (nvCJD) took the lives of dozens of people in

Europe. In experiments with mice, researchers found that prions from human cases of nvCJD caused a disease pattern similar to that caused by prions from cows with BSE. The result suggested that the human infection is linked to BSE.

and has been replaced by barley as the main cereal for livestock feed. Malted barley is the key ingredient in Scotch whisky, a distilled liquor that is one of Scotland's best-known export products. Raspberry growing is concentrated mainly in the central eastern part of the country. Tomatoes were once grown in greenhouses in the Clyde valley, but that industry had all but vanished by the early 21st century. The output of turnips and hay for livestock feeding has fallen, being replaced by an increase in grass silage.

Forestry is a significant activity and has helped to retain population in Scotland's rural areas. Scotland is responsible for about half of the United Kingdom's total timber production and more than two-thirds of its softwood production. The forests are managed by the Forestry Commission, a public body, and by private landowners, including forestry companies. Although the Forestry Commission plants trees throughout the country, it plays a particularly important role in Highland development. The main species used are conifers, including Sitka spruce, Norway spruce, Scotch pine, European larch, and Douglas fir.

The seafood industry has long been vital to Scotland's economy. About two-thirds of the total British fish and shellfish catch is now handled by Scottish ports. Peterhead ranks as Britain's top whitefish port, and Aberdeen and Aberdeenshire are among the United Kingdom's main centres of fish processing. Haddock, cod, herring, sole, and mackerel are the main species caught. Nephrops (langoustine) is the most important shellfish, though scallop, queen scallop, lobster, and several crab varieties are also important. Commercial salmon fishing is important on the west coast from Argyll to the Shetland Islands, and fish farming is also important, especially of salmon and shellfish along the coast and trout in the inland lochs.

RESOURCES AND POWER

Mining and power generation account for less than one-tenth of Scotland's annual GDP. Until the last decade of the 20th century, Scotland's chief mineral resource was coal. The industry reached a peak annual production of 43 million tons in 1913 but subsequently declined drastically. In particular, deep mining became largely uneconomical, and Scotland's last remaining deep-pit coal mine was closed in 2002. Other minerals that have been worked intermittently include gold, silver, chromite, diatomite, and dolomite, but none has been successfully exploited. Although peat is available to a depth of 2 feet (0.6 metre) or more and is spread over some 2,650 square miles (6,880

Ships serving North Sea oil platforms at dock in the port of Aberdeen. Milt and Joan Mann/CameraMann International

square km), its economic value is limited. It is still burned for fuel in the Highlands, but its use has decreased because of the time and labour involved in cutting and drying it.

Britain's North Sea petroleum and natural gas resources began to be developed in the 1970s. The oil fields lie mostly in Scottish waters, but the British government holds their ownership and receives the revenue yield. Large companies have located and extracted the resource, mostly with the aid of American technology. Aberdeen is the centre of the petroleum industry, and the economy of Shetland has also benefited from discoveries in adjacent waters. In addition, natural gas from North Sea wells has replaced manufactured gas in Scotland. Tens of thousands of jobs have been created in Scotland by onshore oil- and gas-related enterprises, such as oil-platform construction and the servicing of North Sea operators. Although the newfound prosperity has been subject to the vagaries of international markets—especially after fossil fuel revenues were severely reduced in the mid-1980s—the petroleum industry continues to provide, directly and indirectly, a great number of jobs in Scotland.

Water is also a valuable resource, especially for generating electricity, and several dams and power stations have been built since the mid-20th century. Coal- and oil-fired stations each produce about one-fourth of Scotland's electric power, and nuclear generation, notably via the station at Torness, east of Edinburgh, accounts for about one-third. Almost one-fifth of Scotland's electricity is generated by renewable resources, and in the early 21st century there was an aggressive push to develop greater renewable capacity. Scotland was at the forefront of research on wave and tidal energy, and it was a global leader in the development and construction of deep-sea offshore wind farms.

MANUFACTURING

Manufacturing and the construction industry contribute more than one-fourth of Scotland's annual GDP. In its industrial heyday Scotland's prosperity was based on such heavy industries as coal, steel, ship construction, and engineering, but these were the industries most exposed to foreign competition and to declines in local production. The structure of Scottish industry has been gradually diversified and modernized, with a reduction in Scotland's dependence on heavy industries and replacement of them with high-technology enterprises and those making consumer goods. As with coal, the 20th-century history of steel and shipbuilding was one of reduction in the number of plants and employees. The sale of the nationalized British Shipbuilders to the private sector accelerated the decline in the number of major shipyards in Scotland. The special facilities built to provide rigs and platforms for exploiting the North Sea oil and gas reserves have experienced fluctuating demand, and some of them have closed. Heavy industry in Scotland received a boost from the emerging wind-energy sector in the early 21st century, and the manufacture and installation of onshore and offshore turbines accounted for thousands of jobs.

Although not matching the older manufactures in terms of employment, the computer, office equipment, and electronics industries have expanded. Much of the investment in those enterprises has come from overseas, particularly from the United States. Electronics and related industries have been a major source of economic growth, employment, and export earnings. Manufacturers in the Midland Valley—which has been nicknamed "Silicon Glen" because of its high-technology sector—have produced many of Europe's computers and electronic machinery. Engineering industries export much of their output, and the textile industries of the Scottish Borders and the Harris tweed in the Hebrides also have a considerable, though reduced, export business.

Distilleries in the Highlands and the northeast produce the Scotch whisky for which the country is internationally famous. Whisky sales have continued to increase despite heavy taxes on home consumption. The appeal of Scotch whisky in foreign countries remains high, and whisky is one of Scotland's leading exports.

Glenlivet whisky distillery, Minmore. © Brian Seed from TSW—CLICK/Chicago

Printing and brewing formerly were well-established industries in Edinburgh and Glasgow but are now in decline.

FINANCE

As a component of the United Kingdom, Scotland uses the British pound sterling as its official currency. Business services and banking account for a large proportion of employment in Scotland. Among the main banking and insurance

TWEED

Rough in surface texture, tweed fabrics are produced in a great variety of colour and weave effects largely determined by the place of manufacture. The descriptions "Scottish," "Welsh," "Cheviot," "Saxony," "Harris," "Yorkshire," "Donegal," and "West of England," for example, cover an extremely wide range of woolen and mixture cloths. Most tweeds are made entirely of wool; but an increasing number consist of blends of wool and cotton, wool and rayon, or wool and man-made fibres, each of which imparts a special property.

The word tweed was not derived from the River Tweed, although the cloth was manufactured in the Tweed Valley. Tweed is usually made by a variation of the basic twill weave, and the old Scottish name for twill was tweel. The name tweed is attributed to a mistake on the part of a London clerk who in 1826, when drafting an order or invoice for tweels, accidentally wrote tweeds, a name that quickly established itself.

The wide range of modified twill weaves in use includes herringbones, diamonds, chevrons, cross twills, and checks, along with an even more extensive variety of stripe, marl, fleck, and mingled heather effects in many tones and hues. The counts of the yarns and the twist and colours employed vary greatly, as do the ends and picks in warp and weft, or filling. Most tweeds are colour woven from dyed yarns, but some are piece-dyed. Technical advances in dyeing raw stock, yarns, and fabrics, together with new techniques in finishing, have resulted in a wide variety of stable and hard-wearing apparel cloths made in different weights.

jobs are legal and computer services, accountancy, and property (real estate) services. Scotland had eight joint-stock banks until the 1950s, when mergers reduced this number to three: the Bank of Scotland, the Royal Bank of Scotland (RBS), and the Clydesdale Bank, each of which retains the right to issue its own notes (currency). By the 21st century, RBS had become one of the world's largest financial institutions, but the ill-timed acquisition of the Dutch bank ABN AMRO in 2007 led to the bank's near collapse and its partial nationalization by the British government. Financial and business services have expanded substantially since the mid-1960s, with Edinburgh becoming second in Britain only to London in this field. The banking sector also has expanded into North America and Europe. Merchant banking facilities are more widely available, and the services historically associated with Scotland, such as the management of unit and investment trusts and life funds, have expanded. About one-third of Britain's investment trusts are managed by firms in Edinburgh, Glasgow, and Dundee, which also have large investments in North America and specialized knowledge of conditions there. Unit trusts are represented in Edinburgh, where some leading British insurance companies also have their headquarters.

SERVICES

Since the mid-1960s there has been a marked shift in employment from manufacturing to services, including tourism, with the service sector accounting for nearly four times the number of jobs as the manufacturing sector. Private services contribute about two-fifths of Scotland's GDP, whereas public services account for more than one-fifth. Retail trade is also an important job creator in Scotland.

Tourism is important in Scotland, with employment particularly strong in the hotel and catering businesses. The majority of visitors come from other parts of Scotland or the United Kingdom, but more than two million annually come from abroad, notably the United States, Germany, France, and Ireland. Among the most popular attractions are Scotland's rural parklands, from those around Greater Glasgow and the Clyde valley to the less-accessible Highlands; the cultural institutions of Edinburgh and Glasgow; the Palace of Holyroodhouse and the country's numerous historic houses; and the Edinburgh, Stirling, Urquhart, and Blair castles. The most popular destination abroad for Scottish tourists, by far, is Spain, including the Balearic and Canary islands; additionally, many travel to other European nations and the United States.

TRANSPORTATION

Public transport was formerly largely state-owned, but much of it has now been privatized. Bus services were deregulated in the 1980s, which led to greater competition, and the Scottish Transport

Group, formed in 1968 to control bus and steamer services on the west coast, was dissolved in 2002. The proliferation of automobiles has made it difficult for bus companies to maintain profitable services in rural areas, where they are being either subsidized by local authorities and the government or withdrawn. Ship services from mainland ports to island towns have been curtailed and replaced by car ferries using short crossings; such ferries operate from several west coast towns to the Hebrides and other islands and from north and east coast ports to the Orkney and Shetland islands.

The Scottish road and bridge network has improved considerably, as some main routes have been upgraded to motorway standard and many single-lane roads in the Highlands have been widened. Improvements in the east and north were speeded up to cope with increased traffic generated by North Sea oil production, and bridges have been built over the Cromarty and Moray firths.

Railway services have been severely reduced since the mid 20th century, when more than 3,000 miles (4,800 km) of track were open to passenger and freight traffic. Many branch lines and stations have been closed, and the route mileage has shrunk to less than two-thirds of the former total.

There has been significant electrification of Scotland's train lines, including for the suburban lines and the main line from London (Euston) to Glasgow.

Scottish ports handle many more imports than exports, as a large proportion of Britain's exports are sent abroad via English ports. Glasgow, the largest port, is under the administration of the Clyde Port Authority. The ports of Grangemouth, Dundee, and Leith, among others, are grouped under the Forth Ports Limited, whereas Aberdeen is independent. Important oil ports are located in Shetland (Sullom Voe), in Orkney (Flotta), and on the east coast. Greenock and Grangemouth are equipped for container traffic, and extensive improvement schemes have been carried out at Leith and other ports. Coastal trade has dwindled because of the competition of motor transport, and inland waterways have never been a commercial success.

Air travel has increased markedly, with a substantial growth in direct services to Europe, including a large number of charter flights. Scotland has major airports at Glasgow, Edinburgh, Aberdeen, and Prestwick on the west coast, which also serves Glasgow. As Prestwick is remarkably fog-free, it is used for transatlantic flights.

CHAPTER 9

SCOTTISH GOVERNMENT AND SOCIETY

Scotland is represented at Westminster in London by 59 members of Parliament in the House of Commons who are elected by plurality votes from single-member constituencies, and all Scottish appointive (life) peers are entitled to sit in the House of Lords. Scotland's head of government is the British prime minister, and the head of state is the British monarch. The country remains subject to the British Parliament in the areas of foreign affairs, foreign trade, defense, the national civil service, economic and monetary policy, social security, employment, energy regulation, most aspects of taxation, and some aspects of transport. The secretary of state for Scotland represents Scotland in the British government's cabinet.

Historically, the British government and its Scottish Office, headed by Scotland's secretary of state, were the sole legislative and executive authorities for Scotland. In a 1997 referendum put forward by the government of Tony Blair, nearly three-fourths of the Scottish electorate favoured the establishment of a Scottish Parliament, which formally began sitting in 1999. The Scottish Parliament, located in Edinburgh, has wide powers over such matters as health, education, housing, regional transport, the environment, and agriculture. It also has the power to increase or decrease the British income tax rate by 3 percent within Scotland. The leading parliamentary party or coalition appoints the Scottish Executive, the administrative arm of the government, which is headed by a first minister.

THE UNITED KINGDOM: NORTHERN IRELAND, SCOTLAND, AND WALES

Legend:
- Cities over 2,000,000
- Cities 200,000 to 2,000,000
- Cities 50,000 to 200,000
- Cities under 50,000
- National capitals
- Country capitals
- International boundaries
- Country boundaries
- Political subdivision boundaries
- Canals
- Bridges
- Waterfalls
- National parks
- Spot elevations in metres (1 m = 3.28 ft)

Polyconic Projection

Key to Political Subdivisions
(shown by number on map)

Scotland
1. SHETLAND ISLANDS
2. ORKNEY ISLANDS
3. WESTERN ISLES
4. HIGHLAND
5. MORAY
6. ABERDEENSHIRE
7. ABERDEEN CITY
8. ANGUS
9. DUNDEE CITY
10. PERTH AND KINROSS
11. FIFE
12. CLACKMANNANSHIRE
13. STIRLING
14. ARGYLL AND BUTE
15. NORTH AYRSHIRE
16. INVERCLYDE
17. WEST DUNBARTONSHIRE
18. RENFREWSHIRE
19. EAST RENFREWSHIRE
20. GLASGOW CITY
21. EAST DUNBARTONSHIRE
22. NORTH LANARKSHIRE
23. FALKIRK
24. WEST LOTHIAN
25. CITY OF EDINBURGH
26. MIDLOTHIAN
27. EAST LOTHIAN
28. SCOTTISH BORDERS
29. SOUTH LANARKSHIRE
30. DUMFRIES AND GALLOWAY
31. EAST AYRSHIRE
32. SOUTH AYRSHIRE

Northern Ireland
33. MOYLE
34. LARNE
35. BALLYMENA
36. BALLYMONEY
37. COLERAINE
38. MAGHERAFELT
39. LIMAVADY
40. DERRY
41. STRABANE
42. OMAGH
43. FERMANAGH
44. DUNGANNON
45. COOKSTOWN
46. ANTRIM
47. NEWTOWNABBEY
48. CARRICKFERGUS
49. NORTH DOWN
50. BELFAST
51. CASTLEREAGH
52. ARDS
53. DOWN
54. LISBURN
55. BANBRIDGE
56. CRAIGAVON
57. ARMAGH
58. NEWRY AND MOURNE

Wales
59. ANGLESEY, ISLE OF
60. GWYNEDD
61. CONWY
62. DENBIGHSHIRE
63. FLINTSHIRE
64. WREXHAM
65. POWYS
66. CEREDIGION
67. PEMBROKESHIRE
68. CARMARTHENSHIRE
69. SWANSEA
70. NEATH PORT TALBOT
71. BRIDGEND
72. VALE OF GLAMORGAN
73. RHONDDA CYNON TAFF
74. MERTHYR TYDFIL
75. CAERPHILLY
76. CARDIFF
77. NEWPORT
78. TORFAEN
79. BLAENAU GWENT
80. MONMOUTHSHIRE

England – Administrative Counties
81. NORTHUMBERLAND
82. CUMBRIA
83. DURHAM
84. NORTH YORKSHIRE
85. LANCASHIRE
86. CHESHIRE
87. DERBYSHIRE
88. NOTTINGHAMSHIRE
89. LINCOLNSHIRE
90. LEICESTERSHIRE
91. STAFFORDSHIRE
92. SHROPSHIRE
93. WORCESTERSHIRE
94. WARWICKSHIRE
95. NORTHAMPTONSHIRE
96. CAMBRIDGESHIRE
97. NORFOLK
98. SUFFOLK
99. ESSEX
100. HERTFORDSHIRE
101. BEDFORDSHIRE
102. BUCKINGHAMSHIRE
103. OXFORDSHIRE
104. GLOUCESTERSHIRE
105. WILTSHIRE
106. SOMERSET
107. DEVON
108. CORNWALL
109. DORSET
110. HAMPSHIRE
111. SURREY
112. WEST SUSSEX
113. EAST SUSSEX
114. KENT

England – Unitary Authorities
115. HARTLEPOOL
116. REDCAR AND CLEVELAND
117. MIDDLESBROUGH
118. STOCKTON-ON-TEES
119. DARLINGTON
120. YORK
121. EAST RIDING OF YORKSHIRE
122. KINGSTON UPON HULL
123. NORTH EAST LINCOLNSHIRE
124. NORTH LINCOLNSHIRE
125. BLACKPOOL
126. BLACKBURN WITH DARWEN
127. WARRINGTON
128. HALTON
129. TELFORD AND WREKIN
130. STOKE-ON-TRENT
131. DERBY
132. NOTTINGHAM CITY
133. LEICESTER
134. RUTLAND
135. PETERBOROUGH
136. MILTON KEYNES
137. LUTON
138. HEREFORDSHIRE
139. SOUTH GLOUCESTERSHIRE
140. BRISTOL
141. NORTH SOMERSET
142. BATH AND NORTH EAST SOMERSET
143. SWINDON
144. WEST BERKSHIRE
145. READING
146. WOKINGHAM
147. BRACKNELL FOREST
148. WINDSOR AND MAIDENHEAD
149. SLOUGH
150. THURROCK
151. SOUTHEND
152. MEDWAY
153. BRIGHTON AND HOVE
154. PORTSMOUTH
155. ISLE OF WIGHT
156. SOUTHAMPTON
157. BOURNEMOUTH
158. POOLE
159. TORBAY
160. PLYMOUTH

England – Metropolitan Counties
161. TYNE AND WEAR
162. MERSEYSIDE
163. GREATER MANCHESTER
164. WEST YORKSHIRE
165. SOUTH YORKSHIRE
166. WEST MIDLANDS
167. GREATER LONDON

LOCAL GOVERNMENT

Local authorities in Scotland are administrative bodies that must act within the framework of laws passed by the European, United Kingdom, and Scottish parliaments. They are responsible for a range of community services, including environmental matters, urban planning, education, roadways and traffic, fire fighting, sanitation, housing, parks and recreation, and elections.

Scotland is divided into 32 council areas, each administered by a local council. The council areas vary considerably in both geographic extent and population. Highland is the largest council area, encompassing 10,091 square miles (26,136 square km), and, at 25 square miles (65 square km), Dundee is the smallest. With a population of roughly 600,000 people, Glasgow is the most populous council area, whereas the least populous is the Orkney Islands, which has about 20,000 residents.

Within the local council areas are hundreds of communities, including towns, villages, and city neighbourhoods.

The Debating Chamber of the Scottish Parliament, Edinburgh. © Scottish Parliamentary Corporate Body 2010

Communities may elect community councils to serve on a voluntary basis and perform a mainly consultative role. Their concerns include environmental and planning matters affecting their communities.

JUSTICE

Scotland has a distinct legal and judicial system that is based on Roman law. The country is divided into six sheriffdoms (Glasgow; Grampian Highland and Islands; Lothian and Borders; North Strathclyde; South Strathclyde, Dumfries, and Galloway; and Tayside, Central, and Fife), each with a sheriff principal (chief judge) and a varying number of sheriffs. There are 49 sheriff courts divided among the sheriffdoms. The most serious offenses triable by jury are reserved for the High Court of Justiciary, the supreme court for criminal cases. The judges are the same as those of the Court of Session, the supreme court for civil cases. An appeal may be directed to the House of Lords from the Court of Session but not from the High Court of Justiciary. The Court of Session, consisting of the lord president, the lord justice clerk, and 22 other judges, sits in Edinburgh and is divided into an Outer House, which hears cases at first instance, and an Inner House, which hears appeals from the Outer House and from lower courts. The Inner House has two divisions, each with four judges. The sheriff courts have a wide jurisdiction in civil cases, but certain actions, such as challenging governmental decisions, are reserved for the Court of Session. They also deal with most criminal offenses, with serious cases tried by jury. The decision whether to prosecute is made by the lord advocate in the High Court and by procurators fiscal in the sheriff courts. District courts, presided over by lay judges, deal with minor criminal offenses. There is also a system for hearing cases involving children.

The lord advocate and the solicitor general for Scotland are the Scottish Executive's law officers, charged with representing the Scottish government in court cases. The lord advocate also serves as Scotland's public prosecutor. Both are appointed by the British monarch on the recommendation of the first minister and with the approval of the Scottish Parliament. The advocate general for Scotland, who is the law officer of the United Kingdom responsible for Scottish matters, acts as an adviser to the British government and to the Scottish lord advocate and solicitor general.

POLITICAL PROCESS

All citizens at least 18 years of age are eligible to vote. Voters in Scotland elect representatives to local councils, the Scottish Parliament, the British House of Commons, and the European Parliament. Terms of office vary for elected officials. Local councillors serve three-year terms, members of the Scottish Parliament four-year terms, and members of the House of Commons and

European Parliament five-year terms. Although local, Scottish, and European elections take place at regular intervals, elections to the House of Commons occur at least once every five years, with the date set by the British government. Non-British European Union citizens are eligible to participate in local and European Parliament elections.

There are 129 members of the Scottish Parliament; 73 are chosen from single-member constituencies and 56 by proportional representation from regional party lists. Coalition governments between the Scottish Labour Party and the Scottish Liberal Democrats were necessary in the initial sittings of the Parliament, as no single party was able to win a majority in the Scottish Parliament. In 2007, however, the Scottish National Party (SNP) formed a minority administration.

Until the middle of the 20th century, Scottish voters split their loyalties about evenly between the Conservative (traditionally known in Scotland as the Scottish Conservative and Unionist Party) and Labour parties, but thereafter into the early 21st century the Labour Party dominated Scottish politics. Indeed, at the 1997 national election the Conservative Party returned no members to the House of Commons. From Keir Hardie, who cofounded the Independent Labour Party in the 1890s, to Ramsay MacDonald, Labour's first prime minister, in the 1920s, to Prime Minister Tony Blair and his successor, Gordon Brown, in the 1990s and early 21st century, many of the most influential Labour Party politicians have either been

J. KEIR HARDIE

James Keir Hardie (born August 15, 1856, Legbrannock, Lanarkshire, Scotland—died September 26, 1915, Glasgow) was the first labour leader to represent the workingman in Parliament as an Independent (1892) and first to lead the Labour Party in the House of Commons (1906). A dedicated socialist, he was also an outspoken pacifist (from the time of the South African, or Boer, War, 1899–1902) and the chief adviser (from 1903) to the militant suffragists headed by Emmeline Pankhurst.

Unmarried at the time of Hardie's birth, his mother, a farm servant, later married a ship's carpenter who was an early trade unionist. In this setting, Hardie became the eldest of a family of nine children, and his childhood, passed partly in Glasgow and partly in the Lanarkshire

Hardie, drawing by Cosmo Rowe; in the National Portrait Gallery, London. Courtesy of the National Portrait Gallery, London

coalfield, was one of great hardship. He never went to school. He began to work at age seven or eight and became a coal miner at 10. In the late 1870s he was fired and blacklisted by the Lanark mineowners for his strike activity. Moving to Ayr, he was chosen secretary of a miners' organization. From 1881 he helped to form miners' unions on a county basis, meanwhile earning his living as a journalist. In his own newspapers, *The Miner* (1887–89) and *Labour Leader* (from 1889), he expressed Christian socialist views on labour and on wider political issues. He founded the Scottish Labour Party in 1888, the year in which he was badly defeated in his first attempt at election to the House of Commons. Successful in the 1892 general election, he was a member of Parliament when, at Bradford, Yorkshire, in January 1893, he participated in organizing the Independent Labour Party (ILP). More a propaganda enterprise than a true political party, the ILP was the first socialist group having a genuine Christian, English, and working-class appeal; it was neither middle class and intellectual (as was the Fabian Society) nor specifically Marxist and thus foreign in inspiration and atheistic.

Following the loss of his Commons seat in 1895, Hardie assisted in planning a Labour Party resembling the Liberals and the Conservatives in parliamentary organization. Delegates at a labour conference in London on February 27–28, 1900, formed the Labour Representation Committee, forerunner of the Labour Party. In the same year, Hardie was returned to Parliament, and, six years later, he was joined in the Commons by 28 other members of the committee, which then became a party organization with an elected leader (at first called the chairman) and party whips. Temperamentally unsuited to the routine administration of a group, Hardie ended his chairmanship in 1907.

As World War I approached, Hardie became primarily concerned with the role of labour in maintaining peace. He sought to bind the Second International to declaring a general strike in all countries in the event of war. His failure in this effort and the decision of a majority of the Labour Party to support British participation in the war caused Hardie to withdraw in disillusion from his colleagues.

Scottish-born or resided in Scotland. The Liberal Democrats have maintained fairly strong support in the Celtic fringes of Scotland, and the SNP, which advocates Scotland's independence from the United Kingdom, has captured a significant share of support since the 1970s. In the 2007 elections the SNP narrowly won the most seats in the Scottish Parliament, but it secured a clear majority in 2011 as Labour continued to rebuild and support for the Liberal Democrats virtually collapsed.

SECURITY

Military planning in Scotland is the responsibility of the British government. Scotland is the site of a number of key military installations, including several belonging to the North Atlantic Treaty Organization (NATO). The Royal Navy has a base at Rosyth on the Firth of Forth, and the Royal Air Force has stations at Lossiemouth and Leuchars. Scottish infantry regiments are still distinguished by their tartans: kilts for the Highland regiments and trousers for those of the Lowlands. The oldest infantry regiment in the British army is the Royal Scots.

The Scottish Parliament and the Scottish Executive, which have a general responsibility for law and order, share control of the police forces with local councils. As in England and Wales, the police do not normally carry firearms, although special units carry guns when dealing with armed or particularly dangerous criminals.

HEALTH AND WELFARE

Health care in Scotland is provided mostly free of charge through the National Health Service. The Scottish Parliament is responsible for health, welfare services, and housing. Scotland's 14 health boards are accountable to the Scottish Executive through the minister for health. The country has some of the highest incidences in Europe of heart disease and lung cancer, which are among the leading causes of death in Scotland, along with other types of cancer and diseases of the respiratory, circulatory, and digestive systems.

HOUSING

Home ownership in Scotland generally has lagged behind that of the rest of the United Kingdom. Owing to policies implemented by the government of Margaret Thatcher in the 1980s that encouraged home ownership, owner-occupied units increased from barely two-fifths of total housing in the mid-1980s to about two-thirds in the early 21st century. Local housing authorities provide about one-fifth of the housing units in Scotland. The housing stock in Scotland varies considerably in size and type. In the latter part of the 20th century, several government-subsidized housing complexes were built on the outskirts of urban areas; however, many of those properties have since become owner occupied or have been taken over by housing trusts.

EDUCATION

Scotland's education system is rooted in tradition. Schools run by the church existed in the Middle Ages, and by the end of the 15th century Scotland already had three universities. Towns were involved in founding schools by the 16th century, and during the 17th century the old Scottish Parliament passed several acts encouraging the establishment of schools. Scotland retained its separate education system following the Act of Union in 1707, and it developed considerably over the next 200 years. In the early 20th century Scotland introduced a single external examination system, founded new secondary schools, and replaced school boards with local education authorities. The state also took over responsibility for Roman Catholic primary and secondary schools; however, the Roman Catholic Church has continued to influence staffing, religious education, and the general ethos of the schools.

The educational system in Scotland was markedly reformed in the 1960s, notably by switching from selective to comprehensive secondary schools. The vocational education system also rapidly expanded during this period, and the number of universities increased from four to eight (St. Andrews, Glasgow, Aberdeen, Edinburgh, Strathclyde, Heriot-Watt, Dundee, and Stirling). New standards were enacted in the 1970s and '80s in an effort to promote further reform and to give parents a greater say in the education of their children. The number of universities increased again in the 1990s as some existing institutions were accorded university status.

Early education is optional and is provided in nursery schools, day nurseries, and play groups, as well as through private child care and other arrangements. The government has a policy of guaranteeing a nursery place to every child age four or five, partially as a means of helping mothers who wish to return to paid employment. School education is compulsory and is provided free for all children between the ages of 5 and 16. Parents have the right to send their children to the school of their choice, although there are some restrictions on this right. Parents can also choose to send their children to private, fee-paying schools. Unlike England, there is no national curriculum, but the "Curriculum for Excellence" practices were introduced in the 21st century to provide a framework

UNIVERSITY OF EDINBURGH

One of the most noted of Scotland's universities, the University of Edinburgh was founded in 1583 as "the Town's College" under Presbyterian auspices by the Edinburgh town council under a charter granted in 1582 by King James VI, who later became King James I of England. In 1621 an act of the Scottish Parliament accorded all the rights and privileges of Scotland's three older universities to the Town's College, after which it gradually assumed the name of the University of Edinburgh. The university remained under the control of the Edinburgh town council until 1858, when it received autonomy under the Universities Act.

The university initially consisted of a liberal arts college and a school of divinity. Schools of medicine and law were established in the early 18th century, and faculties of music, science, arts, social sciences, and veterinary medicine were subsequently added.

Although its faculty of divinity has always been of singular importance to the university, its school of medicine is also renowned. The English naturalist Charles Darwin studied medicine there. The University of Edinburgh has produced a long line of eminent cultural figures, including the novelist Sir Walter Scott, the philosopher and historian James Mill, the essayist and historian Thomas Carlyle, the novelist Robert Louis Stevenson, and the inventor Alexander Graham Bell.

for such matters. Students transfer from primary to secondary school at about the age of 12, and nearly three-fourths continue their studies beyond the leaving age of 16. Postsecondary education is available in further-education colleges or higher-education institutions. Further-education colleges provide vocational education and training and also offer a range of higher-education courses.

Education from preschool to higher education is one of the responsibilities of the Scottish Parliament. Policies are administered through the Scottish Executive Education Department (preschool and school education) and the Scottish Executive Enterprise and Lifelong Learning Department (further and higher education). Many aspects of educational administration are devolved to education authorities and to schools themselves, and further- and higher-education institutions are responsible for much of their own administration. The Scottish Higher Education Funding Council (established in 1993) and the Scottish Further Education Funding Council (set up in 1999) play a key role in allocating funds to institutions in these sectors.

Local authorities are responsible for providing schooling, special educational needs, and the (legally guaranteed) provision of Gaelic teaching in Gaelic-speaking areas. They are also responsible for creating plans that set out a framework for the development of community education in their areas. School boards also play a role in the provision of public education and allow for the election of parents and for their input in the running of their children's school. Both the Roman Catholic Church and the Church of Scotland have the right of representation on local-authority education committees.

Private education is provided outside the state system, and independent—or "public" schools, as they are known—vary considerably in size. Some public schools focus on primary- or secondary-age pupils, while others offer a complete education from preschool to age 18. The highest concentration of public schools is found in Edinburgh.

CHAPTER 10

SCOTTISH CULTURAL LIFE

Scotland's culture and customs remain remarkably vigorous and distinctive despite the country's union with the United Kingdom since the early 18th century and the threat of dominance by its more powerful partner to the south. Its strength springs in part from the diverse strands that make up its background, including European mainstream cultures. It has also been enriched by contacts with Europe, owing to the mobility of the Scottish people since the Middle Ages and the hospitality of Scotland's universities to foreign students and faculty.

DAILY LIFE AND SOCIAL CUSTOMS

Although bagpipes have ancient origins elsewhere and are found throughout the world, they are one of the most recognized symbols of Scottish culture. By the 16th century, various clans had established hereditary pipers, and later the instrument was used in wartime to inflame the

Scottish Highland bagpipe; in the Pitt Rivers Museum, Oxford, England. The Pitt Rivers Museum, Oxford, Eng.

KILT

The knee-length skirtlike garment called the kilt is worn by men as a major element of the traditional national garb of Scotland. (The other main component of Highland dress, as the traditional male garb of Scotland is called, is the plaid, which is a rectangular length of cloth worn over the left shoulder.) The kilt is a length of woven wool that is permanently pleated except for sections at each end and wrapped around the wearer's waist in such a way that the pleats are massed at the wearer's back and the flat, unpleated ends overlap to form a double layer at his front. Both kilt and plaid are usually made of cloth woven with a cross-checked repeating pattern known as a tartan.

The kilt and plaid ensemble developed in 17th-century Scotland from the *féile-breacan*, a long piece of woolen cloth whose pleated first half was wrapped around the wearer's waist, while the (unpleated) second half was then wrapped around the upper body, with a loose end thrown over the left shoulder. Subsequently in the 17th century two lengths of cloth began to be worn for these purposes, and the kilt and plaid thus came to be separate garments.

The plaid and kilt form the only national costume in the British Isles that is worn for ordinary purposes, rather than merely for special occasions. Highland dress is also the uniform of Scottish regiments in the British army, and kilts have been worn in battle as recently as World War II.

passions of soldiers in battle. The form of the kilt, Scotland's national costume, has evolved since the emigration of Scots from Ireland. The modern kilt, with its tartan pattern, became common in the 18th century and served an important role in the formation of a Scottish national identity. Knits from Fair Isle, with their distinctive designs woven from the fine wool of Shetland sheep, are also world famous.

One traditional local custom is the *ceilidh* (visit), a social occasion that includes music and storytelling. Once common throughout the country, the *ceilidh* is now a largely rural institution. Sports such as tossing the caber (a heavy pole) and the hammer throw are integral to the Highland games, a spectacle that originated in the 19th century; the games are accompanied by pipe bands and (usually solo) performances by Highland dancers. Other traditions include Burns suppers (honouring poet Robert Burns), which often feature haggis (a delicacy traditionally consisting of offal and suet boiled with oatmeal in a sheep's stomach) and cock-a-leekie (chicken stewed with leeks). Many Scots consider these games and traditions to be a self-conscious display of legendary characteristics that have little to do with ordinary Scottish life—a show put on, like national costumes, to

HAGGIS

A haggis is actually a large spherical sausage made of the liver, heart, and lungs of a sheep, all chopped and mixed with beef or mutton suet and oatmeal and seasoned with onion, cayenne pepper, and other spices. The mixture is packed into a sheep's stomach and boiled. Haggis is usually accompanied by turnips and mashed potatoes; Scotch whisky is customarily drunk with it.

Haggis is served on Burns Night (January 25, the birthday of the poet Robert Burns, who wrote "Ode to a Haggis") and at the Scottish New Year's celebration Hogmanay, when it is ceremonially presented to the accompaniment of bagpipes.

---

gratify the expectations of tourists and encouraged by the royal family's annual appearance at the Braemar Gathering near Balmoral Castle. Scottish country dancing, however, is a pastime whose popularity has spread far beyond Scotland.

Food and drink have played a central role in Scotland's heritage. In addition to haggis, Scotland is known for its Angus beef, porridge, stovies (a potato-rich stew), shortbreads, scones, cheese (Bishop, Kennedy, Caboc, Lanark Blue), toffee, and game dishes (e.g., salmon, venison, and grouse). The term *whisky* is derived from the Gaelic uisge-beatha, meaning "water of life." Historical references to whisky date from the late 15th century, though its popularity in the country probably goes back even farther. Indeed, throughout Scotland private distilleries proliferated in the 17th century, which led the Scottish Parliament to impose a tax on whisky production in 1644. Today whisky is among the country's leading exports.

THE ARTS

Scottish writers have the choice of three languages—English, Scots, and Gaelic. An early Scottish poet of the 16th century, Sir Robert Ayton, wrote in standard English; one of his poems is thought to have inspired Robert Burns's version of "Auld Lang Syne." Burns is perhaps the foremost literary figure in Scottish history. A poet whose songs were written in the Scottish dialect of English, Burns aroused great passion among his audience and gained a legion of dedicated followers. Hugh MacDiarmid, a nationalist and Marxist, gained an international reputation for his Scots poetry in the first half of the 20th century, and others, such as Robert Garioch and Edwin Muir, followed his lead. Gaelic poets such as Sorley Maclean and Derick Thompson are highly esteemed, as is Iain Crichton Smith, who is also known for his novels in English. Other contemporary novelists, many of whom have earned an

ROBERT BURNS

The national poet of Scotland, Robert Burns (born January 25, 1759, Alloway, Ayrshire, Scotland—died July 21, 1796, Dumfries, Dumfriesshire), was the son of a poor farmer. Early in his life he became familiar with orally transmitted folk songs and tales. His father's farm failed, and a farm he started himself quickly went bankrupt. Handsome and high-spirited, he engaged in a series of love affairs, some of which produced children, and celebrated his lovers in his poems. His *Poems, Chiefly in the Scottish Dialect* (1786) brought acclaim but no financial security, and he eventually took a job as an exciseman. He later began collecting and editing hundreds of traditional airs for James Johnson's *Scots Musical Museum* (1787–1803) and George Thomson's *Select Collection of Original Scotish Airs* (1793–1818); he substantially wrote many of these songs, though he did not claim them or receive payment for them. Among his best-known songs are "Auld Lang Syne," "Green Grow the Rashes, O," "John Anderson My Jo," "A Red, Red Rose," and "Ye Banks and Braes o' Bonnie Doon." He freely proclaimed his radical opinions, his sympathies with the common people, and his rebellion against orthodox religion and morality.

Robert Burns, detail of an oil painting by Alexander Nasmyth; in the National Portrait Gallery, London. Courtesy of the National Portrait Gallery, London

---

international following, include Muriel Spark, Alasdair Gray, Ian Rankin, Kate Atkinson, and James Kelman. Alexander McCall Smith lives in Edinburgh, but he was made famous by his detective stories set in Botswana. Similarly, the Harry Potter books were written in Edinburgh by English novelist J.K. Rowling.

Painting and sculpture flourish and are displayed in numerous galleries and official exhibitions. In the late 20th century there was a popular revival of 19th-century designer and architect Charles Rennie Mackintosh. Scots have also made their mark in motion pictures. Sean Connery, perhaps best known for his portrayal of James Bond, was Scotland's most recognizable film star of the second half of the 20th century; actors Ewan McGregor and Gerard Butler became familiar screen presences in the early 21st century. Glaswegian stand-up comedian and actor Billy Connolly has been a major force in British entertainment since the 1970s. Director Bill Forsyth first gained international acclaim in the 1980s, and his 1983 film *Local Hero* prompted a wave of tourism to the western islands. Scottish filmmaking also enjoyed a renaissance after the success of *Braveheart* (1995), an American production that chronicles Scottish battles with the English in the 13th century and that helped rekindle nationalist aspirations. Other films, such as *Trainspotting* (1996), *Orphans* (1997), *Young Adam* (2003), and *Red Road* (2006) enjoyed wide success, and Scottish films now figure in many international festivals.

Scotland has a wealth of surviving traditional music, ranging from the work songs of the Hebrides to the ballads of the northeast. There has also been renewed interest in such traditional instruments as the bagpipe, fiddle, and *clarsach* (the small Celtic harp). Performers such as the Battlefield Band, Tannahill Weavers, and Dougie MacLean have taken Scottish folk music to international audiences. All aspects of traditional culture are researched, archived, and taught in the Department of Celtic and Scottish Studies of the University of Edinburgh. Scotland has also had a long presence in popular music, with artists such as Lonnie Donegan, a pioneer of pre-rock skiffle music, singer-songwriter Donovan, the Incredible String Band, and Eurythmics. Whereas many Scots had to leave the country to find success, vibrant local scenes in Glasgow and Edinburgh in the 1980s gave rise to such popular groups as Simple Minds and the Jesus and Mary Chain, and later to Teenage Fanclub, Travis, Belle and Sebastian, and Snow Patrol. All of the arts receive support from the Scottish Arts Council, which has a large measure of autonomy from the Arts Council of Great Britain.

CULTURAL INSTITUTIONS

Edinburgh and Glasgow are the cultural capitals of Scotland. Among the cultural institutions achieving high international standing are the Royal Scottish National Orchestra, the Scottish Opera, and the Scottish Ballet, all based in Glasgow. Other major institutions in Glasgow include the Kelvingrove Art Gallery and Museum, the Burrell Collection, and the Riverside Museum. The National Museums of Scotland include the National Museum and the War Museum in Edinburgh, the Museum of Rural Life near Glasgow, the Museum of Flight near Haddington, and the Museum of Costume at Shambellie House near Dumfries. Edinburgh is also the headquarters of the National Library of Scotland, which receives copies of all books published in the United Kingdom and Ireland, and the National Galleries of Scotland, comprising several museums, including the National Gallery of Scotland (with works by Allan Ramsay, Sir Henry Raeburn, and other Scottish painters), the Scottish National Portrait Gallery, and the Scottish National Gallery of Modern Art. Founded in 1947, the annual Edinburgh International Festival, with its Fringe (entertainment on the periphery of the festival), has become one of the world's largest cultural events.

SPORTS AND RECREATION

Sports are an important part of life in Scotland. Association football (soccer) has a wide following and is dominated by the Rangers and Celtic clubs of Glasgow. Rugby football is played especially by private schools and by their former pupils, but in the towns of the Scottish Borders it draws players and spectators from a wider social range. Although Scottish athletes compete as members of the United Kingdom's Olympic team, the country fields national teams for other sports (e.g., football and rugby). Shinty, a hockeylike game, is popular in the Highlands. Curling is another traditional sport, although temperatures are seldom low enough for it to be other than an indoor activity played on man-made ice. Golf, long associated with Scotland though its origins lie elsewhere, is accessible to most Scots through widespread public and private facilities, and the country hosts the annual British Open, one of professional golf's most prestigious tournaments. The Old Course of the Royal and Ancient Golf Club of St. Andrews in Fife is the most famous of many excellent seaside courses. Scotland's landscape is ideally suited to those pursuing hill walking, rock climbing, sailing, and canoeing. Skiing facilities have been developed in the Cairngorms and other areas. Hunting and shooting are traditionally sports of the wealthy, but fishing is popular among all classes, and the country boasts some of the finest salmon fishing in the world.

MEDIA AND PUBLISHING

Edinburgh was once one of the centres of the United Kingdom's publishing industry; however, in the early and mid 20th century, Scottish publishing declined

ROYAL AND ANCIENT GOLF CLUB OF ST. ANDREWS

One of the world's oldest and most influential golf organizations, the Royal and Ancient Golf Club of St. Andrews was formed in 1754 by 22 "noblemen and gentlemen" at St. Andrews, Fife, Scotland, as the Society of St. Andrews Golfers. It adopted its present name (often shortened to the R&A) in 1834 by permission of the reigning British monarch, William IV. The R&A played a major role in the early development of golf. Since 1764 its famed Old Course has been played nine holes out and nine holes back, making the now standard 18-hole round.

In the late 19th century the R&A became the sole authority on rules of the game in Great Britain and the Commonwealth. In 1919 it took over management of the British Open and amateur championship tournaments. It sponsors several international competitions, including the Walker Cup and Curtis Cup matches against U.S. teams. It also maintains close contact with the United States Golf Association and other national federations for purposes of unifying rules of international play.

drastically, especially in the years after World War II, with many publishers moving to London. Only in the 1970s did Scotland's publishing industry begin to revitalize somewhat. Some newspapers are printed in Scotland, but others, which include aspects of Scottish news and sports, are delivered from south of the border. The *Daily Record* and *The Scottish Sun* have the largest circulation in Scotland. *The Herald* (Glasgow) and *The Scotsman* (Edinburgh) continue to serve the west and east coasts, respectively, and their Sunday equivalents, the *Sunday Herald* and *Scotland on Sunday*, are competitors. Other parts of Scotland are served by local papers such as the *Dundee Courier* and *The Press and Journal*. *Scottish Field* and *Scots Magazine* are two well-established monthly publications covering traditional, leisure, and historical interests.

The British Broadcasting Corporation (BBC) produces Scottish news and other programming for radio and television, including some broadcasts in Gaelic. Radio Scotland has largely locally produced programs. There are three independent television companies, including Scottish Television (STV), and several independent radio stations. Somewhat controversially, the Westminster Parliament has retained legislative powers over broadcasting.

CHAPTER 11

EARLY SCOTLAND

Evidence of human settlement in the area later known as Scotland dates from the 3rd millennium BCE. The earliest people, Mesolithic (Middle Stone Age) hunters and fishermen who probably reached Scotland via an ancient land bridge from the Continent, were to be found on the west coast, near Oban, and as far south as Kirkcudbright, where their settlements are marked by large deposits of discarded mollusk shells. Remains suggest that settlers at the Forth estuary, in the area of modern Stirling, obtained meat from stranded whales. By early in the 2nd millennium BCE, Neolithic (New Stone Age) farmers had begun cultivating cereals and keeping cattle and sheep. They made settlements on the west coast and as far north as Shetland. Many built collective chamber tombs, such as the Maeshowe barrow in Orkney, which is the finest example in Britain. A settlement of such people at Skara Brae in Orkney consists of a cluster of seven self-contained huts connected by covered galleries or alleys. The "Beaker folk," so called from the shape of their drinking vessels, migrated to eastern Scotland from northern Europe, probably beginning about 1800 BCE. They buried their dead in individual graves and were pioneers in bronze working. The most impressive monuments of Bronze Age Scotland are the stone circles, presumably for religious ceremonies, such as those at Callanish in Lewis and Brodgar in Orkney, the latter being more than 300 feet (90 metres) in diameter.

ANCIENT TIMES

From about 700 BCE onward there was a distinct final period in Scottish prehistory. This period is the subject of current archaeological controversy, with somewhat less stress than in the past being placed on the importance of the introduction of iron fabrication or on the impact of large new groups of iron-using settlers. One key occurrence in the middle of the 1st millennium was the change from a relatively warm and dry climate to one that was cooler and wetter. In terms of technology, this period was marked by the appearance of hill forts, defensive structures having stone ramparts with an internal frame of timber; a good example is at Abernethy near the Tay. Some of these forts have been dated to the 7th and 6th centuries BCE, which might suggest that they were adopted by already established tribes rather than introduced by incomers. Massive decorated bronze armlets with Celtic ornamentation, found in northeastern Scotland and dated to the period 50–150 CE, suggest that chieftains from outside may have gone to these tribes at this period, displaced from farther south first by fresh settlers from the Continent and later by the Romans in 43 CE. From 100 BCE the "brochs" appeared in the extreme north of Scotland and the northern isles. These were high, round towers, which at Mousa in Shetland stand almost 50 feet (15 metres) in height. The broch dwellers may have carried on intermittent warfare with the fort builders of farther south. On the other hand, the two types of structures may not represent two wholly distinct cultures, and the two peoples may have together constituted the ancestors of the people later known as the Picts.

The houses of these people were circular, sometimes standing alone and sometimes in groups of 15 or more, as at Hayhope Knowe in the Cheviot Hills on the border between modern Scotland and England. Some single steadings, set in bogs or on lakesides, are called crannogs. Grain growing was probably of minor importance in the economy; the people were pastoralists and food gatherers. They were ruled by a warrior aristocracy whose bronze and iron parade equipment has, in a few instances, survived.

ROMAN PENETRATION

Gnaeus Julius Agricola, the Roman governor of Britain from 77 to 84 CE, was the first Roman general to operate extensively in Scotland. He defeated the native population at Mons Graupius, possibly in Banffshire, probably in 84 CE. In the following year he was recalled, and his policy of containing the hostile tribes within the Highland zone, which he had marked by building a legionary fortress at Inchtuthil in Strathmore, was not continued. His tactics were logical if Scotland was to be subdued but probably required the commitment of more troops than the overall strategy of the Roman Empire could afford. The only other period in which a forward policy was attempted was between about 144 and about 190, when a turf wall, the Antonine Wall (named for the emperor Antoninus Pius), was manned between the Forth and the Clyde.

The still-impressive stone structure known as Hadrian's Wall had been built between the Tyne and Solway Firth between 122 and 128, and it was to be the permanent northern frontier of Roman Britain. After a northern uprising, the emperor Severus supervised the restoring of the Hadrianic line from 209 to 211, and thereafter southeastern Scotland seems to have enjoyed almost a century of peace. In the 4th century there were successive raids from north of the wall and periodic withdrawals of Roman troops to continental Europe. Despite increasing use of native buffer states in front of the wall, the Romans found their frontier indefensible by the end of the 4th century.

At Housesteads, at about the midpoint of Hadrian's Wall, archaeologists have uncovered a market where northern natives exchanged cattle and hides for Roman products; in this way some Roman wares, and possibly more general cultural influences, found their way north, but the scale of this commerce was probably small. Roman civilization, typified by the towns and villas, or country houses, of southern Britain, was unknown in Scotland, which as a whole was never dominated by the Romans or even strongly influenced by them.

From about 400 CE there was a long period for which written evidence is scanty. Four peoples—the Picts, the Scots, the Britons, and the Angles—were eventually to merge and thus form the kingdom of Scots.

The Picts occupied Scotland north of the Forth. Their identity has been much debated, but they possessed a distinctive culture, seen particularly in their carved symbol stones. Their original language, presumably non-Indo-European, has disappeared; some Picts probably spoke a Brythonic Celtic language. Pictish unity may have been impaired by their apparent tradition of matrilineal succession to the throne.

The Scots, from Dalriada in northern Ireland, colonized the Argyll area, probably in the late 5th century. Their continuing connection with Ireland was a source of strength to them, and Scottish and Irish Gaelic (Goidelic Celtic languages) did not become distinct from each other until the late Middle Ages. Scottish Dalriada soon extended its cultural as well as its military sway east and south, though one of its greatest kings, Aidan, was defeated by the Angles in 603 at Degsastan near the later Scottish border.

The Britons, speaking a Brythonic Celtic language, colonized Scotland from farther south, probably from the 1st century BCE onward. They lost control of southeastern Scotland to the Angles in the early 7th century CE. The British heroic poem *Gododdin* describes a stage in this process. The British kingdom of Strathclyde in southwestern Scotland remained, with its capital at Dumbarton.

The Angles were Teutonic-speaking invaders from across the North Sea. Settling from the 5th century, they had by the early 7th century created the kingdom of Northumbria, stretching from the Humber to the Forth. A decisive check to their northward advance was administered in 685 by the Picts at the Battle of Nechtansmere in Angus.

CHRISTIANITY

Christianity was introduced to Scotland in late Roman times, and traditions of the evangelizing of St. Ninian in the southwest have survived. He is a shadowy figure, however, and it is doubtful that his work extended very far north.

Firmly established throughout Scotland by the Celtic clergy, Christianity came with the Scots settlers from Ireland and possibly gave them a decisive cultural advantage in the early unification of kingdoms. The Celtic church lacked a territorial organization of parishes and dioceses and a division between secular and regular clergy; its communities of missionary monks were ideal agents of conversion. The best-known figure, possibly the greatest, is St. Columba, who founded his monastery at Iona, an island of the Inner Hebrides, in 565; a famous biography of his life was written by Adamnan, abbot of Iona, within a century of his death. Columba is believed to have been influential in converting the Picts, and he did much to support the Scots king Aidan politically.

St. Aidan brought the Celtic church to Northumbria in the 630s, establishing his monastery at Lindisfarne. At the Synod of Whitby in 664, the king of Northumbria, having to decide between the Celtic and the Roman styles of Christianity, chose the Roman version. There had been differences over such observances as the dating of Easter, but no one regarded the Celtic monks as schismatics. The *Ecclesiastical History of the English People* by Bede the Venerable (died 735), a monk of Jarrow in Northumbria, is a first-rate source for the early Anglo-Saxon history and shows remarkable sympathy with the Celtic clergy, though Bede was a Roman monk.

In the early 8th century the church among the Picts and Scots accepted Roman usages on such questions as Easter. Nevertheless, the church in Scotland remained Celtic in many ways until the 11th century. Still dominated by its communities of clergy (who were called Célidé or Culdees), it clearly corresponded well to the tribal nature of society.

THE NORSE INFLUENCE

Viking raids on the coasts of Britain began at the end of the 8th century, Lindisfarne and Iona being pillaged in the 790s. By the mid-9th century Norse settlement of the western and northern isles and of Caithness and Sutherland had begun, probably largely because of overpopulation on the west coast of Norway. During the 10th century Orkney and Shetland were ruled by Norse earls nominally subject to Norway. In 1098 Magnus III (Magnus Barefoot), king of Norway, successfully asserted his authority in the northern and western isles and made an agreement with the king of Scots on their respective spheres of influence. A mid-12th-century earl of Orkney, Ragnvald, built the great cathedral at Kirkwall in honour of his martyred uncle St. Magnus.

The Norse legacy to Scotland was long-lasting, but in the mid-12th century there was a rising against the Norse in the west under a native leader, Somerled, who drove them from the greater part of mainland Argyll. A Norwegian expedition of 1263 under King Haakon IV failed to maintain the Norse presence in the Hebrides, and three years later they were ceded to Scotland by the Treaty of Perth. In 1468–69 the northern isles of Orkney and Shetland were pawned to Scotland as part of a marriage settlement with the crown of Denmark-Norway. Nonetheless, a Scandinavian language, the Norn, was spoken in these Viking possessions, and some Norse linguistic influence still remains discernible in Shetland.

THE UNIFICATION OF THE KINGDOM

In 843 Kenneth MacAlpin, King Kenneth I of Scots, also became king of the Picts and crushed resistance to his assuming the throne. Kenneth may have had a claim on the Pictish throne through the matrilineal law of succession; probably the Picts too had been weakened by Norse attacks. The Norse threat helped to weld together the new kingdom of Alba and to cause its heartlands to be located in eastern Scotland, the former Pictland, with Dunkeld becoming its religious capital. But within Alba it was the Scots who established a cultural and linguistic supremacy, no doubt merely confirming a tendency seen before 843.

As the English kingdom was consolidated, its kings, in the face of Norse attacks, found it useful to have an understanding with Alba. In 945 Edmund I of England is said to have leased to Malcolm I of Alba the whole of Cumbria, probably an area including land on both sides of the western half of the later Anglo-Scottish border. In the late 10th century a similar arrangement seems to have been made for Lothian, the corresponding territory to the east. The Scots confirmed their hold on Lothian, from the Forth to the Tweed, when, about 1016, Malcolm II defeated a Northumbrian army at Carham. About the same time, Malcolm II placed his grandson Duncan I upon the throne of the British kingdom of Strathclyde. Duncan succeeded Malcolm in 1034 and brought Strathclyde into the kingdom of Scots. During the next two centuries the Scots kings pushed their effective power north and west—William I was successful in the north and Alexander II in the west—until mainland Scotland became one political unit. Less discernible but as important

MACBETH

Macbeth (died August 15, 1057, near Lumphanan, Aberdeen [now in Aberdeenshire]) was the king of Scots from 1040. The legend of his life was the basis of William Shakespeare's tragedy *Macbeth*. Probably a grandson of King Kenneth II (reigned 971–995), Macbeth married Gruoch, a descendant of King Kenneth III (reigned 997–1005). About 1031 Macbeth succeeded his father, Findlaech (Sinel in Shakespeare's play), as mormaer, or chief, in the province of Moray, in northern Scotland. Macbeth established himself on the throne after killing his cousin King Duncan I in battle near Elgin—not, as in Shakespeare, by murdering Duncan in bed—on August 14, 1040. Both Duncan and Macbeth derived their rights to the crown through their mothers.

Macbeth's victory in 1045 over a rebel army, near Dunkeld (in the modern region of Perth and Kinross), may account for the later references (in Shakespeare and others) to Birnam Wood, for the village of Birnam is near Dunkeld. In 1046 Siward, earl of Northumbria, unsuccessfully attempted to dethrone Macbeth in favour of Malcolm (afterward King Malcolm III Canmore), eldest son of Duncan I. By 1050 Macbeth felt secure enough to leave Scotland for a pilgrimage to Rome. But in 1054 he was apparently forced by Siward to yield part of southern Scotland to Malcolm. Three years later Macbeth was killed in battle by Malcolm, with assistance from the English.

Macbeth was buried on the island of Iona, regarded as the resting place of lawful kings but not of usurpers. His followers installed his stepson, Lulach, as king; when Lulach was killed on March 17, 1058, Malcolm III was left supreme in Scotland.

was the way the various peoples grew together, though significant linguistic and other differences remained.

According to the Celtic system of succession, known as tanistry, a king could be succeeded by any male member of the derbfine, a family group of four generations; members of collateral branches seem to have been preferred to descendants, and the successor, or tanist, might be named in his predecessor's lifetime. This system in practice led to many successions by the killing of one's predecessor. Thus, Duncan I was killed by his cousin Macbeth in 1040, and Macbeth was killed by Malcolm Canmore (Duncan's son, later Malcolm III Canmore) in 1057. Shakespeare freely adapted the story of Macbeth, who historically seems to have been a successful king and who may have gone on pilgrimage to Rome.

Until the 11th century the unification was the work of a Gaelic-speaking dynasty, and there is place-name evidence of the penetration of Gaelic south of the Forth. Afterward, however, the Teutonic English speech that had come to Scotland from the kingdom of Northumbria began to attain mastery, and Gaelic began its slow retreat north and west. This is not obscured by the fact that from the 12th century onward Anglo-Norman was for a time the speech of the leaders of society in England and

Scotland alike. By the later Middle Ages the language known to modern scholars as Old English had evolved into two separate languages, now called Middle English and Middle Scots, with the latter focused on the court of the Stewart (Stuart) kings of Scots. After 1603 the increasing political and cultural assimilation of Scotland by England checked the further development of Scots as a separate language.

The persistence of distinctively Celtic institutions in post-12th-century Scotland is a more complex question, as will be seen from the way in which primogeniture replaced tanistry as the system of royal succession. It can be argued, however, that a Celtic stress on the family bond in society persisted throughout the Middle Ages and beyond—and not only in the Highlands, with its clan organization of society.

THE DEVELOPMENT OF THE MONARCHY

Malcolm Canmore came to the throne as Malcolm III in 1058 by disposing of his rivals and thereafter sought, in five unsuccessful raids, to extend his kingdom into northern England. Whereas his first wife, Ingibjorg, was the daughter of a Norse earl of Orkney, his second, Margaret, came from the Saxon royal house of England. With Margaret and her sons, Scotland was particularly receptive to cultural influence from the south. Margaret was a great patroness of the church but without altering its organization, as her sons were to do.

On the death of Malcolm III on his last English raid in 1093, sustained attempts were made to prevent the application of the southern custom of succession by primogeniture. Both Malcolm's brother and Malcolm's son by his first marriage held the throne for short periods, but it was the three sons of Malcolm and Margaret who eventually established themselves—Edgar (1097–1107), Alexander I (1107–24), and David I (1124–53). Such was the force of Celtic reaction against southern influence that Edgar and Alexander could be said to have owed their thrones solely to English aid, and they were feudally subject to the English king. The descendants of Malcolm III's first marriage continued to trouble the ruling dynasty until the early 13th century, but the descendants of his second retained the throne. Until the late 13th century the heir to the throne by primogeniture was always the obvious candidate. It is noteworthy that in charters of about 1145 David's son Henry (who was to die before his father) is described as *rex designatus*, very much like the tanist of the Celtic system. It is thus very hard to date precisely the acceptance of southern custom as exemplified by primogeniture.

DAVID I (1124–53)

David I was by marriage a leading landowner in England and was well known at the English court. He was nevertheless an independent monarch, making Scotland strong by drawing on English cultural and organizational influences. Under

David I, detail of an illuminated initial on the Kelso Abbey charter of 1159; in the National Library of Scotland. By permission of His Grace the Duke of Roxburghe

him and his successors many Anglo-Norman families came to Scotland, and their members were rewarded with lands and offices. Among the most important were the Bruces in Annandale, the de Morvilles in Ayrshire and Lauderdale, and the Fitzalans, who became hereditary high stewards and who, as the Stewart dynasty, were to inherit the throne in Renfrewshire. (After the 16th century the Stewart dynasty was known by its French spelling, Stuart.) Such men were often given large estates in outlying areas to bolster the king's authority where it was weak.

The decentralized form of government and society that resulted was one of the many variants of what is known as feudalism, with tenants in chief holding lands from the king—and having jurisdiction over their inhabitants—in return for the performance of military and other services. An essentially new element in Scottish society was the written charter, setting out the rights and obligations involved in landholding. But the way in which the Anglo-Norman families, in their position as tenants in chief, were successfully grafted onto the existing society suggests that the Celtic and feudal social systems were by no means mutually incompatible, though one stressed family bonds and the other legal contracts. The clan system of Highland Scotland became tinged with feudal influences, whereas Lowland Scottish feudalism retained a strong emphasis on the family.

David began to spread direct royal influence through the kingdom by the creation of the office of sheriff (vicecomes), a royal judge and administrator ruling an area of the kingdom from one of the royal castles. Centrally, a nucleus of government officials, such as the chancellor, the chamberlain, and the justiciar, was created by David and his successors; these officials, with other tenants in chief called to give advice, made up the royal court (Curia Regis). This body became formalized in various ways; by the mid-13th century it might have been meeting as the king's council to discuss various types of business, and before the Wars of Independence the royal court in its capacity as the Supreme Court of Law was already being described as a Parliament. The almost total loss of all the Scottish governmental records from before the early 14th century should not lead one to underestimate the efficiency of the Scottish kings' government in this period. Historians have done much to assemble the surviving royal documents from scattered sources.

MEDIEVAL ECONOMY AND SOCIETY

From David's time onward the burghs, or incorporated towns, were created as centres of trade and small-scale manufacture in an overwhelmingly agrarian economy. At first all burghs probably had equal rights. Later, however, royal burghs had, by their charters, the exclusive right of overseas trade, though tenants in chief could create burghs with local trade privileges. Burghs evolved their own law to govern trading transactions, and disputes could be referred to the Court of the Four Burghs (originally Berwick, Edinburgh, Roxburgh, and Stirling). Many of the original townspeople, or burgesses, were newcomers to Scotland. At Berwick—the great trading town of the 13th century, exporting the wool of the border monasteries—Flemish merchants had their own Red Hall, which they defended to the death against English attack in 1296. Besides commercial contacts with England, there is evidence of Scottish trading with the Low Countries and with Norway in the period before the Wars of Independence.

The church was decisively remodeled by David I and his successors. A clear division emerged between secular and regular clergy according to the normal

Ruins of the cathedral of Moray at Elgin. A.F. Kersting

western European pattern. A complete system of parishes and dioceses was established. But the system of "appropriating" the revenue of parish churches to central religious institutions meant that the top-heaviness in wealth and resources of the church in Scotland was a built-in feature of its existence until the Reformation. Kings and other great men vied in setting up monasteries. Alexander I had founded houses of Augustinian canons at Scone and Inchcolm, while among David's foundations were the Cistercian houses of Melrose and Newbattle and the Augustinian houses of Cambuskenneth and Holyrood. Augustinian canons might also serve as the clergy of a cathedral, as they did at St. Andrews. Prominent foundations by the magnates included Walter Fitzalan's Cluniac house at Paisley and Hugh de Morville's Premonstratensian house at Dryburgh. Later royal foundations included the Benedictine house at Arbroath, established by William I.

From the standpoint of a later age, when the monasteries had lost their

The ruins of the cathedral seen through the West Port of the precinct wall, Saint Andrews. Kenneth Scowen

spiritual force, the piety of David I especially seemed a misapplication of royal resources. But the original monasteries, with their supply of trained manpower for royal service, their hospitality, and their learning, epitomized the stability that it was royal policy to achieve.

From at least 1072 the English church, particularly the archbishop of York, sought some control over the Scottish church; in the face of such a threat, the Scottish church was weakened through having no metropolitan see. But, probably in 1192, the papal bull *Cum universi* declared the Scottish church to be subject only to Rome, and in 1225 the bull *Quidam vestrum* permitted the Scottish church, lacking a metropolitan see, to hold provincial councils by authority of Rome. However, such councils, which might have served to check abuses, were seldom held.

It has been argued that the cultural developments encouraged by the church in pre-Reformation Scotland were not as great as might be expected, but this may be a false impression created because the manuscript evidence has failed to survive. The monasteries of Melrose and Holyrood each had a chronicle, and Adam of Dryburgh was an able theologian of the late 12th century. Surviving Romanesque churches show that Scotland partook of the common European architectural tradition of the time; good small examples are at Dalmeny, near Edinburgh, and at Leuchars, in Fife. Glasgow and Elgin cathedrals are noteworthy, and St. Andrews Cathedral is impressive even in its ruined state. There are also distinguished examples of castle architecture, such as Bothwell in Lanarkshire, and the castles of Argyll may reflect a distinctive mixture of influences, including Norse ones.

DAVID I'S SUCCESSORS

Malcolm IV (1153–65) was a fairly successful king, defeating Somerled when the latter, who had been triumphant over the Scandinavians in Argyll, turned against the kingdom of Scots. Malcolm's brother, William I ("the Lion"; 1165–1214), subdued much of the north and established royal castles there. After his capture on a raid into England, he was forced to become feudally subject to the English king by the Treaty of Falaise (1174); he was able, however, to buy back his kingdom's independence by the Quitclaim of Canterbury (1189), though it should be emphasized that this document disposed of the Treaty of Falaise and not of the less-precise claims of superiority over Scotland that English kings had put forward over the previous century. William's son, Alexander II (1214–49), subdued Argyll and was about to proceed against the Hebrides at the time of his death. His son, Alexander III (1249–86), brought the Hebrides within the Scottish kingdom in 1266, adroitly fended off English claims to overlordship, and brought to Scotland the peace and prosperity typified by the commercial growth of Berwick. In the perspective of the subsequent Wars of Independence, it was inevitable that Scots should look back on his reign as a golden age.

THE WARS OF INDEPENDENCE

With the deaths of Alexander III in 1286 and his young granddaughter Margaret, the "Maid of Norway," four years later, almost two centuries of relatively amicable Anglo-Scottish relations came to an end. A complete uncertainty as to the proper succession to the throne provided Edward I of England and his successors with a chance to intervene in and then to assimilate Scotland. Although the two countries were feudal monarchies of a largely similar type, the English attempt was, in practice, too tactless to have any hope of success. Besides, the struggle for independence disclosed that a marked degree of national unity had arisen among the different peoples of Scotland. Through the Anglo-Scottish conflict, Scotland developed a basic tendency—to seek self-sufficiency and also to look to continental Europe for alliances and inspiration—that persisted at least until 1560.

COMPETITION FOR THE THRONE

Before the death of the Maid of Norway, the Scottish interim government of "guardians" had agreed, by the Treaty of Birgham (1290), that she should marry the heir of Edward I of England, though Scotland was to be preserved as a separate kingdom. After her death 13 claimants for the Scottish crown emerged, most of them Scottish magnates. The Scots initially had no reason to suspect the motives of Edward I in undertaking to judge the various claims. It emerged, however, that Edward saw himself not as an outside arbitrator but as the feudal superior of the Scottish monarch and therefore able to dispose of Scotland as a fief. That Edward's interpretation was disingenuous is suggested by the fact that he had not invoked the old and vague English claims to superiority over Scotland while the Maid of Norway was still alive and he had made a treaty with Scotland on the

SIR WILLIAM WALLACE

One of Scotland's greatest national heroes, William Wallace (born c. 1270, probably near Paisley, Renfrew, Scotland—died August 23, 1305, London) was the leader of the Scottish resistance forces during the first years of the long, and ultimately successful, struggle to free Scotland from English rule.

His father, Sir Malcolm Wallace, was a small landowner in Renfrew. In 1296 King Edward I of England deposed and imprisoned the Scottish king John de Balliol and declared himself ruler of Scotland. Sporadic resistance had already occurred when, in May 1297, Wallace and a band of some 30 men burned Lanark and killed its English sheriff. Wallace then organized an army of commoners and small landowners and attacked the English garrisons between the Rivers Forth and Tay. On September 11, 1297, an English army under John de Warenne, earl of Surrey, confronted him at the Forth near Stirling. Wallace's forces were greatly outnumbered, but Surrey had to cross a narrow bridge over the Forth before he could reach the Scottish positions. By slaughtering the English as they crossed the river, Wallace gained an overwhelming victory. He captured Stirling Castle, and for the moment Scotland was nearly free of occupying forces. In October he invaded northern England and ravaged the counties of Northumberland and Cumberland.

Sir William Wallace, undated engraving. Library of Congress, Washington, D.C. (Digital File Number: cph 3c20690)

Upon returning to Scotland early in December 1297, Wallace was knighted and proclaimed guardian of the kingdom, ruling in Balliol's name. Nevertheless, many nobles lent him only grudging support; and he had yet to confront Edward I, who was campaigning in France. Edward returned to England in March 1298, and on July 3 he invaded Scotland. On July 22 Wallace's spearmen were defeated by Edward's archers and cavalry in the Battle of Falkirk, Stirling. Although Edward failed to pacify Scotland before returning to England, Wallace's military reputation was ruined. He resigned his guardianship in December and was succeeded by Robert de Bruce (later King Robert I) and Sir John Comyn "the Red."

There is some evidence that Wallace went to France in 1299 and thereafter acted as a solitary guerrilla leader in Scotland; but from the autumn of 1299 nothing is known of his activities for more than four years. Although most of the Scottish nobles submitted to Edward in 1304, the English continued to pursue Wallace relentlessly. On August 5, 1305, he was arrested near Glasgow. Taken to London, he was condemned as a traitor to the king even though, as he maintained, he had never sworn allegiance to Edward. He was hanged, disemboweled, beheaded, and quartered. In 1306 Bruce raised the rebellion that eventually won independence for Scotland.

Many of the stories surrounding Wallace have been traced to a late 15th-century romance ascribed to Henry the Minstrel, or "Blind Harry." The most popular tales are not supported by documentary evidence, but they show Wallace's firm hold on the imagination of his people. A huge monument (1861–69) to Wallace stands atop the rock of Abbey Craig near Stirling.

basis of equality, not as a feudal superior claiming rights of wardship and marriage over the Maid.

The claimants to the throne, who had much to lose by antagonizing Edward, generally agreed to acknowledge his superior lordship over Scotland. But a different answer to his claim to lordship was given by the "community of the realm" (the important laymen and churchmen of Scotland as a group), who declined to commit whoever was to be king of Scots on this issue and thus displayed a sophisticated sense of national unity.

The sixth Robert de Bruce and John Balliol, descendants of a younger brother of Malcolm IV and William, emerged as the leading competitors, and in 1292 Edward I named Balliol king. When Edward sought to exert his overlordship by taking law cases on appeal from Scotland and by summoning Balliol to do military service for him in France, the Scots determined to resist. In 1295 they concluded an alliance with France, and in 1296 Edward's army marched north, sacking Berwick on its way.

Edward easily forced Balliol and Scotland to submit. National resistance to English governance of Scotland grew slowly thereafter and was led by William Wallace, a knight's son, in the absence of a leader from the magnates. Wallace defeated the English at Stirling Bridge in 1297 but lost at Falkirk the next year. He was executed in London in 1305, having shown that heroic leadership without social status was not enough. When the eighth Robert de Bruce, grandson of the competitor, rose in revolt in 1306 and had himself crowned Robert I, he supplied the focus necessary to mobilize the considerable potential of national resistance.

ROBERT I (1306–29)

In several years of mixed fortunes thereafter, Robert the Bruce had both the English and his opponents within Scotland to contend with. Edward I's death in 1307 and the dissension in England under Edward II were assets that Robert took full advantage of. He excelled as a statesman and as a military leader specializing in harrying tactics; it is ironic that he should be remembered best for the atypical set-piece battle that he incurred and won at Bannockburn in 1314. The Declaration of Arbroath of 1320 is perhaps more informative about his methods. Ostensibly a letter from the magnates of Scotland to the pope, pledging their support for King Robert, it seems in reality to have been framed by Bernard de Linton, Robert's chancellor. In committing Robert to seeing the independence struggle through, it likewise committed those who set their seals to it. Some of them were waverers in the national cause, whether or not Robert had proof of this at the time, and his hand was now strengthened against them.

In 1328 Robert secured from England, through the Treaty of Northampton, a recognition of Scotland's independence; the following year the pope granted to the independent kings of Scots the right to be anointed with holy oil. However, Robert also died in 1329. By the appropriate standards of medieval kingship, his success had been total, but, because of the nature of medieval kingship, his successor was left with the same struggle to wage all over again.

DAVID II (1329–71)

Robert I's son, David II, has perhaps received unfair treatment from historians contrasting him and his illustrious father. Just over five years of age at his accession, he was soon confronted with a renewal of the Anglo-Scottish war, exacerbated by the ambitions of those Scots who had been deprived of their property by Robert I or otherwise disaffected. In the 1330s Edward Balliol, pursuing the claim to the throne of his father, John, overran southern Scotland. In return for English help, he gave England southern lands and strongpoints not recaptured fully by the Scots for a century. After the Scottish defeat at Halidon Hill near Berwick in 1333, David was forced to flee to France in the following year. Berwick itself fell to the English and was never again in Scottish hands except in the period between 1461 and 1482.

The Scots gradually regained the initiative, and in 1341 David was able to return to Scotland. In 1346, however, he was captured at the Battle of Neville's Cross near Durham. He was released in 1357 for a ransom of 100,000 merks, to be paid in nine annual installments. This ransom, three-fourths of which was eventually paid, constituted a serious burden on Scotland, and there is evidence that Parliament used this national emergency to establish some checks on the actions of the crown. In addition, the representatives of the royal burghs, which were important as an accessible source of finance, established a continuing right to sit in Parliament with the magnates and churchmen from the 1360s on, thus constituting the third of the "Three Estates."

Complex evidence relating to these transactions has been uniformly interpreted in a way discreditable to David, though another interpretation is possible. That he collected revenues more assiduously than he made ransom payments may indicate a reasoned attempt to strengthen the crown financially; and his negotiations, especially of 1363, whereby a member of the English royal house was to succeed him on the Scottish throne, may have been a diplomatic charade. Whatever his faults, David left Scotland with both its economy and its independence intact.

The long wars with England necessarily took their toll, retarding Scotland's economy and weakening the authority of its government. The buildings that have survived from this era are inferior to earlier work, much of which of course suffered damage during the wars. War was increasingly expensive, and taxation was increased drastically to pay David II's ransom. But, again, a rosier picture can be painted, suggesting that the burgesses were able to meet the increased taxation because of increased prosperity through the still-continuing trade with England.

CHAPTER 12

FROM THE 15TH CENTURY TO THE AGE OF REVOLUTION

David was succeeded by Robert II (1371–90), previously the high steward, who was the son of Robert I's daughter Marjory. The next king was Robert II's son John, restyled Robert III (1390–1406). It may be that the future Robert II's conduct was responsible for dissension in Scotland during David II's reign, particularly during his captivity in England.

THE EARLY STEWART KINGS

Neither Robert II nor his son Robert III was a strong king, and some nobles regarded both as upstarts and the latter as of doubtful legitimacy. A long period of monarchical weakness ensued in Scotland, accentuated by a series of royal minorities in the 15th and 16th centuries. Although historians have made much of the turbulence of these times, there were comparable periods of governmental weakness in contemporary England and France, and "bonds of manrent" and other alliances made by the magnates with each other and with their social inferiors should be seen as much as attempts to secure political stability in their own localities as threats to the overall peace of the kingdom.

Robert III's younger brother, Robert Stewart, 1st duke of Albany, was given powers to rule in his brother's name several times, and Robert's son James may have been sent to France in 1406 in order to keep him out of Albany's clutches. However, James was captured at sea by the English, and shortly afterward Robert III died. Following Albany's death in

1420, his son Murdac continued to misgovern the realm until 1424, when James I, then age 29, was ransomed.

The Douglas family was becoming particularly powerful in Scotland. They had been rewarded with the gift of the royal forest of Selkirk and other lands in south and southwest Scotland for loyal service to Robert I. But the growing power of the Douglases in this vital border area posed a growing threat to the crown by the end of the 14th century. At the same time, the Lords of the Isles had attained a stature in the western Highlands that outstripped that of the kings of Scots.

One notable event was the founding of the University of Saint Andrews, Scotland's first university, in 1411. The Wars of Independence led Scottish students to go to Paris rather than to Oxford or Cambridge. But universities were the training grounds of the clergy, and when, in the period 1408–18, Scotland recognized the antipope Benedict XIII after he had been abandoned by France, it became expedient for Scotland to have its own university. The bulls of foundation from Benedict XIII reached St. Andrews in 1414.

James I (1406–37) was an active and able king, keen to once again make the crown wealthy and powerful. Perhaps he was too eager to make up for time lost in his captivity, and thus he prompted the opposition that led to his death. The new posts of comptroller and treasurer were created to gather royal revenues more efficiently. Murdac, 2nd duke of Albany, was executed in 1425, and other powerful men were overawed, even in the far north. The laws were to be revised, and in 1426 a court for civil cases was set up, presaging the later Court of Session.

In 1426, possibly to balance the power of the magnates, it was enacted that all tenants in chief should attend Parliament in person. More realistically, they were, from 1428, permitted to send representatives from each shire. Even this system did not operate until the late 16th century. If James had been inspired during his captivity by the English House of Commons, he was unable to transplant that institution to Scotland. The Scottish Parliament, like that of many other European countries, remained throughout the medieval period the feudal court of the kings of Scots; lacking the distinctive development of the English Parliament, it did not differ essentially in kind from the feudal court of any great magnate. Despite, or perhaps because of, his innovative vigour, James made enemies for himself. His murder in 1437 was part of an attempt to seize the throne for Walter Stewart, earl of Atholl, but the conspirators were executed and James's young son succeeded him.

James II (1437–60) was six years old at the time of his accession. His minority was marked by struggles between the Crichton and Livingston families. During this minority and that of James III, James Kennedy, bishop of St. Andrews, played a statesmanlike part in seeking to preserve peace. James II took a violent line against overambitious subjects. In 1452 he stabbed William Douglas, 8th earl of Douglas, to death, and in 1455 James Douglas, 9th earl of Douglas, was attainted. The main line of the Douglas family never regained its position, though a younger, or cadet, branch of the family, the earls of Angus, was important in the late 15th century. Like his father, James II sought boldly to reassert royal authority, and Scotland lost an able king when he was killed by the bursting of a cannon at the siege of Roxburgh Castle, one of the last Scottish strongpoints in English hands. Roxburgh was subsequently captured by the Scots. Among the cultural advances of the reign was the founding, in 1451 by Bishop William Turnbull, of the University of Glasgow, Scotland's second university.

James III (1460–88), James II's son, acceded at age eight. During a period in his minority he was a pawn of the Boyd family. The Treaty of Westminster-Ardtornish of 1462 showed that John, Lord of the Isles, and the exiled Douglas were prepared to try to carve Scotland into two vassal states of England for themselves. The alliance came to nothing, but the Lords of the Isles were a threat to the territorial integrity of Scotland until their final forfeiture in 1493. Nonetheless, the power vacuum left by their removal was responsible for much of the unrest in the western Highlands thereafter. It was in James III's reign that the territory of Scotland attained its fullest extent with the acquisition of Orkney and Shetland in 1468–69.

As James III came of age, his keeping of company with artists caused grave offense to the nobles he shunned. Although it has been suggested that his fine sensibility did him credit, this is probably an anachronistic view. So serious was James's lack of authority that Berwick fell in 1482 when the nobles, led by Archibald Douglas, 5th earl of Angus, chose—rather than to defend the country against the English—to seize their opportunity to hang some of James's favourites. In 1488 James was murdered while fleeing from a battle against his opponents at Sauchieburn, though it seems that the death of the king was not intended, and he was succeeded without trouble by his son.

15TH-CENTURY SOCIETY

Despite the continuing war and unrest, there is evidence of economic recovery in Scotland during this period. Castle building and the extending of monasteries and cathedrals were widespread; work was done on the royal residences at Linlithgow and Stirling. The building of collegiate churches and of fine burgh churches is additional evidence of prosperity. Both royal burghs, with their share in international trade, and baronial burghs, with their rights in their own locality, were flourishing. The craftsmen threatened to rival the merchants in the running of burgh affairs, but an act of 1469 gave the merchants the majority on the town councils, allowing self-perpetuating cliques to misapply the assets of the burghs—an abuse not remedied until the 19th century. However, the general prosperity that prevailed in Scotland was accompanied by inflation, and a debasement of the coinage added to the troubles of James III's reign.

Interesting Scottish writing from the late 14th century onward, both in the vernacular and in Latin, has survived. John Barbour (1325?–95) wrote in Scots the national epic known as *The Bruce*, considered the first major work of Scottish literature. A Latin history of Scotland was compiled by John of Fordun and continued by Walter Bower, abbot of Inchcolm, in his *Scotichronicon*. Andrew of Wyntoun wrote a history of Scotland titled *Orygynale Cronykil*, one of the few long examples of Middle Scots writing.

Little is left of the corpus of medieval writings in Gaelic. Nonetheless, the sophistication of the western Highland stone carvings of the later Middle Ages suggests that a strong literary culture too was associated with the courts of the Lords of the Isles and other chiefs. *The Book of Deer*, containing the Gospels, has in its margins an 11th-century Gaelic account of Columba's foundation of the monastery of Deer in Aberdeenshire, as well as a series of *notitiae*, or lists of church rights, which provide clues to the nature of Celtic society.

The early 16th-century *The Book of the Dean of Lismore* (the seat of the bishop of Argyll) contains more than 60 Gaelic poems. From the quality of the architecture that has survived from the 15th century, one can infer the existence of paintings and other objects, such as

THE BOOK OF DEER

An illuminated manuscript written in Latin, probably in the 9th century, at a monastery founded by St. Columba at Deer Abbey (now in Aberdeenshire, Scotland), *The Book of Deer* contains 12th-century additions in Latin and an early form of Scottish Gaelic. *The Book of Deer* includes the whole of the New Testament Gospel of St. John and parts of the other three Gospels, an early version of the Apostles' Creed, and a later charter granted to the monks by King David I of Scotland. The illuminations—capitals, borders, and pictures of the Evangelists—resemble those in earlier Irish Gospels. The version of the Gospels is that used in Ireland (combining the Vulgate with earlier readings): the manuscript is clearly a careless transcript of a corrupt text. It was discovered in 1860 in the library of the University of Cambridge.

The 12th-century Gaelic memorandums (the earliest extant Gaelic written in Scotland) provide information on a little-known period of Scottish history—the end of the Celtic period. They give details of clan organization, land divisions, and monastic land tenure and an account of the monastery's foundation.

church furnishings, that have largely disappeared. An outstandingly intricate collegiate church is that at Roslin near Edinburgh, founded by Sir William Sinclair, 3rd earl of Orkney, about 1450. There are fine burgh churches, such as St. John's in Perth and the Church of the Holy Rood in Stirling. Perhaps the outstanding piece of evidence of royal patronage of the arts is the altarpiece for James III's Trinity College Church in Edinburgh, which is almost certainly the work of the great Flemish painter Hugo van der Goes.

In the 14th century the papacy had built up its claims to appoint to the higher offices in the church; in Scotland it had established a system of "provisions," or papal appointments, to vacant offices. This did not merely cut across the rights of rulers, who used the church to provide their loyal bureaucrats with a living, and the rights of other local patrons; it also meant a drain to Rome of money in the form of the tax payable by a cleric "provided" to a vacant post by the pope. James I resisted these developments, and at the same time, in the Council of Basel (1431–49), the conciliarists were seeking to curb papal power in the church; a distinguished member of the Council of Basel was the Scot Thomas Livingston, one of the first St. Andrews graduates.

James also sought to revive the monastic ideal in its early purity and established a house of the strict Carthusians at Perth. A compromise between James I and the pope was probably pending when James was murdered, and his successors tended to let the popes collect their money as long as they "provided" to church offices along lines acceptable to the monarchy. In 1487 James III was granted the concession that the pope would delay promotions to the higher offices for eight months so that the king could propose his nominee.

St. Andrews was made the seat of an archbishopric in 1472, in itself a desirable step. But the first archbishop of St. Andrews secured the honour by supporting the papacy against the king, and, as a result, the appointment was not welcomed in Scotland. Glasgow also became an archbishopric in 1492.

JAMES IV (1488–1513) AND JAMES V (1513–42)

James IV, being physically impressive, cultured, generous, and active in politics and war alike, was well-equipped for kingship. In 1493 he eliminated a potential rival by carrying out the forfeiture of the last Lord of the Isles, and he also dealt severely with unrest on the English border and elsewhere. James and Bishop William Elphinstone of Aberdeen founded King's College, Scotland's third university, in Aberdeen in 1495. This was the great age of Scottish poetry, and, while one of the leading makars, or poets, Robert Henryson (1420/30?–c. 1506), author of *The Testament of Cresseid*, was a burgh schoolmaster, the others were members of the court circle; Gawin

Douglas (1475?–1522), bishop of Dunkeld and kinsman to the earls of Angus, splendidly translated Virgil's *Aeneid* into Scots, and William Dunbar (1460/65–1520), a technically brilliant poet, showed the versatility of which Scots was capable.

After initial disharmony with England, James concluded a "treaty of perpetual peace" with Henry VII in 1502 and married Margaret, Henry's daughter, in 1503. But Henry VIII of England became involved in the anti-French schemes of Pope Julius II, and in 1512 France and Scotland renewed their "auld alliance" as a counterbalance. In 1513 Henry VIII invaded France. James IV consequently invaded England, where he died along with thousands of his army in the rashly fought and calamitous Battle of Flodden.

James's efficiency at home was thus offset by his excessive international ambitions. And both had cost money—for artillery, for a navy whose greatest ship, the *Great Michael*, cost £30,000, and for embassies. The crown granted lands in feu-farm tenure, which gave heritable possession in return for a substantial down payment and an unchangeable annual rent thereafter. In the great European inflation of the 16th century (known traditionally as the "price revolution"), this policy weakened the crown over the long term.

James V (1513–42) acceded to the throne when he was 17 months of age. The factional struggles of his minority were given shape by the division between those who adhered to Scotland's pro-French alignment and those who were determined that the price Scotland paid at Flodden not be repeated. John Stewart, 2nd duke of Albany, was regent until 1524 and favoured France; Archibald Douglas, 6th earl of Angus, maintained a pro-English policy until 1528, when James began his personal rule. James now found Scotland's support in international politics being sought on all sides. In the 1530s he obtained papal financial help in establishing a College of Justice, and he concluded two successive French marriages, each bringing a substantial dowry; his second wife, Mary, daughter of the duke de Guise, became the mother of Mary, Queen of Scots. James's support for the papacy and France alienated some of his subjects, however, and his rule was not simply strict and financially vigorous but rather avaricious and vindictive. Lack of noble support seems to have caused the rout at Solway Moss in November 1542 of a force invading England. This and the deaths of his infant sons led to the death of James, probably from nervous prostration, in December, a week after the birth of his daughter, Mary.

MARY (1542–67) AND THE SCOTTISH REFORMATION

The church in 16th-century Scotland may not have had more ignorant or immoral priests than those of previous generations, but restiveness at their shortcomings was becoming more widespread, and the power structure of the church seemed to preclude the possibility of reform without revolution. The church made a poor showing at the parish level, since by 1560 the bulk of the revenues of nearly 9 parishes in every 10 was appropriated to monasteries and other central institutions. In return for receiving its share of this wealth, the papacy abandoned spiritual direction of the Scottish church; from 1487 royal control over appointments to the higher church offices grew steadily. That this occurred at a time when the church's annual revenue—reckoned at £400,000 in 1560—was 10 times that of the crown readily explains the attraction of church office for unspiritual, career-seeking nobles. Laymen were feued (granted tenure of) church lands, became collectors of church revenues, and were given abbeys as benefices. Church property, particularly monastic property, was effectively being secularized, and if Protestantism offered to the nobles and lairds of Scotland a more spiritually alive church—and one with lay participation—it probably also appealed to them as a system under which they would not have to hand back what they had grabbed.

Particular laymen were as pious as ever, endowing collegiate churches as they had once endowed monasteries, and trenchant criticism of church abuses was expressed in the morality play *Ane Pleasant Satyre of the Thrie Estaitis* by Sir David Lyndsay (c. 1490–c. 1555). Nonetheless, reform from within was probably almost impossible. For example, Archbishop John Hamilton, a would-be reformer who gave his name to a vernacular catechism (1552), belonged to the family who had the most to lose if the careerists were curbed.

Mary began her reign (1542–67) as another Stewart child ruler in the hands of factions. The pro-French party upheld the old church, while the pro-English desired reform. By the Treaties of Greenwich (1543), Mary was to marry Edward, Henry VIII's heir. David Beaton, archbishop of St. Andrews and a papal legate in Scotland from 1544, and Mary of Guise, the queen mother, had this policy rescinded, and the murder of Beaton (1546) and English punitive raids culminating in the Scottish defeat at Pinkie (1547) did not cause Scotland to love England more. France helped Scotland to expel the English, but only in return for such a hold over the country that, by the time of young Mary's marriage to the dauphin in 1558, France appeared to be about to absorb Scotland.

Anti-French feeling and Protestant preaching combined to bring about revolt. In 1559 the reformers took up arms to forestall Mary of Guise's action against them. Despite the preaching of John Knox and others and the plundering of the monasteries, the decisive issues were political and military: Queen Elizabeth I of England sent troops to check French plans in Scotland. Mary of Guise died in June 1560, and, by the Treaty of Edinburgh in July, both France and England undertook to withdraw their troops. With Scotland thus neutralized, England's proximity to Scotland gave it an important advantage over France.

In August 1560 the Scottish Parliament abolished papal authority and adopted a Reformed Confession of Faith, but Mary, still in France, did not ratify this legislation. Still, the organization of local congregations, which had been going on for some years, continued, and the General Assembly emerged as the central legislative body for the church. In the *First Book of Discipline* (1560), Knox and other ministers proposed a striking social program for the church that would provide education and relief for the poor. However, laymen had not despoiled the old church to enrich the new, and, as an interim settlement secured by Mary's government in 1562, the church and crown together were to share but one-third of the old church's revenue.

Mary's husband died in 1560, and in 1561 she returned to Scotland. As a Roman Catholic in a Protestant land and as nearest heir, by descent from Henry VII's daughter, to Elizabeth of England, she had many enemies. Her personal reign was brief and dramatic: she married her cousin Henry Stewart, Lord Darnley (1565); their son, James (the future James VI of Scotland and James I of England), was born (1566); Darnley was murdered (1567); Mary married the adventurer James Hepburn, 4th earl of Bothwell—the instigator of Darnley's murder—prompting Mary's imprisonment and forcing her abdication (1567); and Mary escaped and fled to England (1568). Her task as a ruler was hard—and made more difficult by her own errors of judgment—but she essayed it bravely and was a truly tragic rather than a pathetic figure.

JAMES VI (1567–1625)

James lived through the usual disrupted minority to become one of Scotland's most successful kings. In a civil war between his own and his mother's followers, laird (landed proprietor) and merchant support for James may have been decisive in his eventual victory. Queen Elizabeth detained Mary in England and assisted James Douglas, 4th earl of Morton, regent from 1572, in achieving stability in Scotland.

James's government ratified the Reformed church settlement, and more permanent measures of church endowment were taken. The Concordat of Leith (1572) allowed the crown to appoint bishops with the church's approval. As in Mary's reign, the crown was intervening to prevent the wealth of the old church from being entirely laicized. And if the bishopric revenues were saved from going the same way as the monastic wealth, the crown expected a share in them for its services.

A new presbyterian party in the church, whose members wanted parity for all ministers and freedom from state control, rejected this compromise. Led by

Andrew Melville, a rigid academic theorist, they demanded, in the *Second Book of Discipline* (1578), that the new church receive all the wealth of the old, that it be run by a hierarchy of courts rather than of bishops, and that the state leave the church alone but be prepared to take advice from it. Many historians have seen these demands, as James undoubtedly did, as an attempt to establish a full-blown theocracy. James was not strong enough for out-and-out resistance immediately, and he sometimes made concessions, as in the Golden Act of 1592, which gave parliamentary sanction to the system of presbyterian courts. But he gradually showed his determination to run the church his own way, through the agency of his bishops, who were brought into Parliament in 1600. From 1606 Melville was detained in London, and he was later banished. By 1610 the civil and ecclesiastical status of the bishops was secure. The continued existence of church courts—kirk sessions, presbyteries, synods, and the General Assembly—shows James's readiness for compromise, and he showed a wise cautiousness toward liturgical reform after encountering hostility over his Five Articles of Perth (1618), which imposed kneeling at communion, observance of holy days, confirmation, infant baptism, and other practices.

In the 1580s, as James became personally responsible for royal policy, he faced the need to control unruly subjects at home, nobles and kirkmen alike, and to win friends abroad. He concluded a league with England in 1586, and when Elizabeth executed his mother in the following year as a Roman Catholic threat to the English throne, he acquiesced in what he could not prevent. He thus inherited his mother's claim, and his efforts thereafter to keep in the good graces of Elizabeth and her minister William Cecil were successful. He succeeded peacefully to the English throne in 1603, though his two monarchies, despite his own personal inclinations, remained distinct from each other.

James's policy was one of overall insurance; he avoided giving offense to Catholic continental rulers, and, while he dealt effectively with lawbreakers on the border and elsewhere, he showed marked leniency toward his Catholic nobles, even when the discovery of letters and blank documents (the "Spanish Blanks" affair, 1592) showed that several of them were in treasonable conspiracy with a foreign power. Neither a heroic king, like James IV, nor the pedantic and cowardly buffoon depicted in Sir Walter Scott's *The Fortunes of Nigel*, James VI was a supple and able politician. His theories of divine-right monarchy were a scholar-king's response to an age when the practice and theory of regicide were fashionable. Except perhaps at the very end of his life, James was too realistic to let his theories entirely govern his conduct.

James excelled in picking good servants from among the lairds and burgesses; they were his judges and privy councillors and sat on the Committee of Articles, with which he dominated Parliament. After 1603 they governed Scotland smoothly in his absence. From 1587 Parliament was made more representative by the admission of shire commissioners to speak for the lairds, and the program of James I was thus realized. The privy council had judicial as well as legislative and administrative functions; there were, in addition, the Court of Session for civil cases (it had evolved from the council in the early 16th century and, as the College of Justice, had been endowed with church funds in the 1530s) and justice courts for criminal cases. Local justice and administration continued, however, despite James VI's efforts, to be largely the prerogative of the landowners.

Scotland still had a subsistence economy, exporting raw materials and importing finished goods, including luxuries. However, the luxury imports illustrate that the greater landowners and merchants were gaining in prosperity. Despite the absence of adequate endowment, the Reformed church began to create a network of parish schools, and there were advances in the universities. Melville brought discipline and the latest scholarship to Glasgow and St. Andrews in turn, and there were new foundations at Edinburgh (the Town's College, 1582) and Aberdeen (Marischal College, 1593).

As the continual strife between England and Scotland receded, they drew closer together. Although the national churches in England and Scotland were not identical in structure, they shared a common desire to protect and preserve the Reformation. James VI's accession to the English throne in 1603 as James I encouraged further cultural and economic assimilation. It was far from guaranteeing further political assimilation, but a century of the barely workable personal union of the crowns had increasingly sharpened the Scots' dilemma of choosing between complete union and complete separation.

CHARLES I (1625–49)

James VI's son, Charles I, was raised in England and lacked any understanding of his Scottish subjects and their institutions. He soon fell foul of a restless nobility in a Scotland that lacked the natural focal point of a royal court. The king also caused widespread anger by high taxation, by the special demands made on Edinburgh to build a Parliament House and to provide a cathedral for the bishopric founded there in 1633, and by a Spanish war and a French war that were intended to further English diplomacy but meanwhile disrupted Scottish trading ties. The aristocratic leaders of the opposition found ideal material on which to build clerical and popular support. Charles and his Scottish bishops were fond enough of ritual and splendour in church services to make plausible the (wholly incorrect) suggestion that they were ready for compromise with Rome. The new *Book of Canons* (1635–36) and

Liturgy (1637) therefore offended by their content, as well as by being authorized by royal prerogative alone. The National Covenant (1638) astutely collected national support for the opposition's pledge to resist Charles's innovations. Condemnation of popery was written into it for the benefit of those who feared that Charles might be a crypto-Catholic; others, more sophisticated, welcomed its implicit condemnation of a royal arbitrariness with religion and private rights that was contrary to all Scottish precedent.

The Covenanters humbled Charles in two almost bloodless campaigns, the Bishops' Wars (1639–40), leaving him with no alternative but to ask for money from an English Parliament in which his opponents were strongly represented. Charles had authorized a general assembly of the Scottish church (1638) and a Scottish Parliament (1639); the Covenanters packed these meetings, scrapped all the king's innovations, and abolished episcopacy. Thus, by 1641 there was a revolutionary situation in both kingdoms, and in August 1642 war broke out between Charles and his English opponents. Both sides sought Scottish help, which was soon accorded to the English parliamentary opposition. By the Solemn League and Covenant (1643) the English promised, in return for military aid, to help preserve government by the Presbyterian church in Scotland and, so at least the Scots believed, to set it up in England. James Graham, 1st marquess of Montrose, and others who then left the Covenanting side argued that by this second Covenant, and by certain constitutional constraints they had placed upon the crown, the Scots had gone unwarrantably far beyond the aims of the first Covenant. But those Scots who were prepared to make common cause with the English opposition, even if the English did have a more deep-seated quarrel with their king than the Scots, had reasoned justification, for it was realistic to expect that Charles, as soon as it proved possible, would withdraw concessions made to men whom he regarded as his enemies.

Personal antipathies also helped to split the ranks of the original Covenanters—notably the antipathy between Montrose and Archibald Campbell, 1st marquess of Argyll, who was sincerely devoted to the cause but equally devoted to the advancement of his family. Montrose's military efforts for Charles in Scotland were crushed in 1645, and by 1646 Charles had also lost the war in England. When Charles surrendered to the Scottish army in England, the Scots failed to reach agreement with him and handed him over to the English.

The Scottish contribution to the English war effort had been substantial but not spectacular enough to leave a sense of obligation, and the English army under Oliver Cromwell, who now eclipsed Parliament in English politics, preferred Independency to

Presbyterianism in the church and did not propose to honour the Solemn League and Covenant. A conservative element among the Covenanters in 1647 reached a compromise, or "Engagement," with Charles by which they promised him help in return for the establishment of Presbyterianism in both kingdoms for three years and went to war on his behalf; their ill-planned campaign was crushed at Preston in 1648. The clerics, who had bitterly opposed this compromise, were now able, under the leadership of a few nobles such as Argyll, to purge the Scottish Parliament and army of all those tainted by collaboration with the king. The execution of Charles by the English in 1649 genuinely shocked most Scots, who were prepared to fight for his son, Charles II, once he had been constrained to accept the Covenants and once Montrose had been executed (1650). Cromwell's victory over the Scots at Dunbar (1650) gave more-moderate Scots the ascendancy again, but this brought no better military result. Another, and decisive, defeat at Cromwell's hands came to a Scottish royalist army at Worcester in 1651.

CROMWELL

Cromwell imposed on Scotland a full and incorporating parliamentary union with England (1652). However, this union, maintained by an army of occupation, did not enjoy popular consent. Nevertheless, Cromwell's administration of Scotland was efficient, and his judges, some of them Englishmen, achieved an admired impartiality. Public order was well maintained, even in the Highlands after the collapse of royalist resistance in 1654. Cromwell did not overturn Presbyterianism but ensured toleration for others, save Roman Catholics and Episcopalians (those who believed the Protestant church should be governed by bishops).

THE RESTORATION MONARCHY

The restoration in 1660 of Charles II (1660–85) was welcomed by many moderates in both Scotland and England. Charles had learned much from his father's fate and was prepared to forget many injuries, though his government executed some Scots, including the marquess of Argyll.

In 1662 Charles formally restored church government by bishops, but, like the compromise fashioned under James VI, they were to act in association with synods and presbyteries. Charles seems to have been moved not by rancor toward the Covenanters, who had bullied him in the early 1650s, but merely by a desire to achieve the system that satisfied most people. Many laymen accepted his system, and few nobles opposed it. However, approximately 270 ministers—just over a quarter of the total—were deprived of their parishes for noncompliance, leading to the Pentland Rising (1666), which was easily quashed and was countered by an experimental period of tolerance by the government. Persons who still persisted in attending conventicles were strong only in the southwest and to some extent in Fife and among the small lairds and common people. These men adhered to the "Protester" position, regarding Scotland as still bound by the Covenants. In another trial of strength with the government, they were defeated at Bothwell Bridge (1679). Some Cameronians (the name derives from Richard Cameron, a leading Covenanter) remained, meeting governmental violence with further violence, and in 1690 they refused to join a Presbyterian but uncovenanted Church of Scotland. Their brave and fanatic "thrawnness" (recalcitrance) endeared them to later generations of Scots.

When Charles's brother succeeded as James VII of Scotland and James II of Great Britain and Ireland (1685–88), most Scots showed that they were prepared to support him despite his Roman Catholicism. But he showed his ineptitude by requesting Parliament to grant toleration to Catholics (1686); this stirred up unprecedented opposition to royal wishes in the Scottish Parliament. Nevertheless, although many exiled Scots were at the court of William of Orange in Holland, the collapse (1688–89) of James's regime in Scotland was entirely a result of the Glorious Revolution (1688) in England and the landing there of William.

CHAPTER 13

SCOTLAND SINCE THE 18TH CENTURY

With James VII having fled to France, a Convention of Estates (really the same assembly as Parliament but meeting less formally) gave the crown jointly to the Protestant William of Orange (William III of Great Britain, 1689–1702) and his wife, Mary II (1689–94), James's daughter. William's first major decision was a moderate one: episcopacy was abolished in 1689 and Presbyterianism reestablished the following year. However, a series of crises throughout William's reign exposed his total lack of interest in Scotland and placed a strain on the system that had developed whereby the Scottish ministry took orders not only from the monarch but also from the English ministry.

THE ACT OF UNION AND ITS RESULTS

William fought one war against France (1689–97) and on his death in 1702 bequeathed another (1701–13) to his successor, his wife's sister Anne (1702–14). These circumstances made a union of Scotland and England seem strategically as well as economically desirable. That an Act of Union was achieved in 1707 is at first sight surprising, since intervening sessions of the Scottish Parliament had been in a mood to break the English connection altogether. But by 1707 England's appreciation of its own strategic interests, and of the nuisance value of the Scottish Parliament, was lively enough for it to offer statesmanlike concessions to Scotland and material inducements to Scottish parliamentarians to accept union.

The union was an incorporating one—the Scottish Parliament was ended and the Westminster Parliament increased by 45 commoners and 16 peers representing Scotland. Scotland benefited by gaining free trade with England and its colonies, by the grant of a money "equivalent" of the share of the English national debt that Scotland would assume, and by the explicit safeguarding of its national church and legal system. After Queen Anne's death in 1714, when the Jacobites, supporters of James VII's descendants, missed their best opportunity, the worst crises of the union were past.

JACOBITISM IN THE HIGHLANDS

The Jacobites were seldom more than a nuisance in Britain. An expedition from France in 1708 and a West Highland rising with aid from Spain in 1719 were abortive; bad leadership in the rebellion in 1715 (known as "the Fifteen Rebellion") of James VII's son, James Edward, the Old Pretender, and divided counsels in the rebellion of 1745 ("the Forty-five") led by the Old Pretender's son Charles Edward, the Young Pretender, crippled invasions originating in France that had in any case less than an even chance of success. The government was not always sufficiently prepared for invasions, but the generalship of John Campbell, 2nd duke of Argyll, at Sheriffmuir in 1715 sufficed to check the Jacobites, and that of William Augustus, duke of Cumberland, at Culloden in 1746 dealt the coup de grâce to a Jacobite army.

The Jacobites never had full French naval and military assistance, and support in Scotland itself was limited; not many more Lowland Scots than Englishmen loved the Stuarts enough to die for them. Many politicians, especially before 1714, corresponded with the royal exiles simply as a matter of insurance against their return, and in the dying days of Stuart hopes there were fewer people than there have been since who were struck by the romantic aura surrounding Prince Charles Edward, "Bonnie Prince Charlie." The Stuarts primarily had to rely on the clans of the Gaelic-speaking regions, and Highland support in itself alienated Lowlanders. Not all Highlanders were "out" in the Fifteen or the Forty-five rebellions; such clans as the Campbells and the Munros, the Macleods, and the Macdonalds of Sleat were Hanoverian either because they were Presbyterian or through their chiefs' personal inclinations. However, many clans were Roman Catholic or Episcopalian and favoured a Catholic monarch; they were legitimists and reasonably so, since both James VII and his son, James Edward, the Old Pretender, appreciated Highland problems—problems of an infertile land overpopulated with fighting men who owed personal allegiance to their chiefs and who were partly dependent on plunder to maintain their standard of living.

The years after the Battle of Culloden were characterized by a series of attempts by the chiefs in the late 18th and particularly in the early 19th century to emulate the new capitalist agriculture of the Lowlands, thus creating an impersonal cash relationship with their tenants based on the exploitative employment of the latter—in industries such as the harvesting of kelp (seaweed) for its alkali content—or stimulating recruiting to newly formed regiments of the British army. The roots of this process can be found prior to the defeat of Jacobitism, but the catastrophe of the Fifteen and Forty-five rebellions made the process more rapid and more painful. The atrocities of government soldiers and the repressiveness of government legislation after 1746 were much less important in ushering in the new order than economic and social forces.

Adam Smith, paste medallion by James Tassie, 1787; in the Scottish National Portrait Gallery, Edinburgh. Courtesy of the Scottish National Portrait Gallery, Edinburgh

THE SCOTTISH ENLIGHTENMENT

No straightforward connection can be drawn between the union and the exceptional 18th-century flowering of intellectual life known as the Scottish Enlightenment. Absence of civil strife, however, permitted the best minds to turn, if they chose, from politics and its 17th-century twin, religion, and few of the best minds from 1707 onward were in fact directly concerned with politics. Philosophy, in which 18th-century Scotland excelled, was a proper concern for a country where for generations minds had been sharpened by theological debate. Scottish culture remained distinctive, and distinctively European in orientation. The historian and philosopher David Hume sought to remove Scotticisms from his speech, and the architect Robert Adam gained extra experience as well as income from being able to design buildings in London as well as in Edinburgh. Nevertheless, Adam drew most of his stylistic inspiration from the Classical architecture he had studied in Italy, and Hume, "le bon David," was an honoured member of Continental polite and intellectual society. Hume's *The History of England* (1754–62) made his literary reputation in his lifetime, but it is his philosophical works, such as his *A Treatise of Human Nature* (1739–40), that

DAVID HUME

David Hume (born May 7, 1711, Edinburgh, Scotland—died August 25, 1776, Edinburgh) conceived of philosophy as the inductive, experimental science of human nature. His first major work, *A Treatise of Human Nature* (1739–40), explains the origin of ideas, including the ideas of space, time, and causality, in sense experience; presents an elaborate account of the affective, or emotional, aspects of the mind and assigns a subordinate role to reason in this order ("Reason is, and ought only to be, the slave of the passions"); and describes moral goodness in terms of "feelings" of approval or disapproval that a person has when he considers human behaviour in the light of the agreeable or disagreeable consequences either to himself or to others. The *Treatise* was poorly received, and late in life Hume repudiated it as juvenile. He revised Book I of the *Treatise as An Enquiry Concerning Human Understanding* (1758); a revision of Book III was published as *An Enquiry Concerning the Principles of Morals* (1751). His *Dialogues Concerning Natural Religion* (1779), containing a refutation of the argument from design and a critique of the notion of miracles, was withheld from publication during his lifetime at the urging of friends. From his account of the origin of ideas Hume concluded that we have no knowledge of a "self" as the enduring subject of experience; nor do we have knowledge of any "necessary connection" between causally related events. Immanuel Kant, who developed his critical philosophy in direct reaction to Hume, said that Hume had awakened him from his "dogmatic slumbers." In Britain, Hume's moral theory influenced Jeremy Bentham to adopt utilitarianism. With John Locke and George Berkeley, Hume is regarded as one of the great philosophers of empiricism.

have caused the continuous growth of his reputation since his death.

Adam Smith, author of *The Wealth of Nations* (1776), was the philosopher of political economy. The discipline of history was developed by William Robertson, a Church of Scotland clergyman, principal of the University of Edinburgh, and official historiographer royal for Scotland; his *History of Scotland, During the Reigns of Queen Mary and of King James VI* was published in 1759. Henry Home, Lord Kames, may be singled out from a number of other significant figures to illustrate the versatility characteristic of the times. He was a judge, interested in legal theory and history, an agricultural reformer in theory and practice, a commissioner of the Forfeited Estates (of the rebels of 1745), and a member of the Board of Trustees for Manufactures (which encouraged Scottish industries, notably linen production). In poetry there was a reaction, possibly against union—and certainly against assimilation—with England; revived interest in Scots vernacular poetry of the past was the herald of a spate of new vernacular poetry, which culminated in the satires of Robert Fergusson and the lyrics of Robert Burns. Some of the greatest Gaelic poets, such as Alexander MacDonald, were also writing at this time.

The Scottish educational system, its foundations so securely laid throughout the previous century, made possible this extraordinary cultural outpouring. The Scottish universities enjoyed their heyday, Edinburgh being notable for medicine and preeminent in most other subjects as well. Gradually the regents, who taught students throughout their university course, were replaced by professors specializing in single subjects. That students seldom troubled to graduate was of little disadvantage in an age when appointments depended on patronage. Not bound by a rigid curriculum, students were able to indulge the Scots' traditionally wide intellectual curiosity by attending lectures in a variety of subjects. Scientific study was encouraged, and practical applications of discoveries were given due place. Francis Home, professor of Materia Medica at Edinburgh, studied bleaching processes and plant nutrition; and James Watt, instrument maker to the University of Glasgow for a time, was encouraged by the university to work on the steam engine, to which he was to make crucial improvements.

19TH-CENTURY SCOTLAND

Agitation for constitutional change was considered treasonable by many during the years 1793–1815, when Britain was fighting Revolutionary France. Several advocates of universal suffrage, including a young Glasgow lawyer, Thomas Muir of Huntershill, were sentenced to transportation (exile) in 1793. After repression had broken this first radical wave, postwar industrial depression produced another—the "Radical War" of 1820, an abortive rising of workers in the Glasgow area. Intellectual campaigning of a more moderate sort had greater short-term success. *The Edinburgh Review*, founded in 1802 by a group of young lawyers led by Francis Jeffrey and Henry Brougham (1st Baron Brougham and Vaux), was influential in both radical politics and literature. Edinburgh life was particularly brilliant during the war years, when students unable to study abroad found the University of Edinburgh more attractive than ever. Outstanding in this period was Sir Walter Scott, although not until 1827 was he known to be the author of the Waverley novels. Scott's greatness as a novelist lay in the way he took Scottish society as a whole for his main character, and his best books are a lament for an era that he knew was dying, the organic society of preindustrial Scotland. The other major figure in 19th-century Scottish fiction was Robert Louis Stevenson, who published a wide variety of historical novels, adventure stories, and travel literature before his premature death in Samoa in 1894. His voice, especially from exile, was distinctive. Scottish writing in the 1890s is generally perceived to be sentimental and mawkish, exemplified by the Kailyard novels of Sir James

Barrie, Samuel Rutherford Crockett, and Ian Maclaren; George Douglas perhaps overcompensated for this tendency in *The House with the Green Shutters* (1901), the first realistic portrayal of Scottish life. Gaelic poetry is generally held to have been in decline for much of the 19th century until the work of Iain Mac a'Ghobhainn (John Smith), Uilleam MacDhunlèibhe (William Livingstone), and the political activist Màiri Mhór nan Oran (Mary Macpherson) in the final third of the century.

THE INDUSTRIAL REVOLUTION

From the 1820s the Industrial Revolution was in full swing in Scotland, linked (in a way historians have not altogether disentangled) to a dramatic increase in population. There were perhaps a million people in Scotland at the beginning of the 18th century. By the beginning of the 19th century there were more than 1.5 million, and by the turn of the 20th century the population exceeded 4.5 million. The manufacturing towns showed spectacular increases. Hundreds of thousands of Irish emigrants went to Scotland in the 19th century, beginning prior to but increasing in number during the Irish Potato Famine of 1845–49. In some country regions there was a population decrease as people moved to the towns, to England, or overseas. Part of the overall increase was the result of improved medical care that had lessened the ravages of epidemic diseases by the mid-19th century. Much of the food for the increased population was supplied by progressive Scottish agriculture. Farming in the southeast was celebrated for its efficiency in the early 19th century, and the northeast became famous for its beef cattle and Ayrshire for its milking herds.

The key advance was in heavy industry, which from about 1830 took the industrial primacy from textiles, at a time when industry as a whole had replaced agriculture as Scotland's chief concern. Coal production rose, as did that of iron, with the hot-blast process (1828) of James Beaumont Neilson making Scottish ores cheaper to work. Major canals, such as the Forth and Clyde, completed in 1790, enjoyed a short boom before being rendered obsolete by the railways, of which the Glasgow-to-Garnkirk (1831) was noteworthy for using steam locomotives (rather than horses) from its inception. Above all, Scottish international trade was catered to, and Clydeside's reputation made, by the building of ships. Robert Napier was the greatest of many great Scottish marine engineers. The later 19th century was characterized by the expansion of new heavy industry, such as steel, and technological advances in shipbuilding and marine engineering.

POLITICS AND RELIGION

Parliamentary (1832) and burgh (1833) reform ended fictitious county votes and corrupt burgh caucuses but disillusioned the working classes by failing to extend to them the franchise. As in England, they had to await the 1867 and subsequent Reform Acts. But the great bulk of the Scottish middle classes were delighted with the Whigs, who had brought the reforms. The Whig Party, or Liberal Party (as it became known in the 1860s), dominated Scottish mid-19th-century politics. Liberal Party leader and hero William Ewart Gladstone, of Scottish parentage, was widely admired among Scots for his moral dynamism and fire despite his High Church Episcopalianism.

Ecclesiastical strife was perhaps more important than parliamentary politics in Scottish life in the 19th century. Opposing approaches to the relationship between church and state within the Church of Scotland brought about the Ten Years' Conflict, which was not resolved until a large proportion of the clergy and the laity left the established Church of Scotland in 1843 to form the Free Church of Scotland. This fracture was not healed until the Presbyterian reunion in 1929, and it had profound effects on Scottish life, because the church was the main agency of social welfare (until 1845) under the old Poor Law of Scotland and undertook a similar role in the Scottish education system until 1872.

Trade unions of skilled workers had led an uninterrupted existence since the early 19th century. By the 1880s unskilled workers were being organized. Various factors delayed the permanent organization of the miners until a major leader, James Keir Hardie, emerged from their ranks. Failing to sufficiently engage the Liberals in support of organized labour, he helped form the Scottish Labour Party in 1888. In 1893 Hardie created the Independent Labour Party (ILP) for Britain as a whole, and in 1900 the ILP federated with the trade unions for the purpose of running the Labour Party (given its present name in 1906). However, liberalism continued to dominate Scottish politics until 1922 (the Liberals even won a majority of Scottish seats in the two general elections of 1910), as the labour movement, despite the activity of Hardie, found it difficult to emerge from the shadow of the Liberals.

THE HIGHLANDS

By 1800 the Highlands had become overpopulated relative to the means of subsistence. Many lairds, seeking to support their tenantry through the kelp industry, were ruined when it collapsed in the period from 1815 to 1825. Other landowners introduced sheep, sometimes violently removing their tenants in the "Highland Clearances"—as agents of the Sutherland family did in Strathnaver, Sutherland, about 1810–20. The Potato Famine in the Scottish Highlands that began in the mid-1840s caused distress and encouraged landowners to engage in a new round of clearances and to sponsor large-scale emigration.

By the 1880s Highland subsistence-farming tenants, or "crofters," faced a new problem. Deer forests had replaced sheep runs as the most immediately profitable land use open to landowners, and, as a result, the shortage of land for grazing and arable agriculture was the major grievance of the crofting community. Parliamentary agitation by the crofters, who voted for the first time in 1885, and by their Lowland sympathizers, as well as sporadic outbursts of violence beginning in 1882 (the "Crofters' War"), secured an act of 1886 that gave the crofters security of tenure and empowered a Crofters' Commission to fix fair rents, though it did little to make more land available to crofters. (Further legislation in 1911 and 1919 helped to alleviate this problem.) Unlike their Irish counterparts, the Highlanders sought not ownership of their land but the imposition of certain standards of conduct and responsibility upon their landlords. As the crofting agitation of the 1880s united both Highlanders and Lowlanders, it was a key stage in the forging of a modern Scottish consciousness.

WORLD WAR I AND AFTER

World War I had a great effect on Scottish society; 74,000 Scots were killed and industry mobilized as never before in a coordinated national effort. Clyde shipbuilding and engineering were crucial, and Clydeside was the key munitions centre in Britain. In retrospect, however, the expansion of heavy industry in the 1920s was in fact an overexpansion. The collapse of the wartime boom in 1920 began a period of economic depression in Britain, in which Scotland was one of the worst-affected regions.

Economic distress bred political radicalism. The Liberals were eclipsed, and in most seats the real contest was between the Unionists and Labour, which became Scotland's biggest single party for the first time in the election of 1922. Willie Gallacher, Scotland's only notable communist member of Parliament and an able political theorist strongly influenced by Vladimir Lenin, was at the same time a radical belonging to a revered Scots tradition. In 1930 John Wheatley, who had been minister of health in the first Labour government (1924) and the author of an important housing act, died, thereby depriving left-wingers in the Labour Party of a skilled leader, and counsels of moderation in the party prevented its taking any distinctive initiative on the economic crisis. Ramsay MacDonald, a Scot who had led two minority Labour governments, agreed to form a national coalition government with Conservative and Liberal support in 1931. However, the Labour Party refused to participate, disowned MacDonald, and was heavily defeated at the polls in Scotland as elsewhere.

Another political development that resulted partly from economic distress was the formation in 1934 of the Scottish National Party (SNP), a merger of two previous parties. It had some distinguished supporters, especially literary figures, but it was suspected, sometimes unfairly, of political extremism and made little electoral impact before World War II. The national government of the 1930s was dominated by the Conservatives. While opposed to an independent Scottish legislature, this government furthered the extension of the Scottish administrative system in 1939, installing it in St. Andrew's House in Edinburgh.

The interwar period was one of significant cultural advance and self-confidence in Scotland. In poetry the dominant figure in this renaissance was Christopher Murray Grieve, who published under the pseudonym Hugh MacDiarmid. Important achievements in prose literature were made by Neil Gunn, Edwin Muir, Nan Shepherd, and Willa Muir. James Leslie Mitchell (Lewis Grassic Gibbon) published a trilogy of novels, collectively known as *A Scots Quair* (1932–34), which charted the changes in the social life of the communities of northeastern Scotland. In Gaelic literature poetry continued to be the dominant form, and the lyrical work of Somhairle MacGill-eain (Sorley Maclean) dominated the 20th-century scene.

WORLD WAR II AND AFTER

During World War II Scotland suffered some 34,000 combat deaths, and approximately 6,000 civilians were killed, many in air attacks on Clydeside. In 1943 Tom Johnston, a Labour member of Parliament who acted as secretary of state for Scotland in the wartime national government, helped to create the North of Scotland Hydro-Electric Board, which was one of the most successful government agencies of the period.

In 1945 Labour won a landslide national election victory that gave it 37 of Scotland's 74 seats in Parliament to the Conservatives' 32. Support for Labour gradually ebbed in the early 1950s, however, and in 1955 the Conservative Party took 36 of 71 Scottish seats, its first majority in Scotland. These gains were reversed in 1959, when the Conservatives lost 3 seats in Scotland, despite the party's net gain of 23 seats nationally.

The Scottish economy was relatively healthy from 1945 through the mid-1950s. The Labour governments (1945–51) sought to ensure full employment, and though the Conservatives initially opposed Labour's widespread nationalization of industries—such as the coal mines, the Bank of England, the railroads, and electric power—they eventually accepted the mixed economy and the expanded welfare state. The Scottish Milk Marketing Board helped to boost Scotland's agricultural productivity. However, Scotland's heavy industries—especially coal mining and shipbuilding—began to stagnate in the mid-1950s, and unemployment in Scotland was often twice that in England. In its 1961 report on the Scottish economy, the Scottish Council for Development

STONE OF SCONE

According to one Celtic legend the Stone of Scone (Scottish Gaelic: Lia Fail) was once the pillow upon which the patriarch Jacob rested at Bethel when he beheld the visions of angels. From the Holy Land it purportedly traveled to Egypt, Sicily, and Spain and reached Ireland about 700 BCE to be set upon the hills of Tara, where the ancient kings of Ireland were crowned. Thence it was taken by the Celtic Scots who invaded and occupied Scotland. About 840 CE it was taken by Kenneth MacAlpin to the village of Scone.

At Scone, historically, the stone (which is also called the Stone of Destiny) came to be encased in the seat of a royal coronation chair. John de Balliol was the last Scottish king crowned on it, in 1292, before Edward I of England invaded Scotland in 1296 and moved the stone (and other Scottish regalia) to London. There, at Westminster Abbey in 1307, he had a special throne, called the Coronation Chair, built so that the stone fitted under it. This was to be a symbol that kings of England would be crowned as kings of Scotland also.

The stone, weighing 336 pounds (152 kg), is a rectangular block of pale yellow sandstone (almost certainly of Scottish origin) measuring 26 inches (66 cm) by 16 inches (41 cm) by 11 inches (28 cm). A Latin cross is its only decoration.

Attached to the stone in ancient times was allegedly a piece of metal with a prophecy that Sir Walter Scott translated as

Unless the fates be faulty grown
And prophet's voice be vain
Where'er is found this sacred stone
The Scottish race shall reign.

When Queen Elizabeth I died without issue in 1603, she was succeeded by King James VI of Scotland, who became James I of England (or Great Britain). James was crowned on the Stone of Scone, and patriotic Scots said that the legend had been fulfilled, for a Scotsman then ruled where the Stone of Scone was.

On Christmas morning 1950 the stone was stolen from Westminster Abbey by Scottish nationalists who took it back to Scotland. Four months later it was recovered and restored to the abbey. In 1996 the British government returned the stone to Scotland.

and Industry remarked that "if there is a panacea for Scotland's economic problems we have not found it."

Scottish nationalism was relatively muted in the 1950s, despite the signing of a Scottish Covenant, which called for home rule in Scotland, reportedly by more than two million Scots in 1949, and despite the theft of the Stone of Scone, the ancient stone upon which Scottish kings were traditionally crowned, from Westminster Abbey on Christmas Day

1950 (the stone, which was taken to Scotland, was returned in April 1951).

By the late 1950s Scottish nationalists supported independence or the creation of a devolved assembly, though their demands were opposed by both major parties. Scotland's faltering economy under the Conservatives in 1951–64 helped to increase support for Labour, which defeated the Conservatives by 43 seats to 23 in 1964 and by 46 seats to 20 in 1966. The Liberals and the SNP—both of which supported greater autonomy for Scotland—also made gains in these elections, though the SNP failed to secure any parliamentary seats.

In the 1960s the Labour government of Harold Wilson introduced a plan to modernize Scotland's economy and retrain its workforce for new industries. Despite these efforts, there was considerable pessimism about the country's economic prospects until the early 1970s, when oil was discovered in the North Sea. During the early 1980s a worldwide recession coincided with a collapse in oil prices and a series of closures of large industrial plants in Scotland, contributing to an increase in unemployment and further pessimism. In response, the British government created special agencies to attract new investment, notably from American electronics companies, with the result that by the 1990s Scotland had become one of Europe's major electronics manufacturing centres. Scotland's resource industries—farming, fishing, and forestry—continued to play an important role in its economy, and tourism increased in importance. Revitalization in Glasgow led to its designation as the European Capital of Culture in 1990, and by the end of the 1990s Scotland's "Silicon Glen"—the nickname given to the central part of the country that housed the country's high-tech sector—produced nearly one-third of Europe's computers, four-fifths of its workstations, and two-thirds of its automatic teller machines. Although high-tech plants remained important, confidence in the sector was shaken at the turn of the 21st century by the closure of a number of high-profile plants during the worldwide economic slowdown.

NORTH SEA OIL AND THE RISE OF SCOTTISH NATIONALISM

In the early 1970s the SNP enjoyed some short-lived electoral success, especially as the flow of North Sea oil increased support for Scottish independence. Campaigning for the October 1974 election on the slogan "It's Scotland's oil!," the SNP managed to mobilize a sense of economic grievance and cultural resentment that cut across the traditional class divisions of Scottish politics. The party won more than 30 percent of the Scottish vote and 11 of the 71 Scottish seats in Parliament.

On March 1, 1979, in an effort to stave off militant nationalism, the Labour government of James Callaghan held a referendum to approve its devolution legislation, which was designed to grant Scotland its own assembly with limited legislative and executive powers. Although favoured by a majority (52.9 percent) of the Scots who voted, the referendum failed to win the approval of the required 40 percent of the electorate. The SNP (along with the Liberals and the Plaid Cymru) then withdrew its support from the Labour government, causing it to lose a vote of confidence, and in the ensuing election the SNP lost 9 of its 11 seats in Parliament.

Despite economic and political problems in the 1980s Scottish cultural confidence grew in most areas of artistic activity. Established Scottish writers such as Alasdair Gray and James Kelman pursued new themes in Scottish literature. They were joined by a new generation of younger writers, notably Irvine Welsh, whose novel *Trainspotting* (1993) was made into a successful film.

Throughout the 1980s, when the Conservative government in London enjoyed little support in Scotland, support for greater political autonomy increased. In 1989 the introduction in Scotland of the "community charge," a uniform-rate poll tax intended to replace taxation based on property, produced widespread protests against the Conservatives and Prime Minister Margaret Thatcher. (The poll tax was introduced in England and Wales in the following year.) Partly because of the SNP's strong opposition to the poll tax and Labour's lukewarm response, the SNP's support spiked to 21.5 percent of the Scottish vote in 1992—though it won only 3 seats in Parliament, because of the plurality election system; the Labour Party won 49 seats, the Conservatives 11, and the Liberal Democrats 9. Despite Labour's continued popularity in Scotland, the SNP managed to remain a significant presence.

THE ESTABLISHMENT OF A SCOTTISH PARLIAMENT

After Labour won a landslide victory in the general elections of May 1997—in which the Conservatives lost all their Scottish seats and the SNP took 6 seats in Parliament—the Labour government of Tony Blair called a referendum for establishing a Scottish Parliament with a broad range of powers, including control over the country's education and health systems. Supported by the SNP and the Liberal Democrats—but opposed by the Conservatives—the referendum passed with more than 74 percent of voters in favour; 64 percent also approved giving the body the power to change tax rates.

Despite opposition from the Conservative Party and the House of Lords, the government adopted a proportional representation system for elections to the new Scottish Parliament, which made it possible for the SNP to extend its influence. At the first elections to the Scottish Parliament in May 1999, Labour won 56 seats, the SNP 35, the Conservatives 18, and the Liberal Democrats 17, while the Greens and the Scottish Socialists each took one seat (an independent candidate captured the remaining seat). Labour and the Liberal Democrats formed a coalition government, with Labour's Donald Dewar assuming the title of first minister. Dewar—considered the "father of devolution"—died in 2000 and was replaced by Henry McLeish. McLeish's tenure as first minister was also short-lived, as he was forced to resign the following year because of financial irregularities. Despite being led by three first ministers in the first three years of the Scottish Parliament and severe policy disagreements within the Labour–Liberal Democrat coalition, particularly on education policy, the governing coalition endured, and the Scottish Parliament began to develop into a mature, responsible legislative body, highlighted by its intense but civil debate over war in Iraq in 2003.

In the Scottish Parliament's second election, in May 2003, support for Labour and the SNP dropped (they won 50 and 27 seats, respectively), while the Liberal Democrats and the Conservatives performed at roughly the same level as in 1999. Notably, minor parties increased their seats in the Scottish Parliament significantly, with the Greens winning 7 seats, the Scottish Socialists 6, and independents 4. Still, Labour and the Liberal Democrats continued in coalition. In 2005 the Parliament moved into its permanent building at Holyrood. In the 2007 elections, the SNP staged a historic upset, winning the most seats (47) in the Scottish Parliament to end some 50 years of Labour Party dominance in Scotland; Labour finished second with 46 seats, and the Conservatives placed third with 17. SNP leader Alex Salmond was subsequently elected first minister of Scotland, becoming the first Nationalist to hold the post. Salmond won a second term in 2011 as the SNP surged to secure a majority in the Scottish Parliament. SNP gains came at the expense of Labour and the Liberal Democrats, and Salmond vowed to put forward a vote on Scottish independence by 2015.

Devolution has permitted Scotland to develop distinctive policies, such as on financial support for students and land reform, while in the cultural sphere the establishment of a National Theatre of Scotland filled a gap in the artistic landscape.

CHAPTER 14

Wales: The Land and Its People

Famed for its strikingly rugged landscape, the small nation of Wales—which comprises six distinctive regions—was one of Celtic Europe's most prominent political and cultural centres, and it retains aspects of culture that are markedly different from those of its English neighbours.

The medieval chronicler Giraldus Cambrensis (Gerald of Wales) had topography, history, and current events alike in mind when he observed that Wales is a "country very strongly defended by high mountains, deep valleys, extensive woods, rivers, and marshes; insomuch that from the time the Saxons took possession of the island the remnants of the Britons, retiring into these regions, could never be

entirely subdued either by the English or by the Normans." In time, however, Wales was in fact subdued and, by the Act of Union of 1536, formally joined to the kingdom of England. Welsh engineers, linguists, musicians, writers, and soldiers went on to make significant contributions to the development of the larger British Empire even as many of their compatriots laboured at home to preserve cultural traditions and even the Welsh language itself, which enjoyed a revival in the late 20th century. In 1997 the British government, with the support of the Welsh electorate, provided Wales with a measure of autonomy through the creation of the Welsh Assembly, which assumed decision-making authority for most local matters.

Although Wales was shaken by the decline of its industrial mainstay, coal mining, by the end of the 20th century the country had developed a diversified economy, particularly in the cities of Cardiff and Swansea, while the countryside, once reliant on small farming, drew many retirees from England. Tourism became an economic staple, with visitors—including many descendants of Welsh expatriates—drawn to Wales's stately parks and castles as well as to cultural events highlighting the country's celebrated musical and literary traditions.

Wales, which forms a westward extension of the island of Great Britain, is bounded by the Dee estuary and Liverpool Bay to the north, the Irish Sea to the west, the Severn estuary and the Bristol Channel to the south, and England to the east. Anglesey (Môn), the largest island in England and Wales, lies off the northwestern coast and is linked to the mainland by road and rail bridges. The varied coastline of Wales measures about 600 miles (970 km). The country stretches some 130 miles (210 km) from north to south, and its east-west width varies, reaching 90 miles (145 km) across in the north, narrowing to about 40 miles (65 km) in the centre, and widening again to more than 100 miles (160 km) across the southern portion.

RELIEF

Glaciers during the Pleistocene Epoch (about 2,600,000 to 11,700 years ago) carved much of the Welsh landscape into deeply dissected mountains, plateaus, and hills, including the north-south–trending Cambrian Mountains, a region of plateaus and hills that are themselves fragmented by rivers. Protruding from that backbone are two main mountain areas—the Brecon Beacons in the south, rising to 2,906 feet (886 metres) at Pen y Fan, and Snowdonia in the northwest, reaching 3,560 feet (1,085 metres) at Snowdon, the highest mountain in Wales. Snowdonia's magnificent scenery is accentuated by stark and rugged rock formations, many of volcanic origin, whereas the Beacons generally have softer outlines. The uplands are girdled on the seaward side by a series of steep-sided coastal plateaus ranging in elevation from about 100 to 700 feet

SNOWDONIA NATIONAL PARK

Snowdonia National Park (Welsh: Parc Cenedlaethol Eryri) in Gwynedd county and Conwy county borough, northern Wales, is best known for its mountains, composed largely of volcanic rock and cut by valleys that show the influence of Ice Age glaciers. Snowdon mountain's summit, Yr Wyddfa, in the northwestern part of the park, is the highest peak in England and Wales, with an elevation of 3,560 feet (1,085 metres). A rack-and-pinion railway (opened 1896) runs from Llanberis to the summit. Farther south Cader Idris ("Chair of Idris"), a long mountain ridge, reaches a height of 2,927 feet (892 metres) at Pen-y-Gader. The park has an area of 838 square miles (2,171 square km).

Tourism thrives, stimulated by the possibilities for climbing, hill walking, fishing, and sightseeing. Tourist centres in and near the park include Bala, with recreational facilities on Bala Lake, the largest natural lake in Wales; Betws-y-Coed, noted for its waterfalls, wooded gorges, and picturesque bridges; Blaenau Ffestiniog, where the defunct Llechwedd Slate Caverns are open to visitors; Dinas Mawddwy, with a textile mill and craft shop oriented toward touring shoppers; Dolgellau, overlooked by Cader Idris; the old village of Ffestiniog, on a bluff above the wooded Vale of Ffestiniog; Llanberis, at the foot of Snowdon, facing the massive Dinorwic slate quarries; and the Cardigan Bay resorts of Harlech, Barmouth, and Aberdovey.

Snowdon, viewed from Lake Mymbyr, Gwynedd. G.F. Allen/Bruce Coleman Inc.

(30 to 210 metres). Many of them have been pounded by the sea into spectacular steplike cliffs. Other plateaus give way to coastal flats that are estuarine in origin.

Wales consists of six traditional regions—the rugged central heartland, the North Wales lowlands and Isle of Anglesey county, the Cardigan coast (Ceredigion county), the southwestern lowlands, industrial South Wales, and the Welsh borderland. The heartland, which coincides partly with the counties Powys, Denbighshire, and Gwynedd, extends from the Brecon Beacons in the south to Snowdonia in the north and includes the two national parks based on those mountain areas. To the north and northwest

Coastline, Pembrokeshire Coast National Park. James P. Rowan

lie the coastal lowlands, together with the Lleyn Peninsula (Penrhyn Llŷn) in Gwynedd and the island of Anglesey. To the west of the heartland, and coinciding with the county of Ceredigion, lies the coastline of Cardigan Bay, with numerous cliffs and coves and pebble- and sand-filled beaches. Southwest of the heartland are the counties of Pembrokeshire and Carmarthenshire. There the land rises eastward from St. David's Head, through moorlands and uplands, to 1,760 feet (536 metres) in the Preseli Hills. South Wales stretches south of the heartland on an immense but largely exhausted coalfield. To the east of the heartland, the Welsh border region with England is largely agricultural and is characterized by rolling countryside and occasional wooded hills and mountainous moorland.

DRAINAGE

The main watershed of Wales runs approximately north-south along the central highlands. The larger river valleys all originate there and broaden westward near the sea or eastward as they merge into lowland plains along the English border. The Severn and Wye, two of Britain's longest rivers, lie partly within central and eastern Wales and drain into the Bristol Channel via the Severn estuary. The main river in northern Wales is the Dee, which empties into Liverpool Bay. Among the lesser rivers and estuaries are the Clwyd and Conwy in the northeast, the Tywi in the south, and the Rheidol in the west, draining into Cardigan Bay (Bae Ceredigion). The country's natural lakes are limited in area and almost entirely glacial in origin. Several reservoirs in the central uplands supply water to South Wales and to Merseyside and the Midlands in England.

SOILS

The parent rock of Wales is dominated by strata ranging from Precambrian time (more than 540 million years ago) to representatives of the Jurassic Period (about 200 million to 145 million years ago). However, glaciers during the Pleistocene blanketed most of the landscape with till (boulder clay), scraped up and carried along by the underside of the great ice sheets, so that few soils can now be directly related to their parent rock. Acidic, leached podzol soils and brown earths predominate throughout Wales.

CLIMATE

Wales has a maritime climate dominated by highly unpredictable shifts in Atlantic air masses, which, combined with the diverse range of elevations, often cause local conditions to vary considerably from day to day. Precipitation is frequent and often more than adequate, with annual totals averaging 55 inches (1,385 mm) for the country as a whole. There is no markedly wet or dry season; roughly 4 inches (88 mm) of precipitation are recorded in April, whereas 6 inches (142 mm) are typical in January. Winter snowfall can be significant in the uplands, where snow or sleet falls some 10 days of each year. The mean diurnal temperature is 50°F (10°C), ranging from 40°F (4°C) in January to 61°F (16°C) in July and August.

PLANT AND ANIMAL LIFE

The combination of physical conditions and centuries of human activity in Wales has brought about a predominance of grasslands, varying from mountain grasses and heather to lowland pastures of bent grass (*Agrostis*) and ryegrass. Planted woodlands are also common, including mixed parkland, boundary woods, and commercial plantations.

The remoter parts of Wales shelter some mammals and birds that are extinct or rarely found elsewhere in Britain, including European polecats and pine martens, red kites, and choughs (crowlike birds that breed inland as well as at some coastal sites). Seabirds and shorebirds occur in large numbers, and bottlenose dolphins inhabit Cardigan Bay. There are three designated national parks in Wales—Snowdonia, Pembrokeshire Coast, and Brecon Beacons—and five areas of outstanding natural beauty—Gower (Gŵyr), Lleyn (Llŷn), the Isle of Anglesey (Ynys Môn), the Clwydian Range, and the Wye valley.

ETHNIC GROUPS AND LANGUAGES

Some coastal caves in Wales were occupied about 200,000 years ago, during the Paleolithic Period (Old Stone Age). Additional waves of settlers arrived from continental Europe and lowland Britain during the Neolithic Period (New Stone Age) and Bronze Age, and iron-wielding Celtic peoples invaded after 2000 BCE. The basic culture of these peoples survived the Roman occupation and was later strengthened and broadened by Celtic immigrations from other parts of Britain. Their language, a Brythonic branch of Celtic speech, formed the basis of modern Welsh, while their heroic poetry, dating from the 6th century CE, became the basis of one of the oldest literary traditions of Europe. There were limited Norse incursions during the early Middle Ages, commemorated today mainly in place-names along the coastal fringes. Large Anglo-Saxon and Anglo-Norman groups subsequently entered Wales from the English border and began to dominate the ethnic and linguistic makeup of the country.

Welsh and English are the two major linguistic and ethnic traditions in Wales. The Welsh border region, known historically as the Marches (a patrolled frontier region), in particular is characterized by an amalgam of the Welsh and English cultures. Welsh was still spoken by about half of the population in 1900, but its use thereafter began steadily to decline, and its survival became one of the main cultural and political themes in national life. It is now spoken by about one-fifth of the population, notably in the heartland—the so-called Y Fro Gymraeg ("Welsh-Speaking Region")—where more than four-fifths of the inhabitants of some localities speak Welsh. The proportion is much diminished in South Wales, falling below one-tenth in the extreme southeast. The Welsh Language Act of 1967 placed it on the same legal standing as English. In 1993 the Welsh Language Act was passed; it established in principle the equality of Welsh and English in Wales. It further established the Welsh Language Board "to promote and facilitate the use of the Welsh language" and set minimum standards for the use of Welsh by public bodies, including councils, police, fire, and health authorities, and schools. Some of the duties of the board, upon its dissolution in 2012, were taken up by the newly created position of Welsh Language Commissioner.

RELIGION

The people of Wales have become increasingly secular in outlook, but many are at least nominally adherents to Protestant and Nonconformist churches, Calvinistic Methodism being perhaps the most widespread denomination, especially in Welsh-speaking areas. The Church in Wales, which is widely and evenly distributed throughout the country, has maintained an autonomous clerical hierarchy, including its own archbishop, since being disestablished from the Anglican church in 1920. Roman Catholicism accounts for a small but growing minority, notably in the northeast.

SETTLEMENT PATTERNS

The people of Wales are unevenly distributed in a largely concentric settlement pattern: sparsely populated uplands are at the core, surrounded by bands of gradually increasing population density that culminate on the coasts and the English border. The pattern largely reflects the country's traditional agricultural regions and its more recent urban and industrial developments. Although the central heartland region has lost considerable

CAERNARFON

A Roman fort, Segontium, was built about 75 CE on a low hill southeast of the present town of Caernarfon, in Gwynedd county, Wales, near the west end of the Menai Strait separating the mainland from Anglesey. It became the seat of local chieftains after the

Caernarfon Castle, a popular tourist attraction in Wales. Photos.com/Thinkstock

Roman withdrawal (c. 380–390). A Celtic church was founded there, probably in the 5th century. Norman penetration (11th century) was brief, but it produced a motte (fortified mound), and subsequently the Welsh Gwynedd princes set up a *maenor* ("manor") there. The township was completely transformed by the English king Edward I immediately after his conquest of Wales in 1282–83, for he built a large new stronghold around the motte and a walled borough adjacent to it, with a grid pattern of streets. The borough, to which he granted a charter in 1284, was made the capital of North Wales, and it was at the castle that his son, prince of Wales and later Edward II, was born in 1284. Only since 1911, however, has the castle been used for the investiture of the prince of Wales. Both castle and town walls are exceptionally well preserved and attract many tourists. The castle is one of several structures erected by Edward I in northern Wales that were collectively designated a UNESCO World Heritage site in 1986.

The town has grown considerably beyond the original walls. A small harbour was important mostly in the 19th century as an outlet for slates from nearby quarries.

Caernarfon (Carnarvon) Castle. J. Allan Cash Photolibrary/EB Inc.

population, it retains much of its traditional culture and serves as a hearth for the Welsh language.

The Welsh tribal economy, of semi-nomadic pastoral origin, produced mainly dispersed, isolated farmsteads, with only limited nucleation (clustering of buildings) on some of the larger tribal domains. Missionaries known as the Celtic saints established individual monastic or cell habitations in rural areas following the collapse of the Roman Empire, and some of their dwellings attracted additional settlers because of their favourable sites or positioning. The Anglo-Norman manorial system was introduced into Wales after the conquest of 1282, but nucleated villages became significant only in the eastern and southern peripheries of the country, where physical and political conditions favoured their development. As a result, large numbers of isolated, whitewashed stone cottages and farm buildings still dot the rural landscape, forming a strong underlying element within the Welsh social fabric.

Some four-fifths of the Welsh population live in urban areas; two-thirds of the total reside in the South Wales industrial zone, and many others live in the northeast. Prior to the Norman Conquest there was scarcely any urban development in Wales, but the Normans introduced castle towns (walled towns) that still dominate the contemporary urban landscape—at least in number if not in size. These towns remain and serve commercial, administrative, and social functions; however, their physical appearance often betrays their military and colonial origins.

Superimposed on this earlier urban pattern was that generated by the Industrial Revolution—notably in the south and northeast, where unplanned, overcrowded urban settlements sprang up in zones where coal deposits were being rapidly exploited. The coalfields of South Wales were developed in the 19th century as one of the premier mining regions of Britain, and such urban settlements as Rhondda, with tightly packed rows of terraced housing strung out along narrow valleys, are perhaps among the most widely known characteristics of Wales. The region declined markedly during the Great Depression of the 1930s and with the collapse of the coal and steel industries in the late 20th century. However, South Wales remains the most densely populated and industrialized region in Wales. It is divided into several essentially urban administrative areas including Cardiff, Swansea, Newport, Port Talbot, Neath, Bridgend, Barry, and Caerphilly.

Developments in the 20th century included ferry ports (packet stations) for traffic to Ireland, resort towns in some of the coastal areas, and two designated "new towns"—Cwmbrân in the southeast and Newtown in the middle borderland—which were promoted in an attempt to stem depopulation. Aberystwyth, with its university and the National Library of Wales, is the largest town west of the central heartland region. The region preserves many essentially Welsh elements in its social life because of its somewhat isolated, west-facing location. The middle borderland region, traditionally agricultural, has diversified its economy in an attempt to stem long-standing trends of emigration and depopulation. Settlement in the region's southern half is oriented toward the highly trafficked Severn estuary.

DEMOGRAPHIC TRENDS

The Industrial Revolution dramatically increased the Welsh population from around 500,000 people in the mid 18th century to some 2,600,000 by 1921. In the 1890s alone roughly 130,000 migrants were drawn into the coalfields of South Wales from England, Ireland, Spain, Italy, and elsewhere; many people from rural areas in Wales also migrated to industrial centres. Although new manufacturers and mines provided employment for many Welsh workers, others emigrated, particularly to the northeastern United States.

Heavy industry declined during the 20th century, and agriculture became increasingly commercialized and capital-intensive, producing further emigration from Wales, mainly of younger workers, and leaving behind a disproportionately aged population. In the late 20th century new industrial growth stemmed the population loss, except in South Wales and other coalfield regions. There is now a rough balance between inward and outward migration; however, many of the more recent arrivals have been seasonal vacationers or rural retreaters from metropolitan England, which has produced considerable tensions in traditionally Welsh-speaking areas where up to half the population was born outside Wales. In contrast, nonnatives account for less than one-tenth of the residents of some southern districts. Many African seamen were attracted to South Wales during the industrial boom of the late 19th century, but people of African ancestry now account for only a tiny fraction of Wales's total population. Cardiff is home to one of the oldest black communities in Britain.

CHAPTER 15

THE WELSH ECONOMY

The Welsh economy generally reflects the national trends and patterns of the United Kingdom; however, Wales has higher proportions of employment in agriculture and forestry, manufacturing, and government, and it provides concomitantly fewer jobs in financial and business services. There is active foreign investment in Welsh manufacturing, particularly in its high-technology industries, but Wales's gross domestic product (GDP) per capita and employment rates are far below average for the United Kingdom. The European Union has awarded significant developmental aid to parts of western and southern Wales in order to improve conditions there.

AGRICULTURE, FORESTRY, AND FISHING

Agriculture, forestry, and fishing account for less than 2 percent of the GDP of Wales. Agricultural production mainly centres on the raising of sheep, cattle, pigs, and poultry. Major crops include barley, wheat, potatoes, and oats. Wales's highly variable relief and climate are obstacles to the development of other commercial crops. The Forestry Commission (a government department) owns and operates large estates for the commercial exploitation of timber. Wales has several small ports and hundreds of small fishing vessels, but the overall fishing catch is limited. Major catches include clams, cod, lobsters, and skate.

Sheep and cattle raising dominate the economy of the central heartland. The Lleyn Peninsula and Anglesey have

MILFORD HAVEN

The inlet of Milford Haven (Welsh: Aberdaugleddau) in Pembrokeshire has for many centuries served as a landing and embarkation point on the route from southwestern Wales to Ireland, but the town of the same name was founded only in 1793. It has had a checkered maritime history, suffering a rapid decline of its whaling industry and losing to other ports on the Haven its naval dockyard and Irish packet service, all before 1860. It gained importance as a fishing port by 1900, though, and since 1960 it has become one of Europe's leading oil ports, one of the few places in western Europe able to accommodate the largest tankers. Major refineries were built, and both oil and petroleum products arrive at the port via pipeline.

rich farming areas. Along the Ceredigion coast, fishing and dairying are important, and in Pembrokeshire and part of Carmarthenshire there are numerous low-lying pastures, dairy farms, and fishing ports. Milford Haven, which has a vast natural harbour, is the main fishing port.

RESOURCES AND POWER

Wales has few natural resources beyond coal, agricultural lands, water, and woodlands. Coal is the only significant mineral resource of Wales, but the local coal-mining industry is now precipitously diminished from its previous level (in 2012, for example, only about 1,200 people continued to be employed in coal mining in Wales). The coal deposits of South Wales are far more extensive and contain higher-grade anthracite than those of the northeast. The bulk of this coal is consumed locally by the coal-fired power plant at Aberthaw and by the steelworks at Port Talbot. Nonferrous ores occur in small quantities and are not economically viable. Iron ore deposits, which were important during the early development of the industrial regions, are now exhausted.

There are several hydroelectric projects and reservoirs in Wales for domestic and industrial purposes. About half of the hydroelectric power produced in Wales serves areas in England. Several commercial windmill electricity-generation installations, including some of Europe's largest, were established in the late 20th century in the Welsh highlands. A nuclear power station is located at Wylfa, though it is scheduled for decommissioning.

MANUFACTURING

Manufacturing accounts for nearly one-third of the GDP of Wales, although most heavy industries had declined by the late 20th century. Improvements in the Welsh transportation infrastructure have helped bring diversified manufacturing into the southeast and northeast, including foreign-owned companies specializing in electrical, automotive, and chemical products. Foodstuffs, metals and metal products, beverages, and optical equipment are also important.

SERVICES

Financial and business services, government (including education and health services), hotels, restaurants, and trade account for more than half of the GDP and nearly two-thirds of employment in Wales. Most services are concentrated in Cardiff and other urban areas. Wales does not have its own national currency nor its own central bank; instead it uses the pound sterling and relies on the Bank of England for currency and other financial matters. A large number of commercial banks and insurance companies operate in Wales.

Another important source of income is tourism, particularly around the upland national parks and in the coastal region. The heartland, with its uplands, moorlands, and rivers, provides numerous attractions for tourists. The scenery and accessibility from English population centres make the central lowlands a popular tourist area as well.

TRANSPORTATION

Wales lacks a fully integrated system of transportation, and travel into or out of the country is much easier than internal movement. The main lines of transport in Wales have always been lateral, between west and east—that is, along the respective northern and southern coastal belts and across the centre, where the Severn valley links the borderlands to the English Midlands. Subsidiary lines of communication have also developed from north to south, along the west coast and the border. Cross-country links in the highlands have always been problematic, even following improvements to the road system. Wales has an extensive network of paved roads, particularly along its northern and southern coasts, but the only limited-access motorways link South Wales with the English Midlands and the Bristol area, the latter via bridges over the Severn estuary.

Several railroad lines closed during the 1950s and '60s because of cutbacks in British Rail service. The rail network now follows a pattern similar to that of the roads, with main routes following the north and south coasts. Wales also has several picturesque narrow-gauge railways, which operate largely during the summer tourist season.

Milford Haven, the main ocean port, has become one of the major oil-importing and refining centres in western Europe. Holyhead, on Holy Island off the coast of Anglesey, also has a busy deepwater port. Together with the ferry port of Fishguard, Holyhead links the main rail and road lines with Ireland across the Irish Sea. Various South Wales ports, which formerly handled coal exports, now import iron ore, petroleum, and general cargo; Swansea also provides ferry service to Ireland. Wales has no commercial inland waterways.

Cardiff International Airport handles domestic flights to other parts of the United Kingdom and international flights to several other countries.

CHAPTER 16

Welsh Government and Society

Because Wales is a constituent unit of the United Kingdom, foreign relations and many domestic matters for Wales are determined in London by the British government and Parliament's House of Commons, which includes many Welsh members. Thus, the British prime minister is the head of state and chief executive. However, the National Assembly for Wales (Cynulliad Cenedlaethol Cymru), established in Cardiff in 1999, assumed several responsibilities, including urban and rural development, economic planning, health and welfare, culture, education, transportation, tourism, and environmental matters. Before approval of a referendum in 2011 that extended direct lawmaking powers to the National Assembly, however, the assembly had to ask Parliament for primary lawmaking powers on a case-by-case basis. With passage, the assembly assumed the power to enact laws without first seeking consent from Parliament. Unlike the Scottish Parliament, the National Assembly does not have the power to levy taxes. The 60-seat National Assembly comprises 40 members who are directly elected from the 40 parliamentary constituencies and an additional 20 members who are elected through proportional representation. The National Assembly elects a first minister (formerly known as first secretary), who leads the government with the aid of a cabinet of departmental secretaries.

LOCAL GOVERNMENT

The functions of local government in Wales were long divided among 13 historic counties, which now retain only historic and cultural relevance. Parliamentary reforms redrew the administrative boundaries in 1974 and again in the 1990s. Since 1996 Wales has consisted of 22 unitary authorities, or local governmental units. These are further divided into 14 counties (which generally have some rural component) and 8 county boroughs (generally large population centres). The counties and county boroughs are responsible for all major local governmental functions, including local planning, fire fighting, schools, libraries, social services, public health and sanitation, recreation, the environment, and voter registration.

Community councils form the lowest tier of local government in Wales and consist of localities (cities, towns, and villages) within the counties and county boroughs. They have a range of other rights and duties, including assessing surcharges (precepts) on property taxes, participating in local planning, and maintaining commons and recreational facilities.

JUSTICE AND SECURITY

Unlike Scotland, Wales has no separate justice system. Criminal and civil cases are heard by magistrates' courts and by a circuit of the Crown Court. The Home Office in Whitehall, London, is responsible for police services in Wales, which are administered through local police headquarters or constabularies. The country has no independent defense forces, although three British army regiments are historically associated with Wales—the Welsh Guards, the Royal Welch Fusiliers, and the Royal Regiment of Wales (the latter two were merged into a single unit and dubbed the Royal Welsh in 2006).

POLITICAL PROCESS

The Welsh people historically have tended to support liberal and radical governments and have done so in large numbers—Wales has a consistently higher turnout at the polls than does Britain as a whole. The Labour Party is the largest single political party in Wales; Plaid Cymru, the Liberal Democrat Party, and the Conservative Party have more limited electoral support.

During the 19th and early 20th centuries the Liberal Party promoted the policy of Home Rule and produced such figures as Prime Minister David Lloyd George. The electorate in Wales's industrial regions then began to support socialist Labourites such as Keir Hardie, the British Labour leader and the first independent Labour member of Parliament, who (although Scottish) represented the South Wales constituency of Merthyr Tydfil. Other prominent Labour members of Parliament for South Wales have

NEIL KINNOCK

Neil Kinnock (born March 28, 1942, Tredegar, Monmouthshire, Wales) was the leader of the British Labour Party from 1983 to 1992. The son of a miner, Kinnock was educated at University College, Cardiff, and was then for four years an organizer and tutor at the Workers' Educational Association. In 1970 he was elected to Parliament for the seat of Bedwellty. He soon began a rapid rise in party ranks, thanks to his gift for oratory and to the patronage of party leader Michael Foot. In 1974–75 he served as parliamentary private secretary to Foot, and in 1978 he was named to the Labour Party's national executive committee. During this period he wrote two books, *Wales and the Common Market* (1971) and *As Nye Said* (1980).

Following the election of 1983, in which Labour suffered its heaviest defeat since 1935, the search began for a leader to replace Foot. Although a relative newcomer who had never held even a junior ministerial post, Kinnock in October 1983 was elected leader of the Labour Party at its annual conference, becoming the youngest leader in the party's history. Kinnock initially supported the party's policy calling for the unilateral nuclear disarmament of Britain and the removal of all U.S. nuclear weapons and bases from British soil. Labour lost the 1987 general election to the Conservative Party, though it managed to increase its parliamentary representation somewhat. By 1989 Kinnock had persuaded his party to abandon its radical policies on disarmament and large-scale nationalization. Labour lost the 1992 general election to the Conservatives, and though his party had again increased its numbers in Parliament, Kinnock stepped down from his post as party leader later that year. In 1995 he retired from the House of Commons to become a member of the European Commission and served as its vice president from 1999 to 2004. Kinnock was named a life peer in 2005.

included Aneurin Bevan, Michael Foot, James Callaghan, and Neil Kinnock.

Plaid Cymru, renamed bilingually as Plaid Cymru–The Party of Wales, was founded in 1925 to promote a full parliament for Wales and direct international representation. The party first won a parliamentary seat in a by-election in 1966 and then captured additional seats at local, national, and European elections. Support for the party is concentrated in areas where Welsh is widely spoken. More radical organizations, such as Cymdeithas yr Iaith Gymraeg (the Welsh Language Society), exist on the fringe of the broader nationalist and separatist movement and are disassociated from Plaid Cymru. Some such groups have engaged in civil disobedience to further their ends, while the more extreme factions have carried out attacks on property, most notably on English-owned holiday homes in rural Wales in the 1980s.

HEALTH AND WELFARE

There are great variations in rates of death and illness in Wales, with the highest rates in the southern industrial valleys and poorer inner-city areas. Life expectancy has reached about 75 years for men and 80 for women. Deaths from cancer and heart disease are significantly higher than in England; other leading causes of death include respiratory and cerebrovascular diseases. Social security benefits make up a higher proportion of income in Wales than elsewhere in the United Kingdom, partly because the country traditionally has had higher unemployment rates and because there are pockets of persistently high unemployment within urban South Wales. The highest rates of social deprivation are in such urban and industrialized areas as Merthyr Tydfil, Rhondda, Swansea, and Newport.

HOUSING

As in most areas of the United Kingdom, home ownership significantly increased in the last half of the 20th century. Whereas fewer than half the homes were owner-occupied in the 1950s, by the beginning of the 21st century nearly three-fourths of homes were. Much of that increase occurred in the 1980s, when the government of Margaret Thatcher implemented policies to encourage the tenants of council houses (public houses) to purchase their units. The country's housing stock is relatively modern, with more than one-fourth of all units built since 1970. The Welsh Office of the British government traditionally provided funds for rural housing and other improvements. With the creation of a devolved assembly, however, much of the responsibility for housing was transferred to the Welsh government.

EDUCATION

With its rich cultural heritage, Wales has maintained a tradition of, and respect for, quality education at all levels. The Welsh school curriculum varies considerably from that pursued in England, notably in its stringent requirement for Welsh-language education. Furthermore, approximately one-third of Welsh primary-school pupils and one-fifth of those in secondary school receive all their instruction in Welsh. The demand

University of Wales, Bangor. Velela

for Welsh-language schooling has grown rapidly, particularly in Anglicized parts of South Wales.

Education in Wales was set for major structural changes after the Higher Education Funding Council of Wales recommended to the government in 2010 that Wales consolidate its institutions of higher education into six universities. Most notably, the University of Wales (1893) was scheduled to formally merge over the following decade with Swansea Metropolitan University and University of Wales Trinity Saint David. (The University of Wales Trinity Saint David was itself amalgamated from the University of Wales Lampeter and Trinity University College Carmarthen in 2010.)

CHAPTER 17

WELSH CULTURAL LIFE

Although united politically, administratively, and economically with England since the Act of Union of 1536, Wales has preserved, maintained, and developed a somewhat independent cultural identity. It is the interplay between English and Welsh elements—sometimes united, sometimes independent, and sometimes in conflict—that characterizes contemporary cultural life in Wales. A more distinctive perception of Welsh identity emerged in the final decades of the 20th century, arguably underpinning support for creation of the National Assembly for Wales, which was approved by referendum in 1997.

Wales may be described as possessing a Welsh-speaking, rural north and west and an English-speaking, urban, and industrial south and east. The Welsh-speaking areas long considered themselves culturally Welsh rather than British, and during the 20th century many Welsh thus sought connections to a wider pan-Celtic network of minority groups such as Bretons, Basques, and Galicians. The English-speaking areas, on the other hand, largely rejected definitions of Welsh identity that they believed were too closely allied to the Welsh language, and some promoted an alternative cosmopolitanism. By the early 21st century the divide between the two groups had begun to break down as a wider sense of inclusive Welshness took hold. The process was reinforced by the revival of the Welsh language in South Wales and its widespread presence in the media and classroom.

DAILY LIFE AND SOCIAL CUSTOMS

Daily life in Wales varies markedly by region. Social advantage and deprivation can exist side by side, particularly in parts of South Wales. The population also varies in terms of its cultural diversity, from the cosmopolitanism of Cardiff to the traditionally monolithic industrial communities. Although rural Wales has often been described as a cultural heartland, many of its small towns have lost a measure of their cultural, and especially linguistic, distinctiveness. Nonetheless, many parts of northern and western Wales remain predominantly Welsh-speaking, and people there may live their daily lives largely through the medium of Welsh, perhaps including their places of employment. Children receive Welsh-language instruction at preschool, primary, and secondary levels, and some courses at the University of Wales are taught in Welsh in addition to those focusing on the Welsh language and literature.

Wales celebrates the national holidays of Great Britain. In addition, many institutions have effectively made St. David's Day (March 1), the feast day of the patron saint of Wales, into a Welsh holiday. All Hallow's Eve (Nos Galan Gaeaf) has significance for Welsh nationalists as the beginning of the Celtic new year, though it is popularly celebrated as the American-style Halloween. The country's cuisine exhibits the universalizing tendencies of Western culture (with fast food restaurants and processed foods), though some traditional dishes remain popular, including cawl (a light soup containing lamb), Welsh cakes (small fruit scones cooked on a griddle), bara brith (a rich fruit bread), and laver bread (a red seaweed typically fried with oatmeal and cockles). The Welsh have enjoyed a revival of traditional foods and of organic farming, with notable contributions from migrants to rural Wales, many of them English. The long heritage of some groups with Italian ancestry, particularly in South Wales, is manifest in the large number of family-owned ice cream producers as well as in a few cafés known locally as Bracchis.

MUSIC, LITERATURE, AND FILM

Wales has been popularly called "the land of song," and its traditional culture has been rooted in oral (and aural) art forms, including the spoken and written word and vocal music, particularly choral singing involving multiple parts and complex harmonies.

The singing of *penillion*, simple vernacular songs, to the accompaniment of the triple harp was a feature of Welsh folk culture until the early 18th century, and efforts have been mounted to revive the form. The *cymanfa ganu* ("singing festival") has been a popular expression of religious Nonconformism since the mid 19th century. Some of the most renowned Welsh composers, such as William

DYLAN THOMAS

The Welsh poet and prose writer Dylan Thomas (born October 27, 1914, Swansea, Wales—died November 9, 1953, New York, New York, U.S.) left school at age 16 to work as a reporter. His early verse, as in *The Map of Love* (1939), with rich metaphoric language and emotional intensity, made him famous. In the more accessible *Deaths and Entrances* (1946), with "Fern Hill," he often adopts a bardic, oracular voice. *In Country Sleep* (1952), containing "Do Not Go Gentle into That Good Night," and *Collected Poems* (1952) followed. Thomas's prose includes the comic *Portrait of the Artist as a Young Dog* (1940); a play for voices, *Under Milk Wood* (1954); and the reminiscence *A Child's Christmas in Wales* (1955). His sonorous recitations contributed greatly to his fame. Debt and heavy drinking began taking their toll in the late 1930s, and he died of an alcohol overdose while on tour.

Dylan Thomas, 1952. Rollie McKenna

Williams Pantycelyn, almost exclusively composed hymns, although Walford Davies established himself as a classical composer in the 20th century. The Welsh National Opera (1946) is highly regarded, with soloists of international renown, including Sir Geraint Evans, Dame Gwyneth Jones, Dame Margaret Price, and Bryn Terfel. The Welsh Guards Band, a unit of the British Army, is also a familiar presence at festivals and parades and has released several recordings. Popular and rock music enjoyed a resurgence in Wales in the late 20th century and contributed to a movement playfully dubbed "Cool Cymru." Welsh-language recordings by pop groups are a mainstay of contemporary radio programming and enjoy popularity throughout Britain and abroad. However, the country's most popular recording artist, singer Tom Jones, has recorded his music only in English.

The Welsh literary tradition extends at least to the 6th century CE, flowering with such medieval works as the *Y Gododdin*, a long poem by Aneirin, and the work of Taliesin, available only in a reconstructed version known as the *Book of Taliesin*; with a the great body of Arthurian legend collected by Geoffrey of Monmouth in his *Historia Regum Britanniae* (1135–38; *History of the Kings of Britain*); and with the *Mabinogion*, a collection of tales dating to the 11th century. The translation of the Bible into Welsh in 1588 by the Anglican bishop William Morgan

RICHARD BURTON

Richard Burton in Cleopatra *(1963).* © Twentieth Century-Fox Film Corporation

Elizabeth Taylor and Richard Burton in Who's Afraid of Virginia Woolf? (1966) Courtesy of Warner Brothers, Inc.

The Welsh stage and motion-picture actor Richard Burton (born Richard Walter Jenkins, Jr., November 10, 1925, Pontrhydyfen, Wales—died August 5, 1984, Geneva, Switzerland) was noted for his portrayals of highly intelligent and articulate men who are world-weary, cynical, or self-destructive. He was the 12th of 13 children born to a Welsh coal miner. He studied acting under Philip Burton, a schoolteacher who became his mentor and helped him obtain a scholarship to the University of Oxford. In gratitude to his benefactor, he assumed the professional name Burton. His first stage appearance was in 1943, but subsequent service as a Royal Air Force navigator delayed his career. In 1948 he resumed his stage performances and had his first role in a motion picture, *The Last Days of Dolwyn*. He scored his first real stage triumph in 1949 in Christopher Fry's *The Lady's Not for Burning*.

Burton's first Hollywood film role was in *My Cousin Rachel* (1952). Throughout the remainder of the 1950s he specialized in historical roles in motion pictures, including the leading role in the first wide-screen CinemaScope production, *The Robe* (1953). Burton rose to superstar status during the filming of *Cleopatra* (1963), when he and his American co-star Elizabeth Taylor became lovers. Both of his highly publicized marriages to Taylor (1964–74, 1975–76) ended in divorce. *Who's Afraid of Virginia Woolf?* (1966) and *The Taming of the Shrew* (1967) are the best of the 11 films the couple made together. Burton's other important films include

Becket and *The Night of the Iguana* (both 1964), *The Spy Who Came in from the Cold* (1965), *The Comedians* (1967), and *Equus* (1977).

Burton meanwhile continued to receive critical acclaim for his theatre performances. He acted in Shakespearean productions at London's Old Vic in 1953–56, and he gave a memorable performance of Hamlet in John Gielgud's long-running Broadway production of that play in 1964. Burton also played on Broadway in Jean Anouilh's *Time Remembered* (1957) and portrayed King Arthur in the Broadway musical *Camelot* in 1960 and 1980.

---

inspired a renaissance of Welsh writing, but by the early 18th century most Welsh literature was being written in English. Even with the revival of the Eisteddfod, an assembly of bards and minstrels, in the late 18th century, Welsh continued to lose ground as a literary language. The nationalist movement of the 20th century, however, brought about a resurgence in Welsh literature, though much of it was confined to universities or small journals. Welsh literature, as with so much else in Wales, has been divided between Welsh- and English-language camps. The former has not gained a widespread international reputation, although translations have been published of the plays of Saunders Lewis (a leading figure in the nationalist movement) and the novels and short stories of Gwyn Thomas, Kate Roberts, T. Rowland Hughes, and Caradog Prichard. The Anglo-Welsh literary tradition—writing on Wales and Welshness but through the medium of English—has produced the poets R.S. Thomas and Glyn Jones and the poet and playwright Dylan Thomas. A large number of novelists and poets also chronicled the shifting fortunes of industrial South Wales, particularly during the depression years, as exemplified in Richard Llewellyn's *How Green Was My Valley* (1939) and Rhys Davies's *The Black Venus* (1944).

The power of the spoken word in Wales is also embodied in the figures of Welsh actors, most notably Richard Burton, Sir Anthony Hopkins, and Emlyn Williams (also a playwright), as well as John Rhys-Davies, Rhys Ifans, and Catherine Zeta-Jones. A small Welsh-language film industry was initiated with the release of *Coming Up Roses* (*Rhosyn a Rhith*) in 1985.

VISUAL ARTS

Traditional histories of Wales often suggested that Welsh culture was essentially rural, domestic, and noncommercial and was made more austere by the spread of Puritan Nonconformism and its associated 19th-century religious revivals. Several historians blamed these factors for the apparent failure to develop a "visual culture" in Wales. However, Wales has produced such renowned artists as the 18th-century landscape painter Richard Wilson and the 20th-century modernists David Jones

Ruins of Tintern Abbey, Monmouthshire.
Kenneth Scowen

and Ceri Richards. Revised histories of Welsh visual culture point to a vibrant aesthetic sense, particularly in folk art of various kinds. There are few architectural landmarks in Wales, although a rich and intensely varied tradition of vernacular architecture exists. Tintern Abbey, made famous by William Wordsworth's poem, is one of many (mostly ruined) abbeys, priories, and castles scattered across the Welsh countryside. Wales's Nonconformist chapels, seen as exemplifying an artistically "sober dignity," were stylistically countered by the architect Sir Clough Williams-Ellis in the 1920s, when he began creating Portmeirion, an exuberant Italianate village in North Wales.

CULTURAL INSTITUTIONS

Large numbers of Welsh-speaking artists converge annually in August at the National Eisteddfod of Wales, a competitive and highly individualized festival held alternately in North and South Wales. The Eisteddfod consists of competitions in all aspects of music, literature, drama, and art, together with a series of dramatic performances and concerts, all in the Welsh language; it also boasts a series of fringe activities, including a weeklong rock festival organized by Cymdeithas yr Iaith Gymraeg, a cultural association formed in the 1960s, and attracts a series of broadly political spectacles. The Gorsedd (Bardic Circle), a pseudo-Druidic organization composed of poets and musicians, also conducts its ceremonies at the national Eisteddfod. Founded in 1947, the International Musical Eisteddfod is held in Llangolen each July and highlights dancers and singers from many countries. Local Eisteddfodau are held in towns and villages throughout the year, and the Eisteddfod organized by Urdd Gobaith Cymru (Welsh League of Youth) is one of the largest youth festivals in Europe.

The Welsh Arts Council provides government assistance for literature, art, music, film, and drama. The council helps arrange tours of Wales by British and foreign orchestras and supports art exhibitions, Welsh- and English-language theatre companies and theatres, regional arts associations, and music societies and festivals, particularly those concerned with commissioning new works.

The National Library of Wales (1907) at Aberystwyth, like the British Library, receives copies of virtually all books published in the United Kingdom. It is also the main Welsh reference library and a repository of documents and manuscripts relating to Wales from the earliest times. The National Museum of Wales (1907) is situated in Cardiff; the Museum of Welsh Life, in the castle and grounds of nearby St. Fagans, embraces the antiquities and natural history of Wales along with a comprehensive Welsh art collection; and the Segontium Roman Museum in Caernarfon preserves one of Roman Britain's major forts.

SPORTS AND RECREATION

Rugby dominates competitive sporting culture in Wales, especially among males, and the sport plays a major role in Welsh national identity. Although Welsh athletes compete as members of the United Kingdom's Olympic team, the country fields national teams for other sports (e.g., football [soccer] and rugby). Wales hosted the Rugby World Cup in 1999, and the position of the sport at the heart of national and sporting life was symbolized at that time by the opening of the 72,500-seat Millennium Stadium in Cardiff. Swansea, Cardiff, and Wrexham play football in the English league system, and Wales also has its own league. The national parks are popular locations for outdoor pursuits of all kinds, and Snowdonia is particularly renowned among rock climbers.

MEDIA AND PUBLISHING

The media in Wales has increasingly highlighted a sense of national identity. BBC Wales, which has always had considerable independence from the British Broadcasting Corporation, provides television and radio services in both English and Welsh. ITV Wales, a commercial company, covers Wales and the western part of England. A Welsh-language television channel, S4C (Sianel Pedwar Cymru, or Channel Four Wales), began broadcasting in 1982 after a long campaign against the homogenizing tendencies of English-language television. *The Western Mail* is the national newspaper for Wales, although the *Daily Post* also has a significant readership. In addition to a lively periodical press, there are several other regional and local newspapers and dozens of Welsh-language *papurau bro* ("community papers") produced by volunteers. The Internet has reduced the costs of, and expanded the possibilities for, Welsh-language publishing.

The "Home Union" rugby teams of Wales (red and white) and England (white), compete in the Five Nations Championship, 1986. Sporting Pictures (U.K.)

CHAPTER 18

WALES BEFORE THE NORMAN CONQUEST

Meaningful study of prehistoric Wales has to be pursued against the broader background of British prehistory, for the material remains of the period 3500–1000 BCE, especially funerary monuments, provide regional manifestations of features characteristic of Britain as a whole. The Celtic origins of Britain, probably to be sought in a gradual process within the last millennium BCE, are a matter of continuing scholarly debate. Traditional archaeological and linguistic interpretation emphasizes an influx, from the late Bronze Age onward, of Celtic-speaking peoples, though not perhaps in vast numbers, and a dynamic relationship between continental and insular communities. Modern views emphasize that the ethnogenesis of the Celts must be seen as a complex process of social change and not entirely the result of migrations. As regards their social structure, the metalwork associated with feasting and military prowess, such as that found at Llyn Fawr and Llyn Cerrig Bach, coupled with the broad distribution of fortified sites, typifies the highly stratified but politically fragmented and warlike society that prevailed in Wales down to the Roman period.

ROMAN WALES (1ST–4TH CENTURIES)

Wales in the Roman period shared broadly the experience of other parts of highland Britain, but modern archaeological study has tended to moderate the traditional contrast drawn between military and civil zones. Mediterranean culture is best exemplified in southern Wales, where there were important Roman towns at Caerwent and Carmarthen and villas at a number of other sites. Remains elsewhere consist mainly of the roads and forts of a phase of military occupation that lasted to about 200 CE. But at Caernarfon (Segontium) there was a continuous well-ordered settlement to about 400 CE, and it is likely that civil influences were exerted much more widely than was once thought. Linguistic study suggests that the native language, known to scholars as Brittonic or Brythonic, was infused with Latin terms, though distinction needs to be made between borrowings of the period of Roman rule and the scholarly borrowings of subsequent periods. Early Welsh consciousness of a Roman heritage may owe a great deal to the Latinity sustained in later centuries by the Christian church.

THE FOUNDING OF THE KINGDOMS

The origin of early Welsh political organization must be sought in the period following the cessation of Roman rule in about 400 CE. Native leaders, unable to sustain Roman methods of governance, initiated the processes that were to lead to the founding of a number of kingdoms. The *Historia Brittonum*, an antiquarian compilation dating from the early 9th century, explains the origin of the kingdom of Gwynedd by relating a tradition that Cunedda Wledig migrated from northern Britain to northwestern Wales to expel the Irish who had occupied the area. This may be an example of the origin stories that were current in early medieval Europe, and the *Historia* also contains an early reference to the Welsh claim to Trojan origin, which was to prove an enduring theme in Welsh historical consciousness. Tradition attributes the names of the various parts of Gwynedd, such as Dunoding and Rhufoniog, to a division of the kingdom said to have been made among Cunedda's sons after his death, but these may be the names of territories that were gradually incorporated into the kingdom during a long period of growth. Cunedda's descendants were to rule as kings; a 7th-century representative of the dynasty is commemorated upon an inscribed stone in Anglesey as Catamanus Rex (Cadfan the King).

In southwestern Wales the Irish presence led to the founding of the Irish kingdom of Dyfed, and some Irish influence was felt further afield in the neighbouring lands of Ceredigion, Ystrad Tywi, and Brycheiniog. In the southeast Glywysig and Gwent emerged, to be united, though impermanently, to form Morgannwg. In north-central Wales the kingdom of Powys, originally centred at Pengwern (a place not identified with certainty), was established, and it embraced at least part of the Roman province of the Cornovii, centred at Wroxeter in Shropshire.

EARLY CHRISTIANITY

There are indications of a Romano-British Christian church in southeastern

Wales, but Christian influence may also have penetrated much deeper into Wales in the Roman period. Inscribed stones, though themselves belonging to the 5th or 6th century, carry terms such as *sacerdos* (probably meaning bishop) and *presbyter* (priest), which may reflect a well-established Christian church of early origin. Stones with Irish (or Ogham) inscriptions and Christian symbols in southwestern Wales suggest that the immigrants, if not already Christian upon arrival, were Christianized soon afterward. The extent of the continuity of the early Romano-British church, however, has become the subject of scholarly debate. From the mid-20th century onward historians have argued in favour of discontinuity by stressing the importance of what they considered to be new Gallo-Roman influences exerted on western Britain in the 5th and 6th centuries. According to this view Celtic "saints" coming from the Continent reestablished Christianity by their missionary activities along the western seaways. More recently, however, the view held by an earlier generation of historians that the Christian church had a continuous existence from the Romano-British period has regained support. Scholars defending this position argue that much of the evidence for the missionary activity of Celtic saints was derived from the saints' lives and church dedications of a later date. Basing their arguments on the *De excidio et conquestu Britanniae*, a work by the 6th-century British monk Gildas that suggests a long-established Christian tradition of Romano-British derivation, they postulate that the trade and cultural contacts along the western seaways may have served not to introduce Christianity or to revitalize a lingering faith but to bring to an existing church a form of monasticism that had proved to be an important influence in the development of the Gallic church.

Support for the argument of a "Celtic church" rests upon the church's monastic character. A major church (*clas*, plural *clasau*) was headed by an abbot and bishop who was responsible for daughter houses. The *clas* was not a cloistered community, and its head was responsible for the ordination of priests and the pastoral care of the laity in neighbouring areas. But the hereditary succession to office and to ecclesiastical property that developed with time was among traditional practices, and, even though at places like Llanbadarn Fawr there were ecclesiastical families who maintained a Christian learning of a high order, these practices were considered to be contrary to the teaching of the reformed church.

POLITICAL DEVELOPMENT

The settlement of Anglo-Saxon peoples along the Welsh borderland separated the Brythonic peoples of Wales from those of northern and southwestern Britain. Whereas to the English they were "Welsh" (foreigners), they identified themselves as "Cymry" (compatriots). Offa's Dyke, the great linear earthwork built in the times of King Offa (died 796) of Mercia, represents the demarcation line of English penetration into Wales.

Attempts during the next two centuries to bring the Welsh kingdoms west of the dike into a political unity proved to be only partially successful and impermanent. Rhodri Mawr ("the Great"; died 878), the king of Gwynedd who provided stern resistance to the Viking attacks, brought Powys within his dominion and then briefly extended his sway over two areas in the southwest (lying north and east of Dyfed), namely Ceredigion and Ystrad Tywi, which had previously been united to form the kingdom of Seisyllwg. The period following Rhodri's death proved to be of far-reaching significance. The outlying kingdoms of Wales—Dyfed, Brycheiniog, Glywysing, and Gwent—being subjected to pressure by Rhodri's sons or by Mercia, turned to the kingdom of Wessex and by a formal commendation entered into that allegiance, ultimately expressed in homage and fealty, which each of the kings of Wales owed, individually and directly, to the English monarchy. Anarawd (died 916), a son of Rhodri, subsequently submitted to Alfred (died 899) and completed the formal subjection of the Welsh kingdoms to the English sovereign. Rhodri's grandson, Hywel ap Cadell (Hywel Dda, "the Good"; died 950), starting from a patrimony in Seisyllwg, secured Dyfed by marriage, thereby creating the kingdom of Deheubarth. Eventually Gwynedd

HYWEL DDA

Called the "king of all Wales" in the prologues to the Welsh lawbooks, the chieftain Hywel Dda (died 949 or 950) was indeed deserving of that epithet by the end of his reign. Known in English as Howel the Good, he became ruler of Seisyllwg (roughly the area of Dyfed and the Towy Valley) jointly with his brother Clydog after the death of their father, Cadell (C. 910), but after Clydog's death in 920 he ruled alone. Sovereignty over Dyfed in southwest Wales came to him through his wife, Elen, daughter of Llywarch ap Hyfaidd (died 904), the last king of its dynasty; he acquired Gwynedd, in northwest Wales, and probably Powis, in northeast Wales, on the death of his cousin Idwal Foel ap Anarawd, in 942. Hywel's reign was remarkable for its peacefulness, the result of his consistent policy of subservience to England. Hywel's first recorded act is his homage to Edward the Elder in 918. Thereafter, he often attended the English court, and his name is found as a witness to 12 charters of Athelstan and Edred between 928 and 949. In 928 he went to Rome on a pilgrimage.

Hywel was the only Welsh ruler to issue his own coins. He is remembered chiefly for the codification of Welsh law attributed to him. Although there is no contemporary record of this work, Hywel was certainly responsible for a coordination of preexisting law.

and Powys also came under his rule. Hywel, possibly inspired by admiration for the Wessex court but more probably constrained by the power of King Athelstan (died 939), accepted the status of a *sub-regulus*, or under-king, of the king of Wessex. But, whatever its compulsions, Hywel's policy provoked a reaction (expressed in the poem *Armes Prydein*) that envisaged the formation of a great alliance to withstand the Anglo-Saxon suzerain.

Before the close of the 10th century Maredudd ap Owain (died 999), a grandson of Hywel Dda, brought the northern and western kingdoms once more into a transitory unity. But his death opened a period of prolonged turmoil in which internal conflicts were complicated and intensified by Anglo-Saxon and Norse intervention. The established dynasties were challenged by men who asserted themselves within the kingdoms and exercised ephemeral supremacies. Of these, the most successful was Gruffudd ap Llywelyn (died 1063), who brought Gwynedd, then Deheubarth, and finally (though briefly) the whole of Wales under his dominion. The devastation wrought upon the English borderland, still not erased at the time of the making of Domesday Book (1086), was probably in large measure due to him. His death in 1063 meant that the most powerful ruler of independent Wales was destroyed only a few years before the Norman forces came to the Anglo-Welsh frontier.

EARLY WELSH SOCIETY

The endeavours of the dynasties in the 9th and 10th centuries, though only partially successful with regard to the problem of Welsh unification, had important and lasting consequences. Scholarly activity such as that represented in the *Historia Brittonum* and in annals and genealogies, material relating both to northern Britain and to Wales, may well reflect the attempt of the descendants of Rhodri Mawr to consolidate their position and enhance their prestige. With regard to creative literature, it is likely that the origins of some texts preserved in medieval manuscripts, including some material in triad form (triple groupings of legal, literary, historical, and other materials), may be traced back to this period. The earliest Welsh law texts, though they date from the 13th century onward, attribute the original codification of law to Hywel Dda; and it is possible that a significant development in Welsh jurisprudence took place under the aegis of that ruler. These texts, along with other materials, reveal a society of relatively settled kingdoms ruled by kings (*brenhinoedd*, singular *brenin*) who were endowed with an extensive range of powers, notably the public enforcement of legal obligations.

The kingdoms were normally divided for purposes of royal administration into *cantrefs*. These in turn consisted of groups of *maenors* occupied by the bond or free elements of which Welsh society was composed. The bond population, which was probably larger than once thought and which was concentrated in fairly compact *maenors* in lowland areas that were favourable to an agrarian economy, was organized on conventional manorial principles. In the economy of the upland areas the emphasis was upon a pastoral economy practiced by free communities, which were accorded more extensive *maenors*. As a result of changes that quickened considerably in the 12th century, the *maenor* organization of Welsh society was superseded by new forms designed to ensure a more intensive exploitation of the soil. A smaller unit, the *tref*, or township, then replaced the *maenor*. In the sphere of royal administration the *cantref*, by a process probably already well advanced on the eve of the first Norman invasions, was largely replaced by a small unit, the *commote*, which was to remain, under Welsh and alien lords, the basic unit of administration and jurisdiction throughout the medieval period.

CHAPTER 19

WALES IN THE MIDDLE AGES

The Norman Conquest of England saw the establishment upon the Welsh border of the three earldoms of Chester, Shrewsbury, and Hereford, and from each of these strongpoints advances were made into Wales.

NORMAN INFILTRATION

Norman progress in southern Wales in the reign of William I (1066–87) was limited to the colonization of Gwent in the southeast. Domesday Book contains evidence suggesting that King William and Rhys ap Tewdwr, king of Deheubarth (died 1093), made a compact that recognized the Welsh ruler's authority in his own kingdom and perhaps also his influence in those other areas of southern Wales outside Deheubarth, particularly Morgannwg and Brycheiniog, that still lay outside Norman control. Meanwhile, from Chester and Shrewsbury, the Normans had penetrated more deeply into Wales, so that at Domesday, though the area colonized was limited, Norman lordship had been asserted over numerous *cantrefs* and *commotes* that had previously formed portions of the kingdoms of Gwynedd and Powys. The political situations in the northern and southern parts of the country were reversed during a period of renewed conflict in the reign of William II (1087–1100). Soon after Rhys ap Tewdwr's death in 1093 while opposing the Norman advance into Brycheiniog, the Normans invaded virtually the whole of southern Wales. Advances from several bases along the Welsh border enabled Norman lords to establish the major lordships of Cardigan, Pembroke, Brecon, and Glamorgan. This advance constituted the decisive stage in the creation of the March of Wales; in this land, consisting of lordships, Norman lords and their successors exercised rights founded on the powers previously enjoyed by the Welsh kings but greatly expanded so as to give the lords, under "the custom of the March," extensive powers in their lordships and a large measure of autonomy in their relations with the king of England.

GWYNEDD, POWYS, AND DEHEUBARTH

The crucial years after 1093 saw also the initiation in northern Wales of a period of conflict by which the area was gradually recovered from Norman rule and the kingdoms of Gwynedd and Powys reconstituted as major political entities. Gwynedd, first under Gruffudd ap Cynan (died 1137) and then under his son Owain Gwynedd (died 1170), gained a firm governance that enabled the younger ruler, controlling a kingdom extending from the Dyfi to the Dee, to withstand foreign pressure, which was particularly severe during the reign of Henry II (1154–89). In Powys the rule of Madog ap Maredudd (died 1160) likewise proved to be a period of stability and of expansion eastward beyond Offa's Dyke into lands that had been subjected to alien settlement in both the Anglo-Saxon and Norman periods. In southwestern Wales, too, representatives of the dynasty of Deheubarth for more than 30 years waged a campaign that finally enabled Rhys ap Gruffudd (died 1197), a grandson of Rhys ap Tewdwr, to win from Henry II a recognition of his position. Rhys ruled a land that was not as extensive as the ancient kingdom, for Norman control of the lordship of Pembroke and of other lordships along the southern coastline was conceded, but it nevertheless constituted a considerable dominion.

The three kingdoms of Gwynedd, Powys, and Deheubarth formed by the third quarter of the 12th century a well-defined sphere of Welsh political influence (Wallia, or Pura Wallia) in contradistinction to the sphere of Norman influence (Marchia Wallie). Throughout the remainder of the period of Welsh independence there remained a memory that Wales, outside the March, had consisted historically of three kingdoms ruled from the three principal seats of Aberffraw in Gwynedd, Mathrafal in Powys, and Dinefwr in Deheubarth. The rulers of these three kingdoms formulated a concept of Welsh kingship in which indigenous elements were blended with the new influences at work in the feudal monarchies. Each ruler, still known as a king (*rex, brenin*) but later to be styled prince (*princeps, tywysog*) or lord (*dominus, arglwydd*), governed an autonomous territory for which he did homage and fealty to the king of England.

Political stability enabled these territories to recover from the depredations of the Norman period, and the rulers sought to increase the resources of their demesne lands both by exploiting the labour services of bondmen and by providing some bondmen with more favourable tenurial conditions as an incentive to the colonization of marginal lands. With regard to lands held by freemen, a trend toward more intensive agricultural exploitation and a more precise definition of fiscal obligations may explain the description in late medieval land surveys of territorial assets vested in lineages that often traced their descent from a 12th-century ancestor. The endowment of some privileged proprietors with extensive estates facilitated, despite continued adherence to partible succession, the growth of a class of landowners who were linked with the rulers by ties of service and provided the personnel of their administration.

A renewed cultural vitality is noticeable in the Latin scholarship of this period and in a flowering of the literary tradition, exemplified in prose and in eulogistic poetry. *The History of Gruffydd ap Cynan*, probably written in the reign of his son Owain Gwynedd, provides a classic statement of the political and cultural values of independent Wales. Emphasizing the stability and prosperity of an ordered society, it provides an indigenous counterpoint to the more critical view of Welsh society embodied most notably, despite his subsequent identification with the cause of an independent Welsh church, in the works of the Welsh historian Giraldus Cambrensis.

In ecclesiastical affairs, the early Norman period saw the inauguration of a process by which the *clas* organization was replaced by arrangements consonant with the practice of the reformed church. The four territorial dioceses of Bangor, St. David's, Llandaff, and St. Asaph were created, and a parochial organization was gradually established. The church structure was a creation of the Normans, and the bishops appointed to Welsh sees owed a profession of obedience to Canterbury. Even so, Bernard, bishop of St. David's in 1115–48, claimed the status of an archbishop and, in furthering his campaign, appealed to the historical legacy of an early independent Welsh church. His bid was revived at the end of the century by Giraldus Cambrensis. But no less significant than Giraldus' endeavour was the resistance of the clergy of Bangor, who, acting under the protection of Owain Gwynedd at a time of national resistance toward the end of his reign, steadfastly refused to meet the demands of Thomas Becket, archbishop of Canterbury, that the newly elected bishop should swear fealty to Canterbury. The lay powers found adherents in the Cistercian Order; houses such as Margam and Tintern, situated in the March, had close associations with their marcher patrons. The offshoots of the Cistercian monastery of Whitland, notably Strata Florida and Aberconway, were handsomely endowed by the Welsh rulers, who in return were supported in their political endeavours.

LLYWELYN AP IORWERTH

In each of the three kingdoms of Gwynedd, Powys, and Deheubarth, the death of its powerful ruler was followed by a contested succession. In Powys and Deheubarth the unity of the kingdom was never restored; but with the emergence to power in the late 12th century of Llywelyn ap Iorwerth (died 1240), a grandson of Owain Gwynedd, Gwynedd was united once more under the strong hand of a single ruler. Llywelyn's aggression against neighbouring territories incurred resistance, which King John turned to his advantage in a campaign in 1211 whereby the prince of Gwynedd was subjected to humiliating terms. But availing himself of a general Welsh reaction to John's measures for the permanent subjugation of the country, Llywelyn directed a sustained campaign in which his former adversaries participated. Llywelyn achieved a dominant position among the princes, which, while the contest with John persisted, augured the forging of a Welsh polity by bonds of homage and fealty to himself. But, though he remained a powerful influence over the other Welsh princes and thereby minimized the crown's involvement in the affairs of Wales, Llywelyn was unable to secure a formal royal recognition of the territorial and conceptual achievements of the period of conflict. Llywelyn's aspirations for a wider Welsh principality based upon the supremacy of Gwynedd then centred upon David ap Llywelyn, his son by Joan, daughter of King John. David was designated as Llywelyn's heir in preference to his elder but bastard son, Gruffudd, and the Welsh dynasty looked to the English monarchy to ensure an unchallenged succession. In the event, the crown was able to use the dissension between the two sons and the disparate ambitions of the other Welsh princes to restrict David's power to Gwynedd alone. During the war of 1244–46 David contended for a broader influence, but his promising endeavour was cut short by his early death in 1246, without heir.

In the following year his nephews Owain and Llywelyn, two of the four sons of Gruffudd, entered into a treaty obligation by which the crown decreed the partition of a truncated Gwynedd into two parts, with the prospect of further division to provide for the younger brothers. But between 1255 and 1258 Llywelyn ap Gruffudd (died 1282), one of the four brothers, asserted his supremacy first in Gwynedd and then farther afield. In this he was helped by the preoccupation of the English crown with the baronial conflict that led to the Provisions of Oxford in 1258. The prince secured a hegemony that was formally acknowledged by Henry III in 1267 by the Treaty of Montgomery, in which Llywelyn's style, "prince of Wales," first assumed in 1258, and his right to the homage and fealty of the Welsh lords of

Wales were recognized. Llywelyn had thereby brought into being a Principality of Wales composed of the lands that had formed the 12th-century kingdoms of Gwynedd, Powys, and Deheubarth as well as parts of the March. Historically, this meant the reversal of a situation, for which there were several centuries of precedent, whereby the increasingly fragmented territories under Welsh rule had been fiefs held directly from the king of England. The opportunity to consolidate the governance of the principality proved to be brief. Friction between Llywelyn and Edward I led in 1277 to a war in which the prince, isolated by the withdrawal of his vassals' fealty and confronted with the great resources and superior organization of England, was forced to accept terms that restricted his power to Gwynedd west of the Conwy. By 1282 a deterioration in relations between Edward and a number of Welsh princes resulted in renewed conflict. Although Llywelyn may not have been the instigator of the rebellion, he placed himself at its head. In his negotiations with Archbishop Pecham late in 1282 he forcefully expressed the aspirations that had inspired his great endeavour to secure the internal unity of Wales and to stabilize its relationship with England. Shortly afterward, on December 11, Llywelyn was slain in combat, and the resistance, though sustained by his brother David ap Gruffydd (died 1283) for several months, finally collapsed in the summer of 1283.

THE EDWARDIAN SETTLEMENT

Edward I provided for the security of his conquests by means of a program of castle building, initiated after the war of 1277 and subsequently extended to include the great structures of Conwy, Caernarfon, Harlech, and, later, Beaumaris. Each castle sheltered a borough where English colonists were settled. The king's arrangements for the governance of Llywelyn's former lands in northwestern Wales were embodied in the Statute of Wales (1284). Three counties (shires)—Anglesey, Caernarvonshire, and Merioneth—were created and placed under the custody of a justice of North Wales. In northeastern Wales a fourth county, Flintshire, was attached to the earldom of Chester. In southwestern Wales the counties of Cardiganshire and Carmarthenshire, under the custody of the justice of West Wales, were formed out of lands over which royal power had been gradually extended by a process completed upon the failure, in 1287, of the revolt of Rhys ap Maredudd, the last of the princes of the dynasty of Deheubarth. Structurally, the shires that formed the Principality of Wales were similar to those of England, and certain common-law procedures were introduced into their courts, but the shires remained outside the jurisdiction of the central courts of Westminster and they did not elect representatives to Parliament. The March of Wales was extended through the creation by royal charters, out of parts of Gwynedd and Powys, of the lordships of Denbigh, Ruthin, Bromfield and Yale, and Chirk. In his relations with two of the major barons of the older March, Gilbert de Clare of Glamorgan and Humphrey de Bohun of Brecon, Edward showed a determination to assert the sovereignty of the crown over the March and to eradicate abuses of the Custom of the March such as the claim, defiantly expressed by Gilbert, to the right to wage war in the March. But neither Edward nor his successors attempted any far-reaching changes in the organization of the March, and political fractionization persisted over the next two centuries.

REBELLION AND ANNEXATION

Both the crown and the marcher lords employed in the administration of their lands Welshmen drawn from an administrative class that had been fostered by the princes themselves. Those of the principality revealed a particular loyalty to Edward II in the political crises of his reign, and their continued attachment to his cause even after his deposition created a tense situation in 1327. During the 14th century there were occasional variances, but the identity of interest established between the crown and the leading Welshmen proved durable. Even so, the community endured both

OWEN GLENDOWER

Owen Glendower (born c. 1354—died c. 1416), the self-proclaimed prince of Wales, whose unsuccessful rebellion against England was the last major Welsh attempt to throw off English rule, became a national hero upon the resurgence of Welsh nationalism in the 19th and 20th centuries. A descendant of the princes of Powys, Glendower (Welsh: Owain Glyndwr, or Owain Ap Gruffudd) inherited several manors in northern Wales. He studied law in London and then served with the forces of Henry Bolingbroke, an opponent of King Richard II and afterward King Henry IV. When he returned to Wales, he found that England's oppressive rule had crippled the Welsh economy and aroused popular resentment. In September 1400, a year after Bolingbroke usurped the throne, Glendower's violent feud with a neighbour, Reynold, Lord Grey of Ruthin, touched off an uprising in northern Wales. The insurgency quickly became a national struggle for Welsh independence. Glendower formed an alliance with Henry's most powerful opponents, and by 1404 he had control of most of Wales. Styling himself prince of Wales, he established an independent Welsh Parliament and began to formulate his own foreign and ecclesiastical policies. In 1405, however, the tide of battle turned against him. He was twice defeated by Henry IV's son, Prince Henry (later King Henry V), and his allies in England were crushed. Reinforcements sent by France could not save his cause. By 1408–09 Prince Henry had captured Glendower's main strongholds, but the rebel was active in guerrilla fighting as late as 1412.

the economic difficulties encountered over wide areas of Europe at this time and the specifically Welsh problems created by the fact that an important phase in the transition from early medieval social arrangements coincided with the pressures exerted by an alien and fiscally extractive administration. At the very end of the century the deposition of Richard II, who had influential Welshmen among his partisans, released from allegiance to the monarchy a group that, associated with Owen Glendower (Owain Glyndwr), raised a great rebellion that drew its strength from the community as a whole. In the period 1400–07 the royal government lost control of the greater part of Wales, and in some areas the insurrection remained unextinguished several years later.

The rebellion, however, quickened certain processes that were to lead ultimately to the enfranchisement provided by Tudor legislation. In northern Wales particularly, the availability of civil actions by English law led to an early but unrequited demand for English land law. After the rebellion the disabilities incurred by reason of Welsh nationality were underlined. Although often expressed in literature in militant terms and, during the years of dynastic conflict, manipulated by the protagonists of York and Lancaster, the aspirations of the community were focused in a demand for English denizenship. First individual petitioners looked for enfranchisement, and then whole communities in northern Wales secured from Henry VII, by negotiation and payment, charters conferring upon them English land law and other advantages. A realization by the crown of its inability to reverse a decline in the financial yield of its Welsh lands, an experience shared by the marcher lords, contributed to Henry VII's policy.

CHAPTER 20

WALES FROM THE 16TH TO THE 21ST CENTURY

In 1536 Henry VIII's government enacted a measure that made important changes in the government of Wales. Whereas the Statute of Wales (1284) had annexed Wales to the crown of England, the new act declared the king's wish to incorporate Wales within the realm.

UNION WITH ENGLAND

One of the main effects of the 1536 Act of Union was to secure "the shiring of the Marches," bringing the numerous marcher lordships within a comprehensive system of counties. For the first time in its history Wales was to have uniformity in the administration of justice. Welshmen were to enjoy the same political status as Englishmen, and the common law of England, rather than Welsh law, was to be used in the courts. Wales also secured parliamentary representation by the election of members for shires and boroughs. The implementation of the act was set aside until more detailed provision was made by a second act in 1543. Statutory recognition was now given to the Council of Wales and the Marches, which exercised a jurisdiction over both Wales and four border counties of England. But the council fell into abeyance during the Civil Wars and was finally abolished after the Glorious Revolution (1688–89).

In 1543 the Courts of Great Sessions were also created, modeled on the practice already used in the three counties that, since 1284, had formed the principality of North

Wales (Anglesey, Caernarvonshire, and Merioneth), but with 12 counties now grouped into four judicial circuits and the 13th, Monmouthshire, linked with the Oxford circuit. The Great Sessions remained the higher courts of Wales until 1830 when, despite considerable opposition, they were abolished. Finally the Courts of Quarter Sessions were instituted in the manner in which they were already held in England, with the administration of the law vested in justices of the peace. Besides their judicial functions, the justices undertook a wide range of administrative duties, which they continued to fulfill until, with the reform of local government by the Local Government Act of 1888, the county councils were established.

THE REFORMATION

Enacted in the wake of Henry VIII's break with Rome, the union legislation, stressing the need for uniformity with the realm, required those who participated in administration under the crown to use the English language. The need to secure the Protestant faith, however, was to lead to an acknowledgement that the Welsh language had to be used in public worship. William Salesbury and Richard Davies were among a group of distinguished scholars, motivated both by Protestant conviction and passionate concern for the nation's cultural heritage, who realized that the provision of the Scriptures and the Book of Common Prayer in Welsh was essential for the promotion of the faith and the vitality of the language. A petition to the Privy Council led to an act of Parliament in 1563 that required the translation of the Bible and the Book of Common Prayer into Welsh by 1567. Translations of the New Testament and the Book of Common Prayer were indeed published in 1567. The New Testament included an introductory essay by Davies that interpreted the establishment of the Protestant faith as a restoration of the true religion, which had flourished in Wales before the corrupt faith of Rome had been imposed upon its inhabitants. The demands of the Elizabethan government and the aspirations of the Welsh Protestant humanists were met in full when William Morgan's translation of the entire Bible appeared in 1588. Alone among the Celtic nations in securing the Scriptures in the vernacular within half a century of the Reformation, the Welsh people had scored a success of profound significance for the future of the language and the sense of nationhood. Scholarly devotion to the language, also shown by Catholic exiles such as Gruffydd Robert, was accompanied by new interest in Welsh antiquities, and the work of the 16th-century historians Humphrey Llwyd, David Powel, George Owen, and their successors conserved the heritage of the Middle Ages and laid the foundations of modern historical scholarship.

SOCIAL CHANGE

Wales in the mid-16th century probably had a population not much above 250,000, though it was by then growing once more after a period of prolonged stagnation. Towns, though often prosperous, remained small, and Wales possessed no major urban and commercial focus. Although industrial enterprises had an effect upon the economy of certain localities and some Welshmen were enriched by entrepreneurial ventures outside Wales, income was largely derived, directly and indirectly, from pastoral and arable farming. During the 16th and 17th centuries gentry estates were enlarged and consolidated, and the holdings of innumerable proprietors were absorbed into the larger estates. Consequent changes in tenurial status, the growth in population, and inflation created intense problems that were only partially relieved by the enclosure of waste areas and the cultivation of marginal lands. While more and more land was concentrated in fewer hands, smaller proprietors who retained their stake in the soil were often forced to divide their holdings and convert summer dwellings, hitherto used by shepherds in summer months, into permanent homesteads. Many were forced off the land altogether, and it was not until the late 18th century that industry became a major outlet for a rural population that the land could not sustain.

Social trends and the interplay of indigenous and foreign influences were reflected in domestic architecture. The timber-framed hall house, already characteristic of the eastern borderland and of the northern parts of Wales in the late Middle Ages, continued to represent a strong vernacular tradition. But the varying scale and refinement of the houses told of a growing disparity in wealth. In some areas, notably in Glamorgan and Monmouthshire, where a tradition in masonry houses had long existed, vernacular characteristics were increasingly set aside in favour of a new type of Renaissance house. Some houses were built on a scale that indicated the emergence of a class of great landowners who were to stand apart from Welsh society at large on account not only of their wealth but also of their intermarriage with English and Scottish families.

POLITICS AND RELIGION, 1640–1800

On the eve of the Civil War in 1642 there was much sympathy for the royalist cause in Wales. But the parliamentarians also found adherents among some landowners, such as Robert Devereux, 3rd earl of Essex, and Thomas Myddelton, as well as among individuals committed to the Puritan cause, such as the writer Morgan Llwyd and the zealous soldier John Jones of Maesygarnedd. It was mainly in the border counties and in Pembrokeshire, however, that Puritan influence and commercial contacts served to win support for the parliamentary cause. The imposition of parliamentary power on Wales and the sequestration of royalists' property incurred resentment, and Puritan missionaries found themselves labouring in what they believed to be a dark corner of the land. The Act for the Propagation of the Gospel in Wales (1650) set up a coercive authority encompassing both political and religious life, but state intervention remained largely unproductive.

Nonetheless, the Interregnum saw the formation of Dissenting congregations, which were to lay the foundations for some of the abiding influences of modern Welsh life. The most radical were the Quakers who, making particular headway in Montgomeryshire and Merioneth, penetrated not only Anglicized border territory but also the heart of the Welsh-speaking areas. Incurring the animosity of churchmen and other Dissenters alike, they were repressed with a severity experienced only by Roman Catholics and forced into emigration to Pennsylvania, in large numbers. On the other hand, small gathered churches of Congregationalists and Baptists, whose theology was Calvinist and whose belief and personal conduct were governed by a strict code expounded in their church covenant, established the Dissenting tradition within rural communities and small towns.

In the 18th century Methodism became a new and potent influence. Launched by a revival movement of great intensity in the years after 1735, Methodism was sustained within the established church by means of local societies and a central association. The combined influences of the old Dissent and the new Methodism, however, eventually transformed the religious adherence of the Welsh people at the expense of the established church. Although served by innumerable men of learning and devotion, among them Griffith Jones, whose circulating schools contributed immeasurably to the growth in literacy, the church was racked by poverty and inadequate leadership. Thus the Methodist secession from the Anglican church made the ultimate triumph of Nonconformity inevitable.

Methodism and Dissent were not the only influences at work in 18th-century Wales. The resilience of a native culture no longer able to depend upon traditional sources of patronage showed itself in a patriotic fervour to preserve a cultural heritage threatened by progressive Anglicization. Although its proponents drew upon Welsh scholarly achievements, notably those of Edward Lhuyd, Wales had no academic institutions capable of appraising critically the work of romantic antiquarians who looked back to Celtic myth and British druidism. Yet despite its shortcomings, the 18th-century cultural movement was an important expression of a preindustrial society's resourcefulness in protecting its heritage. One of its key figures was

Edward Williams (Iolo Morganwg), whose endeavours encompassed a vast range of literary and historical studies and who also represented the political radicalism inspired by the French Revolution. Radical convictions were held only by a small minority, some of them eccentrics and others distinguished expatriates, but their endeavours marked a significant stage in the emergence of a distinctively Welsh political consciousness.

THE GROWTH OF INDUSTRIAL SOCIETY

By 1800 Wales was rapidly ceasing to be a land whose people were almost entirely dependent upon a rural economy. Industrial development, already present in certain localities, now took place on a larger scale. There was considerable development in the coalfield of northeastern Wales; in the southwest, in Swansea, copper smelting, in particular, served to make the town an important metallurgical centre, and for a period it also could count fine porcelain among its range of manufactures. The main industrial expansion occurred, however, with the growth of substantial ironworks on the northern rim of the South Wales coalfield in Glamorgan and Monmouthshire. Not hitherto served by any major urban centres, the area now became densely populated, largely as a result of immigration from other areas of Wales. A natural increase in population accelerated considerably by the late 18th century, with an estimated population for Wales of 450,000 in 1750 rising to 587,245 by 1801. The population continued to grow, again mainly by natural increase, to 1,163,139 by 1851 and to 2,012,875 by 1901. It was only in the following decade that immigration into Wales occurred on a massive scale. In this period 126,529 persons, the majority of whom came from outside Wales, migrated into Glamorgan and Monmouthshire alone, further enlarging the population of the counties that had benefited most from the internal migration of the earlier decades.

Industrial growth made it possible for large numbers of people whom the rural economy could not sustain to find a livelihood within Wales, and the industrial communities of Glamorgan and Monmouthshire contained a substantial Welsh-speaking element throughout the 19th century. Merthyr Tydfil grew rapidly to become the main urban centre of a new industrial society, but it sadly lacked the facilities normally associated with settlements of a more gradual growth. Conditions in the mining areas were harsh; workers were subjected to long hours and low wages, their children were often forced to work at the mines from a young age, and their families lived in wretched and overcrowded circumstances. It was in Merthyr Tydfil that industrial and social unrest, first expressed in wage-related disputes and sporadic rioting in several areas, erupted into a serious rising in 1831. In the

REBECCA RIOTS

Occurring briefly in 1839 and again with greater violence from 1842 to 1844 in southwestern Wales, the disturbances known as the Rebecca Riots were in protest against charges at the tollgates on the public roads. The attacks, however, were symptomatic of a much wider disaffection caused by agrarian distress, increased tithe charges, and the Poor Law Amendment Act of 1834.

Rebecca Riots, drawing from the Illustrated London News, *February 11, 1843.* © Photos.com/Thinkstock

The rioters took as their motto words in Genesis 24:52: "And they blessed Rebecca, and said to her, '…may your descendants possess the gate of those who hate them!'" Many of the rioters were disguised as women and were on horseback; each band was under a leader called "Rebecca," the followers being known as "her daughters." They destroyed not only the gates but also the tollhouses, the raids being carried out suddenly and at night, usually without violence to the tollkeepers.

Emboldened by success, the Rebeccaites in 1843 turned their attention to other grievances. The government dispatched soldiers and police to South Wales, and the disorder was quelled. An act of 1844, known as Lord Cawdor's Act, amended the turnpike trust laws in Wales and lessened the burden of the tollgate system.

following years the workers' main channel for expressing their aspirations was Chartism, which found its most forceful manifestation in the insurrection at Newport in 1839. Rural Wales, too, was subject to social unrest, and between 1839 and 1844 the Rebecca Riots, ostensibly directed against the exaction of road tolls, gave expression to the underlying difficulties of the tenant farmers of southwestern Wales.

Improved economic conditions from the middle years of the century onward ushered in a period of comparative quietude in industrial Wales. A new phase in industrial growth, brought about by the exploitation of the steam-coal reserves of Glamorgan and Monmouthshire during the last decades of the century, created new valley communities that drew immigrants both from rural and industrial settlements in Wales and from elsewhere. The growth in coal exports led to the building of docks on the coast between Newport and Swansea, notably at Cardiff, while increasing dependence on imported ore led to the relocation of the growing steel industry to areas in close proximity to the coast.

POLITICAL RADICALISM

Wales only gradually embraced the radicalism that came to be regarded as its traditional political allegiance. The political exigencies of the years of the French wars of the Napoleonic period forced the Methodists, in particular, into a passivity that was underlined by a sterner interpretation of Calvinist theology. Political passions were aroused, however, by the moral indictment of the Welsh nation, and especially its Nonconformity, carried in the Report of the Commissioners for Education in 1847. The Welsh, especially the women, were portrayed as depraved and immoral, backward and ignorant. Even the more able ones among them were thought to be impeded by their theological wrangling and often by their lack of English. The growth of a Welsh-language periodical press from its largely denominational origins into a distinctively radical force proved an important influence in rural and industrial Wales alike. By the later years of the 19th century, following the franchise reforms of 1867 and 1884, the hegemony of Welsh Liberal Nonconformity was well established. The passing of legislation specifically concerned with Wales, such as the Welsh Intermediate Education Act (1889) and the Church Disestablishment Act (1914), was a parliamentary success matched in cultural life by the founding of three university colleges and the federal University of Wales and the securing of a royal charter for the establishment of the National Library of Wales and the National Museum of Wales. The attempt by Welsh Liberal associations to secure a representative assembly reached its peak with the Home Rule movement of 1886–96, but it was wrecked by dissension within the associations.

THE 20TH CENTURY AND BEYOND

By 1900 there were signs that the Liberal-Nonconformist supremacy would be gradually undermined. Traditional beliefs were challenged, and the experience of World War I created new tensions. The massive flow of workers into the steel and coal areas, largely from outside Wales, affected the composition, and hence the language, of the industrial communities, and immigration coincided with a new era of industrial unrest and political militancy. The miners' efforts at combination led in 1898 to the founding of the South Wales Miners' Federation; the coal owners strengthened their position by forming powerful combines. Despite fierce resistance, the miners won their campaigns for an 8-hour day and a minimum wage. Within the federation a new militancy, expressed in the policy document entitled the *Miners' Next Step* (1912), espoused an industrial unionism with syndicalist tendencies. These influences, though potent in the Rhondda Valley, did not pervade the coal industry, nor did they shape the steelworkers' and tinplate workers' unions. After the war syndicalist influence was subsumed in orthodox communism, or, more generally, in democratic socialism. By 1922 the Liberal Party in South Wales had lost its hold upon the industrial communities to the Labour Party, whose influence was felt both at Westminster and in local government. In the northeast and in the slate-quarrying communities of northwestern Wales, which also experienced prolonged and enervating industrial disputes, an allegiance to radical Liberalism gradually evolved into adherence to Labour.

Economic depression between the world wars, made particularly acute by the collapse of the export market upon which the Welsh economy so heavily depended, brought massive unemployment. Wales lost about 430,000 people by emigration to England and to areas overseas. The war years of 1939–45 brought substantial industrial recovery, and upon the cessation of hostilities strenuous efforts were made to modernize the basic industries of steel and coal and to achieve a diversification of industry in general. Even so, coal production continued to fall, and in the industrial areas the exodus of workers and their families showed no signs of abating. To be sure, the rural economy benefited from government subsidies that facilitated investments in land improvements and new buildings as well as from advisory and marketing agencies. However, the working population continued to fall, even in the rural areas.

Labour continued to retain the political allegiance of the Welsh electorate. After World War II the party registered gains in rural Wales and held as many as 32 of 36 Welsh seats until 1966. Their position was not maintained, however. Plaid Cymru, which was founded in 1925 as the

Welsh Nationalist Party, achieved a measure of influence that was not reflected in successes at parliamentary elections until 1966. It captured its first parliamentary seat in a by-election at Carmarthen that year, though it lost the seat in 1970. The party subsequently won three seats in northwestern Wales in October 1974. The Conservative Party also made gains at Labour's expense, several members being returned in constituencies where boundaries were redrawn to take account of the growth of suburban communities. In the late 1970s and early '80s the Conservatives made even greater gains, winning 14 of 38 Welsh seats in 1983. By the late 1980s, however, Labour was again dominant, and it maintained that dominance into the early 21st century.

The Welsh Language Society, founded in 1962, brought a measure of militancy to the cause of preserving the language and was among the influences that spurred a more positive response to the problem of its continuing decline, including the Welsh Language Act of 1967. In 1964 the Labour government honoured a pledge to appoint a secretary of state for Wales with departmental responsibility, and subsequent Labour and Conservative administrations promoted an extensive transfer of functions to the Welsh Office. Demands in Wales and Scotland for an elected assembly with devolved powers led to the appointment of a Royal Commission on the Constitution, which recommended devolution for both countries in 1973. An act providing Wales with a measure of devolution was passed at Westminster in 1978, but devolution was overwhelmingly defeated—by a margin of nearly 4 to 1—in a referendum held the following year.

Support for devolution and the protection of Welsh identity increased in 1979 with the election in London of a Conservative government, which enjoyed only minority support in Wales. A new phase of immigration in rural Wales in the 1980s and increased economic vulnerability to the global free market prompted renewed and more cohesive efforts to conserve Welsh heritage. In 1982 a Welsh-language television channel was created, and in 1993 the government passed another Welsh Language Act. The Welsh Language Board, established under the provisions of the 1993 act, promoted the use of the Welsh language and sought to give Welsh equal legal weight with English in the conduct of government business.

A second referendum on the creation of a Welsh assembly, held under the new Labour government of Tony Blair, was barely approved (50.3 percent) on September 18, 1997. The assembly was given responsibility for administering public services and implementing regional policies on education, health care, and economic development, among other areas. Its first elections—which were held under a system of proportional representation rather than under the plurality system used for Westminster elections—took place in May 1999 and produced a minority Labour government headed by Alun Michael, who assumed the title "first secretary." Although Labour won 28 seats, a resurgent Plaid Cymru took 17 seats, including several in Labour's traditional strongholds; the Conservatives won 9 seats and the Liberal Democrats 6. In 2000 Labour's Rhodri Morgan became first secretary; later that year the position's title was formally changed to first minister. Morgan remained in that office when Labour won the elections of 2003 and 2007, with Plaid finishing second both times.

In March 2011 another milestone in devolving government for Wales was passed when a referendum granting the Welsh assembly the power to enact laws without first seeking consent from Parliament was approved by 63.5 percent of those voting. Two months later assembly elections were held, with Labour winning 30 seats, 1 short of an absolute majority. The Conservatives finished second, ahead of Plaid Cymru and the Liberal Democrats.

Conclusion

Four people walk into a bar: an Englishman, a Northern Irishman, a Scotsman, and a Welshman... It sounds like the beginning of a well-worn joke, but if the name of that bar were the Early 21st Century and if it were in London, the meaning of the resultant metaphor would hinge on who walks out of that bar: four Britons? Or an Englishman, a Northern Irishman, a Scotsman, and a Welshman? As Northern Ireland, Scotland, and Wales embrace varying degrees of autonomy, their relationship to the entity that is the United Kingdom raises an important question: just how united is it? And, perhaps even more important, what is its future?

This volume has shown again and again the fierce sense of national identity and pride possessed by the peoples of Northern Ireland, Scotland, and Wales. It has also described the distinctive histories and cultures of each place, all of them unique in myriad ways. An important element of each of their stories has been a struggle to escape the dominance of the English, but equally important is the history of their shared accomplishments within the United Kingdom—a long mutual history that included the formation of a British Empire on which it was once said that the sun never set. That legacy was celebrated in the opening ceremony of the Olympic Games in London in 2012, with film footage of singing children from each of the four constituent parts of the United Kingdom and reenactments of proud accomplishments of British history, from the Industrial Revolution to the establishment of the National Health Service. Together, athletes representing the United Kingdom claimed 65 medals at that Olympics.

The question ultimately may not be whether the whole of the United Kingdom is greater than the sum of its parts but whether it is possible to find a formula that allows the people of Northern Ireland, Scotland, and Wales, as well as those of England, to fulfill their national political, cultural, and economic aspirations while still trying to forge a more perfect union.

Glossary

ANGLICAN Of or relating to the established episcopal Church of England and churches of similar faith and order in communion with it.

CELT A member of the early Indo-European peoples distributed from the British Isles and Spain to Asia Minor.

COMMONWEALTH The English state from the death of Charles I in 1649 to the Restoration in 1660.

EARL A member of the British peerage ranking below a marquess and above a viscount.

ECCLESIASTICAL Of or relating to a church especially as an established institution.

ECUMENICAL Promoting or tending toward worldwide Christian unity or cooperation.

ESTUARY A water passage where the tide meets a river current.

GAELIC Of, relating to, or constituting the Goidelic speech of the Celts in Ireland, the Isle of Man, and the Scottish Highlands.

GLEY A sticky clay soil or soil layer formed under the surface of some waterlogged soils.

HOUSE OF COMMONS The lower house of the British Parliament.

HOUSE OF LORDS The upper house of the British Parliament.

LORD A British nobleman.

MONARCH A person who reigns over a kingdom or empire.

PARISH A subdivision of a county often coinciding with an original ecclesiastical parish and constituting the unit of local government.

PARLIAMENT An assemblage of the nobility, clergy, and commons called together by the British sovereign as the supreme legislative body in the United Kingdom.

PLANTATION Forced settlements in early 17th-century Ireland by English and Scottish settlers.

PODZOL Any of a group of zonal soils that develop in a moist climate especially under coniferous or mixed forest and have an organic mat and a thin organic-mineral layer above a light gray leached layer resting on a dark horizon that is marked by illuviation and enriched with amorphous clay.

PRESBYTERIAN Characterized by a graded system of representative ecclesiastical bodies (as presbyteries) exercising legislative and judicial powers.

PROVINCE An administrative district or division of a country.

REPUBLIC A government in which supreme power resides in a body of citizens entitled to vote and is exercised by elected officers and representatives responsible to them and governing according to law.

ROMAN CATHOLIC Of, relating to, or being a Christian church having a hierarchy of priests and bishops under the pope, a liturgy centered in the Mass, veneration of the Virgin Mary and saints, clerical celibacy, and a body of dogma including transubstantiation and papal infallibility.

RUGBY A football game in which play is continuous without time-outs or substitutions, interference and forward passing are not permitted, and kicking, dribbling, lateral passing, and tackling are featured.

SECT A dissenting or schismatic religious body.

SECULAR Not overtly or specifically religious.

SHIBBOLETH A word or saying used by adherents of a party, sect, or belief and usually regarded by others as empty of real meaning.

BIBLIOGRAPHY

NORTHERN IRELAND

GEOGRAPHY

Social and economic conditions are discussed in James H. Johnson, *The Human Geography of Ireland* (1994). An introduction to the economy is provided in Paul Bew, Henry Patterson, and Paul Teague, *Northern Ireland—Between War and Peace: The Political Future of Northern Ireland*, 2nd ed. (2000). The political situation is treated in Brendan O'Leary and John McGarry, *The Politics of Antagonism: Understanding Northern Ireland*, 2nd ed. (1996); and Colin Coulter, *Contemporary Northern Irish Society: An Introduction* (1999). The visual arts are the subject of Liam Kelly, *Thinking Long: Contemporary Art in the North of Ireland* (1996). Sporting life is discussed in John Sugden and Alan Bairner, *Sport, Sectarianism, and Society in a Divided Ireland* (1993).

HISTORY

General historical surveys include Jonathan Bardon, *A History of Ulster*, new updated ed. (2001). Helpful studies of specific historical events and periods include M. Perceval-Maxwell, *The Scottish Migration to Ulster in the Reign of James I* (1973, reissued 1999); Philip S. Robinson, *The Plantation of Ulster: British Settlement in an Irish Landscape, 1600–1670* (1984, reissued 1994); and Marianne Elliott, *The Catholics of Ulster: A History* (2000, reissued 2002). Discussion of 20th-century problems includes Padraig O'Malley, *The Uncivil Wars: Ireland Today*, 3rd ed. (1997); and Paul Bew, Peter Gibbon, and Henry Patterson, *Northern Ireland, 1921–2001: Political Forces and Social Classes*, rev. and updated ed. (2002). John D. Brewer and Francis Teeney, *Religion, Civil Society, and Peace in Northern Ireland* (2011), examines the role of churches in peace building. Two good introductions to contemporary politics are Paul Dixon, *Northern Ireland: The Politics of War and Peace* (2001); and Jonathan Tonge, *Northern Ireland: Conflict and Change*, 2nd ed. (2002). A useful collection of essays on post–Good Friday Agreement Northern Ireland is Rick Wilford (ed.), *Aspects of the Belfast Agreement* (2001). Two views of the IRA's campaign can be found in Peter Taylor, *Provos: The IRA and Sinn Fein* (1997; also published as *Behind the Mask: The IRA and Sinn Fein*, 1999); and M.L.R. Smith, *Fighting for Ireland?: The Military Strategy of the Irish Republican Movement* (1995, reissued 1997).

SCOTLAND

GEOGRAPHY

A good review of the geography of Scotland is Chalmers M. Clapperton (ed.), *Scotland, a New Study* (1983). The people of Scotland are discussed in Nathaniel Harris, *Heritage of Scotland: A Cultural History of Scotland & Its People* (2000); and James McCarthy, *An Inhabited Solitude: Scotland, Land and People* (1998). Jeremy Peat and Stephen Boyle, *An Illustrated Guide to the Scottish Economy*, ed. by Bill Jamieson (1999), is an accessible account of the economy. Accounts of Scottish politics include Christopher Harvie, *Scotland and Nationalism: Scottish Society and Politics, 1707 to the Present*, 3rd ed. (1998); Christopher Harvie and Peter Jones, *The Road to Home Rule* (2000); and Brian Taylor, *The Scottish Parliament* (1999; also published as *The Road to the Scottish Parliament*, 2002). Scottish national cultural heritage is explored in diverse works, including David Daiches (ed.), *A New Companion to Scottish Culture*, rev. and updated ed. (1993; previously published as *A Companion to Scottish Culture*, 1981); and John Purser, *Scotland's Music: A History of the Traditional and Classical Music of Scotland from Earliest Times to the Present Day* (1992). Architecture is addressed in Miles Glendinning, Ranald MacInnes, and Aonghus MacKechnis (eds.), *A History of Scottish Architecture: From the Renaissance to the Present Day* (1996). Art and painting are treated in Duncan Macmillan, *Scottish Art, 1460-2000* (2000). Scottish literature is the subject of Cairns Craig (ed.), *The History of Scottish Literature*, 4 vol. (1987-89).

HISTORY

A comprehensive reference work on all aspects of Scottish history is Michael Lynch (ed.), *The Oxford Companion to Scottish History* (2001), which contains an excellent bibliography. Less detailed but still informative is Fitzroy MacLean, *Scotland: A Concise History*, rev. and expanded with a new chapter by Magnus Linklater (2012). Although readers should be aware that the opinions of historians diverge to a great extent on Scotland's early history, that period can be studied in G.W.S. Barrow, *Kingship and Unity: Scotland, 1000-1306*, 2nd ed. (2003); and Ian D. Whyte, *Scotland Before the Industrial Revolution: An Economic and Social History, c. 1050-c. 1750* (1995). The early modern period of Scottish history can be explored through T.C. Smout, *A History of the Scottish People, 1560-1830* (1969, reissued 1998), which was seminal when first issued and is still a rewarding read. A comprehensive survey of the modern period is T.M. Devine, *The Scottish Nation, 1700-2000* (1999, reissued 2001). William Ferguson, *Scotland, 1689 to the Present* (1968, reissued 1987), remains very valuable on political and intellectual history of the 18th and 19th centuries. Shorter studies include David Allan, *Scotland in the Eighteenth Century: Union and Enlightenment* (2002); John F. McCaffrey, *Scotland in the Nineteenth Century* (1998); and W.W. Knox, *Industrial Nation: Work, Culture and Society in Scotland, 1800-Present*

(1999). Twentieth-century Scottish history is examined in T.M. Devine and R.J. Finlay (eds.), *Scotland in the Twentieth Century* (1996), which contains a series of thematic essays; Christopher Harvie, *No Gods and Precious Few Heroes: Twentieth Century Scotland*, 3rd ed. (1998); and I.G.C. Hutchison, *Scottish Politics in the Twentieth Century* (2001).

WALES

GEOGRAPHY

Harold Carter and H.M. Griffiths (eds.), *National Atlas of Wales* (1980, reissued 1989), provides wide-ranging coverage, with explanatory text in both English and Welsh. Christopher Winn, *I Never Knew That About Wales* (2007), offers interesting insights. Paul Cloke, Mark Goodwin, and Paul Milbourne, *Rural Wales: Community and Marginalization* (1997), addresses the changing and problematic nature of rural Wales. Harold Carter, *The Towns of Wales*, 2nd ed. (1966); and D. Huw Owen (ed.), *Settlement and Society in Wales* (1989), consider the growth, functions, and morphology of urban areas. Social and economic themes are profiled in David Dunkerley and Andrew Thompson (eds.), *Wales Today* (1999), a collection of essays; and in Ralph Fevre and Andrew Thompson (eds.), *Nation, Identity, and Social Theory: Perspectives from Wales* (1999). Language issues are analyzed in John Aitchison and Harold Carter, *A Geography of the Welsh Language, 1961–1991* (1994), and in *Language, Economy, and Society: The Changing Fortunes of the Welsh Language in the Twentieth Century*, updated ed. (2000).

HISTORY

General historical surveys include John Davies, *A History of Wales*, new ed. (2007); Henry Weisser, *An Illustrated History of Wales* (2002); and Gwyn A. Williams, *When Was Wales?: A History of the Welsh* (1985). The early period is examined in Colin Renfrew, *Archaeology and Language: The Puzzle of Indo-European Origins* (1987). The Middle Ages are covered in John Edward Lloyd, *A History of Wales from the Earliest Times to the Edwardian Conquest*, 2 vol. (1911; available also in many later editions), a classic work still not superseded; and R.R. Davies, *Conquest, Coexistence, and Change: Wales, 1063–1415* (1987). The key works for modern Welsh history are Glanmor Williams, *Recovery, Reorientation, and Reformation: Wales, c. 1415–1642* (1987); Geraint H. Jenkins, *The Foundations of Modern Wales: Wales 1642–1780* (1987); and Kenneth O. Morgan, *Rebirth of a Nation: Wales, 1880–1980* (1981). Valuable specialist histories include Ieuan Gwynedd Jones, *Communities: Essays in the Social History of Victorian Wales* (1987); and Meic Stephens (ed.), *The Oxford Companion to the Literature of Wales* (1986), includes historical information on people.

Index

A

Aberdeen, 53, 59, 63, 64, 68, 104, 109
Adam, Robert, 115
Adams, Gerry, 47
Agnew, Elaine, 30
Agricola, Gnaeus Julius, 86
Aidan, St., 88
Anglo-Irish Agreement, 45
Anglo-Irish Treaty, 41
Anglo-Irish War (Irish War of Independence), 41
Antonine Wall, 87
Armagh, 3, 11, 29, 31, 33
Asquith, H.H., 41
Ayton, Robert, 80

B

bagpipes, 78–79, 82
Balliol, John de, 96, 97, 122
Barbour, John, 103
Belfast, 3, 9, 11, 14, 15, 17, 18, 19, 20, 21, 23, 24, 25, 26, 28, 29, 30, 31, 32, 39, 42, 47
Bell, Alexander Graham, 50, 76
Best, George, 31
Blair, Tony, 44, 69, 73, 124, 172
Bloody Sunday, 43–44
Book of Deer, The, 103
Boyne, Battle of the, 28, 38
Brontë family, 29
Burns, Robert, 50, 79, 80, 81, 116
Burton, Richard, 147–148

C

Caernarfon, 133–134, 161
Cardiff, 128, 135, 139, 145, 150
Carlyle, Thomas, 50, 76
Carnegie, Andrew, 50
Carrickfergus, 10, 14, 35
Charles I, 58, 109–111
Charles II, 111–112
Christianity, 33, 57, 58, 88, 152–153
Columba, St., 88, 103
Connery, Sean, 81
Connolly, Billy, 81
Cromwell, Oliver, 37, 110, 111

D

David I, 91–93, 94
David II, 98–99, 100
Deheubarth, 154, 155, 157, 158, 160, 161
DeLorean, John, 15
Derry/Londonderry, 3, 11, 14, 17, 21, 24, 26, 29, 31, 38, 43, 44
Douglas, Barry, 30
drumlins, 5–6, 10
Dundee, 55, 59, 67, 68, 71

E

Easter Rising, 41
Edinburgh, 51, 59, 65, 67, 68, 69, 72, 82, 83, 104, 109, 115, 117, 121
Edinburgh, University of, 76, 117
Edward I, 95–97, 122, 133, 161–162
Elizabeth I, 10, 36, 106, 107, 108, 122
Elizabeth II, 20, 47
European Union, 12, 16, 19, 56, 136

F

Flodden, Battle of, 105
Forsyth, Bill, 81–82
Free Church of Scotland, 58, 119

G

Galway, James, 30
George, David Lloyd, 41, 140
Gladstone, William Ewart, 40, 119
Glasgow, 56, 57, 59, 67, 68, 71, 73, 82, 83, 97, 104, 109, 117, 118, 123
Glendower, Owen, 162, 163
Good Friday Agreement, 19, 20, 21, 23, 24, 25, 46, 47
Government of Ireland Act, 18, 41
Gwynedd, kingdom of, 152, 154, 155, 157, 158, 160, 161, 162

H

Hadrian's Wall, 87
haggis, 79, 80
Hardie, J. Keir, 73–74, 119, 140
Heaney, Seamus, 3, 29
Heath, Edward, 19, 44, 45
Henry VII, 105, 107, 163
Henry VIII, 105, 106, 164, 165
Hume, David, 50, 115–116
Hutcheson, Francis, 49
Hywel Dda, 154, 155

I

International Fund for Ireland, 12
Irish language (Gaelic), 8, 27
Irish Republican Army (IRA), 20, 21, 23, 24, 41, 43, 44, 45, 46, 47

J

Jacobites, 114–115
James I, king of Scotland, 100–101, 104, 109
James II, king of Scotland, 101–102
James III, king of Scotland, 102, 103, 104
James IV, king of Scotland, 104–105
James V, king of Scotland, 104–105
James VI, king of Scotland (James I of England), 35, 36, 76, 107–109, 111, 122
James VII, king of Scotland (James II of England), 10, 28, 38, 40, 112, 113, 114
John, king of England, 35, 160

K

Kames, Henry Home, Lord, 116
kilts, 79
Kinnock, Neil, 141
Knox, John, 57, 106, 107

L

Lewis, C.S., 29
Llywelyn ap Iorwerth, 160–161
Londonderry/Derry, 3, 11, 14, 17, 21, 24, 26, 29, 31, 38, 43, 44

M

Macbeth, 90
MacDiarmid, Hugh, 80, 121
Mackintosh, Charles Rennie, 81
mad cow disease (bovine spongiform encephalopathy), 61, 62
Mary, Queen of Scots, 105–107
Maze prison, 25
McAdam, John, 50
McAleese, Mary, 20
McGuinness, Martin, 47
Milford Haven, 137, 138
Morrison, Van, 3, 30

N

Ness, Loch, 52, 53
Ninian, St., 57, 88
Northampton, Treaty of, 98

Northern Ireland, cultural life of
- the arts, 28–31
- cultural institutions, 31
- daily life and social customs, 28
- media and publishing, 32
- sports and recreation, 31–32

Northern Ireland, economy of
- agriculture, forestry, and fishing, 12–14
- finance, 16
- labour, 17
- manufacturing, 14–15
- resources and power, 14
- services, 16
- trade, 16
- transportation, 17

Northern Ireland, government and society of
- education, 26
- health and welfare, 25–26
- housing, 26
- justice, 21–22
- local government, 21
- political parties, 22–23
- political process, 22–23
- security/military, 24–25

Northern Ireland, history
- disintegration of stability, 43–45
- Home Rule, 40–42, 45
- power-sharing agreements and the establishment of a fragile peace, 45–47
- precarious coexistence, 42–43
- prior to Government of Ireland Act, 33–37, 38–40

Northern Ireland, land and people of
- climate, 6–7
- demographic trends, 11
- drainage, 6
- ethnic groups and languages, 7–8
- plant and animal life, 7
- relief, 3–6
- religion, 8–9
- settlement patterns, 9–11
- soils, 6

O

Olympic Games, 31, 83, 150, 173
Orange Society/Orange Order, 27, 39, 40

P

Paisley, Ian, 47
Potato Famine, 10, 118
Powys, kingdom of, 152, 154, 155, 157, 158, 160, 161, 162
Protestantism
- in Northern Ireland, 8–9, 18, 19, 20, 21, 22, 23, 26, 27, 28, 29, 30, 33, 36, 37, 38, 39, 40, 41, 42–45, 46–47
- in Scotland, 106–107
- in Wales, 132, 165

Provisional IRA, 45

R

Real IRA, 20, 46
Rebecca Riots, 169, 170
Reformation, 57, 93, 94, 105–107, 109, 165
Rhodri Mawr, 154, 155
Robert I, 10, 96, 97–98, 101
Robert II, 100
Robert III, 100
Robinson, Peter, 47
Roman Catholicism
- in Northern Ireland, 8–9, 19, 20, 21, 22, 23, 26, 27, 28, 29, 30, 31, 33, 37, 38, 39, 40, 41, 42–45, 46–47
- in Scotland, 57, 75, 77, 107, 108, 111, 112, 114
- in Wales, 132

Royal and Ancient Gold Club of St. Andrews, 83
Royal Ulster Constabulary, 24, 43

S

Saint Andrews, University of, 76, 101
Salmond, Alex, 125
Saville Report, 44
Scotch whisky, 63, 66, 80
Scotland, Church of, 57–58, 77, 116, 119
Scotland, cultural life of
   the arts, 80–82
   cultural institutions, 82
   daily life and social customs, 78–80
   media and publishing, 83–84
   sports and recreation, 83
Scotland, economy of
   agriculture, forestry, and fishing, 60–63
   finance, 66–67
   manufacturing, 65–66
   resources and power, 63–65
   services, 67
   transportation, 67–68
Scotland, government and society of
   education, 75–77
   health and welfare, 75
   housing, 75
   justice, 72
   local government, 71–72
   political process/political parties, 72–74
   security/military, 74–75
Scotland, history of
   early Scotland, 85–99
   from the 15th century to the age of revolution, 100–112
   since the 18th century, 113–125
Scotland, land and people of
   climate, 55
   demographic trends, 59
   drainage, 54
   ethnic groups, 56
   language, 56–57
   plant and animal life, 55–56
   relief, 52–54
   religion, 57–58
   settlement patterns, 58–59
   soils, 54–55
Scots language, 56, 57, 59, 80
Scott, Sir Walter, 49, 76, 108, 117, 122
Scottish Covenant, 122
Scottish Enlightenment, 115–117
Scottish Gaelic language, 56–57, 58–59, 77, 80
Severus, 87
Sinn Féin, 20, 21, 23, 41, 45, 46, 47
Smith, Adam, 49, 116
Snowdonia National Park, 129, 131
Spark, Muriel, 50, 81
Stevenson, Robert Louis, 76, 117
Stiff Little Fingers, 30–31
Stone of Scone, 51, 122
Sunningdale Agreement, 45
Swansea, 128, 135, 138, 142, 150

T

Táin (*The Book of the Dun Cow*), 34
Thomas, Dylan, 146, 148
tourism
   in Northern Ireland, 16
   in Scotland, 67, 82
   in Wales, 128, 129, 133, 138
tweed, 66
Tyrone, Hugh O'Neill, 2nd earl of, 35, 36

U

Ulster
   in the 18th century, 38–40
   English and Scottish plantations, 35–36
   Gaelic Irish and Anglo-Normans, 34–35
   Home Rule, 40–42
   mythic history, 33–34
   religion and social structure, 36–37
Union, Act of (1536), 128, 144, 164
Union, Act of (1707), 75, 113
Union, Act of (1800), 19, 39

W

Wales, Church of, 132
Wales, cultural life of
   cultural institutions, 149–150
   daily life and social customs, 145
   media and publishing, 150
   music, literature, and film, 145–148
   sports and recreation, 150
   visual arts, 148–149
Wales, economy of
   agriculture, forestry, and fishing, 136–137
   manufacturing, 137–138
   resources and power, 137
   services, 138
   transportation, 138
Wales, government and society of
   education, 142–143
   health and welfare, 141–142
   housing, 142
   justice and security, 140
   local government, 140
   political process/political parties, 140–141
Wales, history of
   in the Middle Ages, 157–163
   before the Norman Conquest, 151–156
   from the 16th to the 21st century, 164–173
Wales, land and people of
   climate, 131
   demographic trends, 135
   drainage, 130
   ethnic groups and languages, 131–132
   plant and animal life, 131
   relief, 128–130
   religion, 132
   settlement patterns, 132–135
   soils, 130–131
Wallace, William, 96–97
Watt, James, 50, 117
Welsh language, 128, 132, 142–143, 144, 145, 148, 149, 150, 165, 170, 172
Williams, Edward, 168
Wilson, Harold, 123
World War I, 14, 41, 71, 120–121, 170
World War II, 3, 14, 43, 56, 59, 61, 79, 84, 121–123, 171

MAR 1 9 2014